COACHING

FOR

ATTORNEYS

**Improving Productivity and
Achieving Balance**

Cami McLaren | Stephanie Finelli

COACHING
FOR
ATTORNEYS

**Improving Productivity and
Achieving Balance**

Cover design by Andrew Alcala/ABA Publishing.

The materials contained herein represent the opinions of the authors and/or the editors, and should not be construed to be the views or opinions of the law firms or companies with whom such persons are in partnership with, associated with, or employed by, nor of the American Bar Association or the Section of Dispute Resolution unless adopted pursuant to the bylaws of the Association.

Nothing contained in this book is to be considered as the rendering of legal advice for specific cases, and readers are responsible for obtaining such advice from their own legal counsel. This book is intended for educational and informational purposes only.

Printed in the United States of America.

21 20 19 18   5 4 3 2

Library of Congress Cataloging-in-Publication Data

McLaren, Cami, author.
    Coaching for attorneys : improving productivity and achieving balance / by Cami McLaren; Section of Dispute Resolution, American Bar Association.
        pages cm
    Includes bibliographical references and index.
    ISBN 978-1-62722-359-1 (alk. paper)
    1. Practice of law--United States. 2. Personal coaching--United States. 3. Law--Vocational guidance--United States. I. Finelli, Stephanie J., author. II. Title.
    KF298.M35 2014
    340.68'3--dc23

                                                                                    2013050021

Discounts are available for books ordered in bulk. Special consideration is given to state bars, CLE programs, and other bar-related organizations. Inquire at Book Publishing, ABA Publishing, American Bar Association, 321 N. Clark Street, Chicago, Illinois 60654-7598.

www.ShopABA.org

For Barbara Fagan

Master
Model
Mentor
Friend

Contents

Chapter 8

Chapter 9
Purpose and Vision

About the Authors

Cami McLaren is the owner of McLaren Coaching, a business dedicated to providing support for attorneys and law firms in creating a way of practice that makes life more fulfilling overall, that generates excellence in business and balance in life. She works throughout the country with bar associations, law firms and individual attorneys. Before starting her coaching practice, she attended McGeorge School of Law in Sacramento and practiced law for sixteen years. Find her on the web at www.mclarencoaching.com.

She lives in Sacramento.

Stephanie Finelli is a licensed attorney practicing in Sacramento, California. She is a 1994 graduate of University of California, Davis King Hall School of Law. Following a one-year fellowship at the Criminal Justice Legal Foundation, she was an associate attorney with Freidberg Law Corporation until 2003 when she formed the Law Office of Stephanie J. Finelli. She focuses on appeals and civil litigation, mainly in the areas of contract and business disputes and family law. She donates her time mediating disputes for the local superior and appellate courts, has served for the past several years as an officer of the appellate section of the Sacramento County Bar Association, and currently serves on the advisory committee and as a mentor for the McClatchy High School Law and Public Policy Academy. She is an avid long-distance runner who has completed numerous marathons and ultra-marathons.

Acknowledgements

Many people were involved in the ultimate production of this book. We are grateful to them all.

In preparing for this book, Cami interviewed many attorneys to find the areas of coaching that they felt were most needed and would be best addressed in this type of book. Those people were: Dean of McGeorge School of Law (at that time), Elizabeth Parker; Sacramento attorneys Wendy Taylor, David Allen, and Tasha Paris; San Ramon attorney James Greenan; Stockton Workers' Comp Judge W. Kearse McGill; Boston attorney Donna Truex; and retired Orange County attorney Joan Virginia Allen.

For their help reviewing portions of the book and giving legal and non-legal opinions about the grammar, writing style, relevance, and appropriateness for attorneys: Gail Blanchard-Saiger, Sonya Grant Zindel, Lorraine Abate, Karen Romero, and Lena Rumps. In particular, I want to thank Matthew Long, a Santa Barbara attorney who allowed me to use his vision process in the Purpose and Vision chapter. You guys are amazing!

Above and beyond all contributions to this book was Joan Virginia Allen, Cami's mother, also an attorney and woman of many talents, who gave tirelessly of her editing and analytic abilities; who took time to read, call, talk, advise, mentor and edit, and who read each and every page of this book more than once.

Cami would also like to thank:

I am grateful to my mom, not just for her editing abilities and willingness to put so much time enthusiastically into this project, but for being so very encouraging as we moved forward in this process and, come to think of it, so encouraging to me in all areas of my life. Your belief in me is what inspires me to leap when I cannot see the net.

Thank you to my sister, Wendy, for being a true friend and for pushing me down the coaching road.

Thank you from the bottom of my heart to the two women who helped me believe I could coach and teach in the first place: To Joyce Christie who asked me just a single question, "what is your purpose?" that led me to realize my deep desire to be "in front of the room" inspiring, teaching, coaching, and empowering other people to have what they want; who challenged me to "stretch" in ways I believed impossible and left me realizing how much really is possible. And to Barbara Fagan, Master Coach, who taught me to be a coach, and then to be a better coach; who pushed me to be in front of the room;

who always saw in me more than I saw in myself; took a stand for any dream I declared; who modeled for me the way to be a professional coach, to start, build, grow, and sustain a coaching company in integrity with my own standards; and who was (and is) there whenever I call, as mentor and friend. Many of the coaching tools I share in this book originated in some way from her and her company, Source Point Training.

To Shannon Stone, Jerry Green, Maria Maione, and Marcia Burditt; and to Linda Cummings, Shirl Woodruff, and Luke Pritchard, all of whom supported me through coach training and continue to this day. To Robert Sims, Joyce Glick, Andrea Voirin, and Kelly Mobeck, true friends who also challenged me to the next level of coaching and teaching, and who always make themselves available to me whatever I want or need. With friends like these, all things are possible!

To all of my clients, each of whom gave me the great honor of allowing me to support them in becoming what they wanted to be—building and growing firms, sole practices, hobbies, non-profit companies, relationships—and in the process, supported me in learning how to be effective with hiring partners, managing partners, sole practitioners, associates, mediators, judges, and counsel.

To Gita for being a resource and inspiration as author, and a real friend.

To Stephanie: wow, a whole book. First the treehouse, and now this. They said it couldn't be done. With different styles, strengths, challenges, and obstacles, somehow we pulled it off. I could not have done this (any of it) without you; and for this I am truly grateful.

To my boys: Graham, my heart's delight, you never cease to amaze me with your creativity, strength, and leadership. Thank you for your support and for being the bright shining star that you are for me and for so many people. To Connor, my fact-checker, knowledge-base, sports guy. I appreciate you for paying attention and for caring so deeply. You mean a great deal to a great many people. You have made my life more exciting and fun!

Steph would also like to thank:
To my parents, Pamela and Louis Finelli, who always told me I could do anything I set my mind to. You were right.

To Pam Jones, one of my dearest friends. You provided emotional support and insights, especially during those long runs. You are a better runner than you think you are.

To Dianne Meyers and all of the Wrong Distance Runners who gave me support, encouragement, and well-needed ego boosting. You guys are awesome.

I would also like to thank every client I have ever had the honor of representing; every opposing counsel I have had the opportunity to "do battle" with; and every judge, arbitrator, and mediator I have ever appeared before. Each of you has had a hand in shaping who I am as a lawyer and as a human being. Without those experiences—including the "difficult" ones—I would not be the lawyer I am today. I have learned many lessons from you, and will continue to do so.

This book would never have been finalized (at least not in its current form) without the proofreading, editing, and suggestions of Cami's mother, Joan Allen. As with everything she does, when Joan decided she would help, she put her whole self into it. Thank you not only for your work on this book, but for all the love, patience, kindness, and wisdom that you and Willis have provided over the years.

Cami: Thank you. I am always honored to be your "go to" person. Your coaching has been invaluable, not only in writing this book, but in my practice and in my life. Thank you for the opportunity to assist in this book. You are a model of constant and never-ending improvement.

To Graham and Connor, for being such good sports about the time and attention needed to write, re-write, edit, and discuss this book.

Introduction

From Cami

Earlier this year, I spoke to a class at my alma mater—McGeorge School of Law, in Sacramento, California. I was speaking to an evening class, taught by adjunct professors—prominent attorneys in Sacramento, one of whom was a sole practitioner; the other had spent his career in a large firm. The class was called "The Business of Lawyering" and its purpose was to teach attorneys how to open and run a successful law practice. I spoke that night on Communication Skills and Trust-Building Skills for attorneys. These are skills you will find within the pages of this book. These are skills I teach at law firms and bar associations throughout the state of California. When I graduated from McGeorge in 1991, no such class was offered.

As I walked out of the class with the professors, one of them said to me, "Law schools make lawyers. They don't make anything else. And that's a problem."

The truth is that when you leave law school, you are only prepared to research, write, and argue. You are only prepared to practice law. You aren't prepared to open your own office. You aren't prepared for the conflict that comes with litigation. You aren't prepared for the long hours expected of you as an associate. Tools not taught in law school include communication skills, interpersonal skills, trust-building with clients and other counsel, time management skills, stress management, and life-balance skills. Yet to be successful in this high-stress line of work, all of these skills are necessary.

When I left law school in 1991, I had a hard time finding a job. In Sacramento at that time, there was an abundance of attorneys looking for work. To make ends meet while I was job hunting, I took on independent contract work. As weeks turned to months and I paid my bills through contracting with other attorneys and law firms to provide research and writing, I came to find that I had a freedom not experienced by my colleagues who were working as associates for law firms. Eventually, I stopped looking for a "real job," and I continued working as a contract attorney. I built a successful business working for other attorneys in small and mid-sized firms. I continued in this business for sixteen years. At times, my contract was to work for several weeks in a law office out of town. I quickly realized that was not for me. Many times, my contract included preparing for, and participating in, trial or arbitration, which meant that I worked very long days. I really enjoyed this work, but when trial ended, I realized each time, I would not want to do this work full time. By paying attention to how I felt and how much I valued freedom and down time, I invented a job that worked very well for me. I kept steady hours, working from home, Starbucks, or the law library.

When, after sixteen years, I became trained as a business coach, I decided I would like to coach attorneys. The main reason I made this choice was from my experience practicing with colleagues who were unhappy, burned out, and overworked. I realized that I had created a way to practice law that worked for me. I always had time for myself and my family. Thus I realized, "practicing law does not have to be hard." And I came to develop my theory of accountability in the practice of law—we each get to decide how hard we want to work and how many hours we want to put in. If you don't like what you are doing, do something else. There are many more ways to approach your practice than you ever could imagine.

And so my goal in coaching attorneys, and in writing this book, has been to bring tools, ideas and skills to attorneys to assist them in practicing in their own way—the way that is most fulfilling for each individual attorney. For in the end, when we feel good about what we are doing, our work is better, our health is better, and our family life is better. A happy, satisfied, fulfilled attorney is simply a better attorney.

But remember this—a tool is just a tool. You might buy a computer to draft documents. But if you don't learn how to use the computer—and actually use it—nothing will get drafted. The same is true with this book. It is full of tools. The way you use them involves opening your mind to a different way and putting the tools in practice. So open the box and read the instructions—learn to use the computer.

Capture your success,

Cami

From Stephanie

When Cami approached me and said she wanted to write a book about coaching for attorneys, and she asked for my help, I was excited. I always wanted to be a writer, but then decided to channel those energies into law-and-motion work and appellate briefs. So being part of an actual book intrigued me.

What was especially compelling about this book, and why I was able to make an effective contribution, is that it addresses a subject more attorneys need to embrace to enhance their practices: coaching. Coaching has greatly improved my practice and my life. I personally have employed several different coaches during my career, and I have seen first-hand the positive changes I have been able to make. Through coaching, I have been able to reach new and different levels in my practice. Coaching has helped me add balance to my life and efficiency and effectiveness to my practice.

My part in this has been to provide real-life examples based on my experience in practicing law and interacting with many different attorneys over my almost twenty-year legal career. What I have seen in the legal profession during that time is that most lawyers are harried, stressed-out, and overwhelmed. There is always too much to do and not enough time to do it. Many of us feel like hamsters in a wheel, running as fast as we can and never getting anywhere. For litigators (like me), the entire job is marked by conflict: conflict with the courts, opposing counsel, and often even our own clients. Lawyering is one of the few professions in which conflict is not only the norm, but often the goal. I see people whose desire to "win" exacts a great toll on their personal lives and their health. And yet the vast majority of attorneys I know and meet are good, hard-working people who strive to make a difference, and who went into the profession with the desire to help people. I saw this book as a way to help them. And it helped me in the process.

I am proud to have been a part of this book. The teachings are invaluable. Putting them to use is the key. There will always be unreasonable opposing counsel, over-demanding clients, and judges who just don't seem to "get it." But by reading this book and implementing the practices herein, you are taking a huge step toward taking control of your life, your practice, and your part in our honorable profession.

Enjoy,

Stephanie

Chapter 1

How to Use This Book or "Taking a Stand"

I. How to Use This Book

Congratulations! If you are reading this book, you are already demonstrating a commitment to practicing law in a new and innovative way that will respect who you are as a person; that will bring excellence to your practice, balance to your life; and that will ultimately have you feeling better and working more productively!

Just some notes as you prepare for your journey: For the most part, you can skip around and read the chapters in whatever order seems appropriate to you. These chapters are largely designed to stand alone. Some chapters may refer to other chapters, in which case you may want to read them in conjunction with one another.

Interspersed with the material are brief case studies. These will be in boxes, separate from the text. The purpose of these case studies is to provide real-world examples of how to use the tools. Additionally, near the beginning of each chapter, there will be a list of reasons to read that particular chapter and/or sample scenarios that set forth examples of the types of situations that would benefit from applying the tool(s) presented in that chapter. In this way, you will be able to quickly see which chapters will be most useful to you, depending on what challenges or situations you are facing at any given time.

We wrote this book together, utilizing Cami's expertise as a performance coach, having spent many years coaching attorneys, and Steph's experience as a practicing attorney—first as an associate in a law firm and then as a sole practitioner and later with an associate and staff. For clarity, we write in the first person plural, that is, "we." When we wish to distinguish ourselves for purposes of sharing experiences, we specify who is speaking by writing either "*Steph*" or "*Cami*." When you see this designation, you are reading a personal experience written by one of us.

This book is based on the following principle: *commitment shows up in action.* If you want to create change, you need to be committed to creating change. That means taking action. Simply put, if you want to create change you **must** take action. Many people believe they can create change by wishing for change and hoping for it and talking about it and thinking about it. But change is only created by taking action. Throughout this book you will find ways not only to become self aware and discover where you are, but tools to use and actions to take to create the change you want. If you want to create change for yourself, take the action steps. Very little will change if you read this book and love everything in it and think about it and recommend it to all your friends, but take no action. Change will occur for you only if you act on what you have learned.

If you have decided to act upon what you learn here, congratulations and buy a notebook! Dedicate this notebook to your exploration of your life as an attorney. Use it to do the exercises in the book and to journal and reflect as you take this journey. Use it to make promises to yourself in order to take action and move forward.

Let's get started. Our first tool is noticing "drift" and taking a stand. You will need to do this in order to make change in your practice. Noticing your drift and the drift of those you associate with is a fundamental starting point.

II. Taking a Stand

The Drift

Cami: I learned the concept of "the drift" from my mentor coach, Barbara Fagan.[1] I met Barbara in a leadership program in 2007, in a hotel conference room in San Francisco. I remember her standing in the middle of a carpet that had a pattern that looked a bit like a river with stones throughout. "We all have a drift," she said. And she elaborated, "We all have individual drifts, as well as collective drifts, such as family drifts, company drifts, and cultural drifts."

"The drift" is the norm—what occurs when we are not acting consciously and purposefully. It acts like a river pulling us along. We are always in the drift, whether it is our individual drift or a collective drift. The only way to make change is to figuratively take a stand. This requires consciousness. As Barbara stood in the middle of the carpet-river, she demonstrated by stepping on to one of the "stones."

"What is an example of someone who stood out of the drift?" she asked. I had just read Nelson Mandela's autobiography, *Long Walk to Freedom*. I offered him as an example, and she asked, "What was the drift he was dealing with?" After Mandela left prison, the black population in South Africa wanted him to run the country without his former oppressors. They wanted him to exclude the white South Africans from the government. Mandela made a values-based choice. His message was about inclusion. It always was—when he was fighting the government, when he was in prison, and continuing after his release. He

---

1.   Go to www.sourcepointtraining.com to learn about personal growth and coach trainings facilitated by Barbara and the phenomenal team of trainers at this company where I also received my coach training.

stayed in prison after he could have left as a stand for inclusion, and once blacks were in power, he remained a stand for inclusion. The way he rebuilt his country was to include all people, even those who had imprisoned him. This required him to take a powerful stand for inclusion against a strong "drift" on the part of his supporters for retribution.

Taking a stand requires courage and conviction and is a consciously-made choice that can have challenging ramifications. It is what I call a "values-based" decision. (See chapter 5 for a complete examination of values and how individuals and firms can learn and apply their values.)

Anthony

Anthony works in a small busy firm specializing in insurance defense litigation. When he started at the firm, he quickly learned that whenever a meeting was called, no one showed up until at least ten minutes after the time the meeting was scheduled to start. Many participants did not arrive until close to twenty minutes after the meeting was scheduled to start. When Anthony first started at the firm, what struck him was that no one ever mentioned the lateness, and the latecomers—even those arriving well after the meetings had begun—did not apologize or even mention their tardiness.

The "drift" in Anthony's firm is "we are all too busy to be on time; we are running as fast as we can; and we arrive as soon as we can." This is based on a belief/attitude that "we are doing important work and the work takes a lot of time."

Another interesting aspect of this community drift is that, since everyone is always late, there is no point in being on time. Anthony, normally a stickler for timeliness, noticed that he began to arrive late as well. As with any community drift, people begin to realize, consciously or not, that "I do not need to be on time because no one else will be." The result is conformity. The antidote would be to take a stand, to speak up, to bring it to light and talk about it. Instead, the most we hear is grumbling and complaining and even the complainers don't show up on time because it is "no use". This is the conversation of the drift.

Why it is Useful to Know Your Drift

The drift in a group fosters mediocrity. What might be possible in Anthony's firm if they began to examine their drift with regard to time and lateness?

The reason we believe *you* should know your personal drifts (and we all have several) is that they are detrimental to forward progress. They are also unconscious. Becoming conscious of them is the important first step. Being conscious of your drifts will allow you to notice when you are in them. Knowing when you are in them will allow you to take a stand when something is important to you and your drift is keeping you from getting it.

Cami: I tend to be a linear and analytic thinker. This can be a strength. But under pressure, my drift is to over-analyze and over-think and take too much time making decisions. Now that I know this about myself, I can catch myself when it happens and ask myself, "Have I analyzed this enough?," interrupting my tendency to overthink and choosing instead to act.

Steph: One of my drifts when I get under stress is to start talking loudly and quickly. In some situations, it causes people to pay attention to what I am saying. But it usually causes others to either stop listening or become anxious themselves. This gets in the way of my relationship with my clients, because when I am in this "drift," they are afraid to tell me if they don't understand what I'm saying. Often when I am in this drift, my clients do not feel like they can interrupt me. As a result, we do not always have clear communication. This drift therefore interferes with my ability to fully connect with my clients in a way that enables us both to be heard and understood by the other. I find it difficult to interrupt this drift, as it occurs when I am stressed and overwhelmed and thus not thinking very clearly. What helps is for me to stop talking, close my eyes, and take a deep breath. I find in that short moment, I am often able to quiet and slow my voice. In this way, I interrupt the drift so that I can hear my clients better, and I can speak in a way that they can better understand me.

How Can You Recognize Your Drift?

Because it is often easier to identify the group drift than your own, you may wish to begin by identifying the drifts of groups in which you are a member. If you belong to a group with a particular drift, you can be assured that you have it too, in one form or another. One way you can identify a group drift is by noticing the common non-working behaviors within the group.

Glossary of Terms

For purposes of this book, in order to look at results we generate, decisions we make, and our behaviors we employ, all without judgment, we will use the following terms:

Working: a behavior, decision, or choice that produces an outcome you desire.

Non-Working: a behavior, decision, or choice that produces an outcome you do not desire.

Note there is a Glossary at the back of this book with the coaching terms we use most often.

Cami: One of my clients shared that the drift in his firm was people did not take problems seriously. If he raised a serious issue, they would joke and laugh and walk away. The drift was to be dismissive of issues and act as if they did not matter. He realized this was getting in the way of their being able to discuss more serious firm issues and generate change.

I asked him, "How do you support this drift?" At first, he didn't see it. Then he said, "I guess sometimes I joke with them too. And I may act in a way that makes them think I want to joke around rather than be serious." He realized there is a time and a place for humor, and if he wanted others to take him seriously, he had to be more serious himself and take a stand out of the drift of turning everything into a joke. In this way, he discovered he had his own drift of using humor in challenging situations.

Mary

Mary is on the board of a non-profit. She notices that this group has a tendency to come up with good ideas during the meetings, but the group does not often follow through with their ideas. For example, when the group was planning a celebration for one of its departing members, and the topic was food, they discussed various alternatives, from having volunteers make food to paying a caterer, to certain places that might donate catering or provide it at cost. But when it came to actually calling the caterers, no one volunteered to do it, and the topic soon changed. Once the meeting ended, there was no action plan. Mary realized that she contributed to the drift in the group by not asking who would do the calling, or volunteering to do it herself. She also realized this occurs in her own life—that she very often has good ideas about her family, her practice, even herself, but fails to implement them. By observing the drift of the Board, she learned an important drift of herself that sometimes keeps her from accomplishing what she wants in her practice—talking about good ideas, but neglecting to follow through.

Chuck

Chuck is an officer of his local county bar association's family-law section. The group regularly holds meetings in which family-law attorneys can mingle and discuss their practices. He has noticed that very often these meetings turn into gripe sessions about clients and about how awful it can be to practice family law. Sometimes the complaining gets on Chuck's nerves, but very often he finds himself agreeing with what is said and adding to it by bringing up his own frustrations, often exaggerating to make his situation appear even worse than it is. Chuck notices this is a drift he has in other aspects of his life, often coming home complaining about traffic or the weather and making it seem worse than it really is. By looking at the drift of the bar association, he realized his drift is to complain rather than take action.

Patrick

Patrick has a wife and three kids. All five people love to talk and share their stories and experiences. Often, when one person is talking, the other four are either waiting for the speaker to be done so they can talk, or they are interrupting. With all five wanting to talk, it is rare that anyone listens. Patrick realizes that he is a part of this drift: while he is genuinely interested in his wife and kids, he is often only half-listening to them because he is waiting for his turn to talk. Patrick realizes he not only does this at home with his family, but with his friends, his clients, and opposing counsel. By noticing the drift in one environment, he learns about himself and sees that his drift carries over to other areas of his life—both personal and professional.

In all of our examples and case studies, the drifts—both collective and individual—result in non-working behaviors that lead to unwanted results. Anthony's unwanted result is that he is often late to his appointments outside the office, when office meetings run over because people are not on time. Mary often does not act on good ideas, because she is waiting for someone else to take action. Chuck does not change many things, because his pattern is to complain instead. Patrick feels stressed around his family.

In order to make change, you must stand for what you want. If you say you want something to be different, but you do not take a stand for the change, the drift will carry you along, and nothing will change. This concept is the first chapter in this book because it is a fundamental precept to which we will refer throughout this book. We will suggest many places in which you can make change in order to have the practice you want and the life you want. In this book, we will offer you the opportunity to create awareness of yourself and your behaviors, and will offer you the tools to make changes. But *you* will need the courage and the commitment to make those changes. This will require you to honestly look at yourself and at your communities so you can take a stand and pull yourself out of the drift. As such, it is valuable now—as you are getting started—to recognize as many of your drifts as possible. As you move forward in this process and put new practices in place, you will discover even more of your personal drifts.

By definition, you are where you are due to a prevailing drift. Why is it that so many children are brilliant and resourceful but if they grow up in families that do not value education, they often will not use their brilliance to get an education and break out of the pattern? This is because the prevailing drift in their families is that education is not important; it is secondary to other things like working or having leisure time or taking care of family. In these families, those who do decide to stay in school and go to college and even graduate school must take a very strong stand because consciously or unconsciously the family will often be trying to pull them back into its drift. In fact, in such families, the one bucking the drift may be the butt of jokes or their families will consciously or unconsciously put obstacles in their path toward an education. When you realize that where you are in life is largely due to the prevailing drift around you, you will also realize that you *cannot* make change comfortably—you must go against the flow.

Picture the drift as the flow of the current. Your group is in the river together, floating downstream with the current. This creates a level of comfort. If one person decides to make a change, it will create resistance ("waves" in the river). There is thus a tendency for the others to want to pull the person back in. And there is a tendency for that person to want to get back in and be surrounded by the others. This is why the collective drift can be so powerful: in order for change to be "comfortable," everyone would have to make it at once. And this is highly unlikely. Change is uncomfortable. You may as well get used to it.

The General Community Drift of Lawyers

After surveying and interviewing many lawyers and making our own observations about lawyers and law firms, we have noted many recurring drifts. Below are examples of drifts that often prevail in law firms and for individual lawyers. Obviously, this is very general and does not apply to all lawyers or all firms. The prevailing drifts in many legal communities include the following:

- Practicing law is hard
- Practicing law takes a lot of time; you will never be caught up and certainly not ahead
- If you have any spare time, it should be filled with completing at least one more task
- If you have any spare time, you are not working hard enough
- Your own fulfillment is secondary to that of the client or the firm
- Stress—sometimes debilitating, I-can't-cope-with-this stress—is just part of the job
- It's OK to be late for meetings, depositions, anything but court
- Everything is urgent
- There isn't enough time to explain fully to associates and staff what senior attorneys need
- There isn't enough time to plan a strategy for a complex case
- If I am not nervous and worried, I am not doing a good job
- If I take a break from work to eat my lunch, I am wasting time and probably not committed to my job
- If my desk is clean and organized, I don't have enough to do
- Working on the weekend is expected, a good thing, and shows you are committed to your job

What do you recognize in your firm? In yourself? Where does this drift get in your way? Where are you taking a stand? Where do you want to take a stand?

We will warn you now (and many times later) that making change in the legal community requires a strong stand.

Cami: When I first began my coaching practice with attorneys, I had a phrase on my fliers that said, "practicing law doesn't have to be hard." And one of my former bosses said to me, "Yes it does. If you do it right, it is hard." I have never heard a truer statement of the lawyer drift. It is a drift many of us are very committed to. If you are not open to the idea that practicing law can be fulfilling, that you could have time for other aspects of life, that you could remain connected to your family and have time for yourself, you should put this book down. Change requires a strong stand. As you change and bring change to your firm, you may encounter resistance. It's just the drift, the status quo. Don't let it stop you.

Conclusion

The reason most self-help books do not sustain lasting change is because they are considered a "good idea" but there is no "call to action." In other words, there is no way to internalize and effectuate lasting change. One of the benefits of hiring a coach is having someone who will assist you in internalizing the concepts behind real change and applying them to your life and business in a way that creates lasting change. If you were to hire Cami as your coach, one thing she would do is *challenge you.* Throughout this book we will challenge you. Short of hiring a coach, the best way to internalize these concepts is to read this book and do the exercises. These exercises are designed to help you internalize the concepts by *using the concepts.* The best way to get maximum results from this book is to do more than simply read it. Use this book as your coach. Take each challenge that we lay down. Here is our first challenge to you—be committed and take this on in earnest. Some ideas are:

1. Buy a journal and do all of the exercises in this book;
2. Spend time regularly with the book and the exercises, perhaps at a certain time every day;
3. Bring these ideas into your firm;
4. Get a group of attorneys and work on the book together, creating an accountability system where each of you promises to make at least one change or try a new tool each week, and report back to the group. Accountability is one of the greatest benefits of hiring a coach. You can get this benefit in a group if you are committed to truly holding one another accountable in a rigorous manner. Sure, you can be compassionate, and you should, but do not let people slide! It does not serve them.

Start with the homework below and embark on the journey!

Homework

1. **What is your firm drift? How do you know? In order to discover, ask yourself the following questions and journal the answers:**
   a.   What is not working in this system?
   b.   What bothers me most about this group of people?
   c.   What bad habits do we all share?
   d.   When we take on a project together what typically gets in our way/slows us down?

2. **What is your family drift? How do you know?**
   a.   What is not working in this system?
   b.   What bothers me most about how we are in our family?
   c.   What bad habits do we all share?
   d.   When we take on a project together what typically gets in our way/slows us down?

3. **What are your own personal drifts?**
   Hint: Look at the previous two questions for ideas. Keep a list of your personal drifts on a few pages in your journal. Add to this list as you discover more. This is not an exercise in beating yourself up. It is an exercise in creating awareness. Be kind to yourself and be curious about yourself. In the chapter on accountability we discuss the concept of neutrality. You may want to read that now. Neutrality is very important when asking yourself what traits you possess that sabotage you.

4. **Talk to someone in one or more of your groups about "drift."**
   Teach them the concept (if you can teach it, you will also learn it). Ask them what they see as the prevailing drifts in this group. Ask yourself if this is also your personal drift. If so, add it to your list.

Chapter 2

What Do You Want From This Book? Creating a Well-Formed Outcome

"You have brains in your head. You have feet in your shoes. You can steer yourself in any direction you choose. You're on your own. And you know what you know. You are the guy who'll decide where to go."
Theodore Geisel, aka Dr. Seuss, *Oh, the Places You'll Go*

Why Read This Chapter?

1. You are going to read this book and you want to be intentional and purposeful in getting something useful from the experience.
2. You do not set well-defined goals in your business and you would like to start, but you're not sure how.
3. At the end of each year, you wonder how you got the results you have. Can you improve them? Can you replicate them? You realize you are not being intentional about getting what you want in your business.

John

John has been working entirely too much lately. He has not been sleeping enough, has not been exercising at all, and has not seen his family as much as he would like. At first, he kept waiting for projects to be finished so he could take a break, but that does not appear to be happening any time soon. He is nervous about talking to the senior partner about his problem, as he is concerned the firm will look down on him for not being able to keep up and that it will affect his pay and possibly his job security.

Rita

Rita hates her job. She cannot stand being a litigator. She hates the long hours, can't stand the confrontational nature of litigation, and is too stressed out to really enjoy life. The problem is that the pay is excellent and she has "rewarded" herself for a job she hates by living a fairly lavish lifestyle. She is not sure what to do and not even sure what she wants.

Tony

Tony's firm is downsizing, and he is the low man on the totem pole. He has been practicing for several years and believes he has enough of a grasp on the law to open his own practice, but the thought terrifies him. He is afraid he will not be able to get and sustain a client base, that he will not understand (or want to deal with) the business aspects of running his own firm, and he wonders if he is enough of a self-starter to work diligently and productively without a boss.

Introduction

What is intention? Webster's Dictionary defines it as "attention;" "a plan of action;" "an aim that guides action; the import, significance, or thrust of something." Synonyms include aim, design, end, goal, intent, meaning, plan, point, purpose, target, and view. Intentional means "deliberately done." Much has been written on the concept of intention, as it has come recently to be seen as a power that we bring to bear on what we want to accomplish—something unseen that fuels our actions. For now, know this: in order to have what you want, you must be intentional. You will not accidentally fall into your goals. And to be intentional, you must know what your goals are. The more clearly defined are your goals, the greater the opportunity to be fully intentional and to manifest them in the shortest period of time.

Well Formed Outcome, or "WFO," is a concept described and explored in the study of Neuro-Lingusitic Programming, or "NLP." In essence, NLP is the study of how human thought, language, and behavior shape our reality. One of the most important concepts, especially in the realm of coaching, is that people can change how they perceive and react to various events through simple processes. Cami is a trained and certified NLP practitioner, and many of the concepts and practices in this book have their origins in NLP.

As we explained in the beginning, this book is designed to be interactive. You will get the most value out of this book by doing the work in both writing and action. We don't change things in our lives by thinking about them; we change things in our lives by doing something different. Reading the words in the book and even understanding the concepts will not be enough to create significant change. So take time with this chapter—it may be the most important thing you do in this book. Figure out what you want. You picked up this book for a reason. Take some time to think about that reason and then sit down with this chapter and answer the questions below. Unique to this chapter, there will be questions to answer throughout, not just homework at the end. So let's get started!

What Do You Want From This Book?

"Would you tell me, please, which way I ought to go from here"
"That depends a good deal on where you want to get to," said the cat.
"I don't much care where..." said Alice.
"Then it doesn't matter which way you go," said the cat.

Lewis Carroll, Alice in Wonderland

If you don't know what you want from reading this book, then you may not get what you want. The same is true in all areas of life: if you don't set out with a plan or an intention, you will get whatever you get. If you become clear about what you want and articulate it, then reading this book will be an intentional experience. You will actively move toward your goal, with ownership for achieving it. This is distinct from waiting to see what arrives. If you hired Cami as your coach, she would ask you what you want. If you said, "I don't know," she would assist you in finding out *before* starting a coaching relationship. Approach this book as if it was a coaching relationship. The WFO is a map. It specifies your destination. There is a difference between getting in your car and driving wherever the road takes you and getting in your car with the intention of arriving in

Texas. The general intention of going to Texas is also distinct from the intention of going to a specific town in Texas. The WFO is designed to determine your specific destination before you start driving.

Anything you want, in any area of your life, can be hastened by the use of a WFO. Our minds are wired to look for answers. Our minds are very powerful. We automatically spend our energy on whatever has our attention. As such, it is useful to consciously decide where to place our attention; this is a way to harness that power and consciously put your energy toward your dreams. This is an intentional way to approach life, as opposed to the lackadaisical way we often come at it. Many times in life we wait to see what will happen, and then react to it. Sometimes we have the courage to *want* or *wish* or *hope* for something; it is rare that we *intend* something. Deciding specifically what we want is a powerful tool and always the best place to start. The more precisely and positively you can define what you want, the more you program your brain to seek out and notice possibilities, and the more likely you are to get what you want. Opportunities exist when they are recognized as opportunities. (O'Connor & Seymour, *An Introduction to NLP.*)

So let's start here. Where do you want to be in your practice? We recognize this is a pretty broad question. If you are having a hard time deciding what you want, here are some thoughts to get you going:

1. What could be improved in your practice?

_____

_____

2. What opportunities are there for you to increase effectiveness in communication with staff, opposing counsel, spouse?

_____

_____

3. What could be improved in the areas of work/life balance?

_____

_____

4. What is possible in terms of growing your practice?

_____

_____

5. Are you clear which area suits you best?

_____

_____

6. Are you looking for a different type of a career?

_____

_____

Once you have an idea of the area, or areas you want to work on, we can begin the process of developing your WFO. There are several basic elements to creating your WFO. Here are a few:

1. What do you want?
2. When do you want it?
3. How will you know when you have it?
4. What is the time-frame for achieving your outcome?

See the inset box for an outline of the entire process. Details are provided below.

Well-Formed Outcome

1. What do I want?
   - Picture what it will be like for you. Describe it in great detail. What do you see and feel when you think about it? Now describe it in writing.
2. How will I know when I have what I want?
   - What will I see?
   - What will I hear?
   - What will I feel?
3. Context—where, when, and with whom do I want it?
4. Is my outcome a large global outcome or is it of manageable size?
5. What is the timeframe for all my outcomes?
6. Why do I want my outcomes?
   - Why?
   - What will having this outcome get me?
7. Ecology
   - What would I have to give up to achieve my outcome?
   - What activities might I have to let go? (External)
   - What relationships might I have to drop or change to have my outcome? (External)
   - What beliefs are in the way of having my outcome fully? (Internal)
   - What attitudes do I need to change or let go of? (Internal)
8. How will I get it? Action Plan:
   - External resources I need?
   - Internal resources I need?
   - External resources I have?
   - Internal resources I have?
   - All of the actions I have already taken toward my WFO?
   - Future Pace
   - What is my first step?

Now let's break down the WFO process.

1. What do I want?

"When you are clear, what you want will begin to show up in your life, and only to the extent you are clear."

Janet Attwood, co-author of The Passion Test

First, you must state *what you want.*

State it in the positive. Take a moment now and state your goal. Very important: state it in the form of what you DO want rather than what you do NOT want. Our subconscious minds do not respond to the word "don't" or "not." This is why when, we are focusing on NOT spilling our coffee or NOT falling down, we get exactly what we don't want: our brains are focused on spilling coffee or falling down.

We get what we focus upon. If we state our goals in terms of what we do not want, we are focused on the problem. When we state our goals in terms of what we do want, we are focused on the solution, the path ahead. When we focus on what we DO want, we start to see it much more clearly, and as a result, we begin to see the opportunities arising to obtain what we want.

For example, imagine that my office is cluttered and this is beginning to really bug me. So I focus on the thought, "I HATE clutter and the office is driving me crazy." Every day I come in to my office, and I say "Oh my goodness, this is awful, how can I live like this, work like this; this clutter is driving me nuts!" And I continue to focus on it in this way. What do I want? To be *clutter*-free. Not to have such a *mess*. Not to have to look at *all this stuff*! Notice how the central object in each statement, which has all the emotion in it, is the clutter, the mess, the stuff—exactly what I DON'T want. But if we get what we focus upon, then is it any surprise the clutter only continues and gets worse?

When I work with my coach, she will ask me the following questions. Answer these for yourself:

1. What *do* I want?

_____

_____

2. Close your eyes and picture what it will be like for you. Describe it in great detail. What do you see and feel when you think about it? Now describe it in writing.

_____

_____

Cami: Now I begin to get a sense of what I want: I want my office to be neat and tidy. This is the goal ahead. Now, instead of focusing on the clutter and how I trip over files when I walk around my office, I can picture the floors clear, maybe some additional shelving, a desk that I can actually see. Now I can move to the next piece: describing it.

Note: It's okay if the biggest thing in your mind is what you don't want. This is a fine starting point. Many of us find it much easier to identify what we don't want. But in order to move forward, we must identify what forward is. If you are stuck on what you don't want, here is another exercise to determine what you want: List in great detail what you don't want and why you don't want it. Write it all out on the left side of a piece of paper. Then draw a line down the middle of the paper and for every point on the "don't want" side, make a corresponding entry on the right side where you describe in detail the opposite of what you don't want. When you are done with this process, it is important that you cross out all the entries of what you don't want. Now you know what you want!

2. How will I know when I have what I want? (State it in Sensory-Terms.)

The next step is to state your outcome in sensory-based terms—what will you see, hear, and feel when you have it? You may also ask what will you smell and taste, if that is appropriate.

Using the above example—a clean office—and focusing on what I *do* want, I start to SEE open spaces, additional shelving, storage containers, labels, organized and free space; I start to FEEL peace and relaxation and energy to start my workday; and I can HEAR in my head an internal conversation of pleasure and satisfaction, as well as my even footfall across a tidy room.

Now think about how you will know when you have what you want from reading this book. What will you see, hear, and feel? It can be useful to close your eyes and imagine actually having it. The more fully you imagine and describe your outcomes, the more your brain can rehearse it and notice opportunities to achieve it. It is useful to commit what you want to writing. Remember: we get what we focus on. The more you state what you want, write it down, and talk about it, the more you will focus on and move toward it. Be very specific and detailed in your description. Likely there will be a physical sensation as you describe it in specific detail, as your mind and body begin to experience having what you want. This is another NLP premise—imagination and memory run the same neural pathways. Imagining in detail affects our brain and body as if we already have what we want. This will further assist your brain in seeing opportunities to move toward what you want.

1. How will I know when I have what I want?

_____

_____

2. What will I see?

_____

_____

3. What will I hear?

_____

_____

4. What will I feel?

_____

_____

3. Context—where, when, and with whom do I want it?

Now is the part where you describe the context of your WFO, including where this outcome takes place, when it occurs, and with whom you share it. Thus, as you are describing the outcome you want, be sure to answer these questions as well:

1. **Where will I be when I have it?** (For example: I will be at work, in my firm when I have my clean office.)

---

2. **When do I want to have it?** (For example: I want to have it within one week.)

---

3. **Who will be involved?** Perhaps I need to enlist others. Perhaps I will ask my spouse to agree to my spending time cleaning on the weekend; or I will hire an organizer; or ask my secretary to hold my calls for part of the day. This is beginning to get into the "how" but it is useful to consider on a superficial level, without creating intricate plans at this point, who might be involved. This will give you a higher level of specificity in your description.

---

4. Ask yourself any other questions that will assist you in painting a very clear and specific picture. (For example, what practices will I need to put in place to keep order in those sections once I tidy them up, and to keep them tidy?)

---

4. Is my outcome a large global outcome or is it of manageable size?
"The secret of getting ahead is getting started. The secret of getting started is breaking your complex, overwhelming tasks into small, manageable tasks, and then starting on the first one."
Mark Twain

It is important to look at the "chunk size" of your outcome. "Chunking" is another NLP concept that describes the size of the task ahead, and whether it may or should be broken into smaller tasks of more manageable sizes. For example, if your goal is to have a firm with ten associates, and it is currently just you, this might be too big a chunk size for you. Chunk size is an individual thing, and you will know if it is too big because the outcome will feel daunting, and your energy will wane when you think about working on it. By the same token, if your chunk size is too small, you may lose motivation.

It is fine to have a large goal, just as it is fine to eat an entire steak. But to eat the steak, you will need to cut it into bite-size pieces. Depending on how you like to eat, you may be more comfortable with big bites or smaller ones. Too big and you can choke. Too small and the steak is unsatisfying. In this way, if your WFO feels too big, you can employ this NLP technique of "chunking down."

If you have as your ultimate goal a firm with ten associates, it may be that you wish to chunk that down to hiring one attorney and one secretary as a first step. On the other hand, if hiring one attorney and one secretary is your long-term goal, you can chunk that down to (1) consistently generating a certain amount of money; (2) growing your client base; and (3) perhaps hiring someone on an independent contractor basis. When it begins to feel easy and doable, then you know that you have chunked down sufficiently. Then your next question becomes what is the first step?

How do you feel about the ease or difficulty of achieving your goal? Is it too big? If yes, how can you chunk it down? In other words, what are some of the steps along the way to your ultimate goal, your WFO?

_____

_____

After chunking, think about how each piece feels. If it still feels too daunting, then chunk down further. In the end you will have a list of many of the elements of your goal.

Cami: For instance, with my office-cleaning example, I may have the following "chunks":

A. Get out my calendar and block the time to do it—half hour per day feels doable.
B. Ask my spouse if he or she is okay with me taking time on certain weekends to clean my office.
C. Spend my first half hour chunk of time looking at the office and making a list of what needs to be done and the order in which I want to do it.
D. Use my blocked time on one section at a time. Perhaps my first goal is to install shelving. Another may be to contact a storage facility or shredding company. And so on.

5. What is the time frame for all of my outcomes?

Perhaps your outcome is to increase the amount of money you make. Be very clear about the specific amount and *by when*. How much money do you want to bill this month? Next month? The next fiscal year? Remember the more precise you are, the easier it will be to achieve your outcome.

By when do I want each outcome complete?

1. _____

2. _____

3. _____

4. _____

6. Why do I want my outcomes?

"Efforts and courage are not enough without purpose and direction."

John F. Kennedy

Now you have thoroughly defined your "what", let's move on to *why*. "Why" is a critical piece to maintaining motivation.

Often, we spend time working toward a goal only to realize we are not truly committed to having it. When we lose energy to continue on our path toward a stated goal, it is usually because we realize it is not that important to us. Let's face it—our goals are often challenging and require dedication, energy, and commitment. The best way to maintain this energy and commitment is to have a compelling purpose. Why do you want to achieve your goal? When you articulate why you want it, how does it feel to you? Is it a good reason that resonates with your core and will sustain you over the long haul? If not, reconsider your goal. Find something you feel excited about.

Cami: Why do I want a clean office? If I realize that it is because I grew up with a mother who frequently reminded me of the importance of being neat, I may decide a clean office is not truly a big deal to me. On the other hand, if I ask why I want a clean office and I realize I can think better and my blood pressure lowers when my office is neat, this may be a very compelling reason.

For another example, if your outcome is to have ten associates working for your firm, ask yourself why you want it. It may turn out you want it because you consider "success" as a lawyer to mean having associates who work for you. Upon closer examination, you may realize this definition of success is not really important to you. If you realize up front that this is your reason, you may find that it will not keep you motivated in the long run. If, however, you want associates because you have a lot of work and you love working with others and you want to build a practice that serves many people, this will be your motivation moving forward. If that feels powerful and motivating as a purpose, it will give you the energy to keep moving toward your goal.

Why do I want my outcomes?

_____

_____

To help you identify purpose, you might also ask, what will having this outcome get you? Knowing what you are really after is also valuable in giving you the energy to move forward. What is your ultimate purpose in achieving this outcome? Make sure your outcome is worthwhile—that is, something that truly has a useful, positive impact on your life whether directly or indirectly, by enhancing the lives of others around you.

Cami: Back to my office, when I ask why do I want this outcome, I believe that it will make me feel good when I arrive to work; I will be able to find things easily and quickly; and I will want to spend more time in my office. These are compelling reasons for me.

What will having this outcome get me?

---

7. Ecology

Ecology is another NLP concept that looks at all aspects of one's life, and assumes there is a reason why you do not yet have what you want. The concept of ecology presumes that the reason you do not have what you want is that you would have to give something up to have it or that you believe (rightly or wrongly, consciously or unconsciously) that some area of your life would be adversely affected by the change.

Is there is any part of you not aligned with the desired outcome? Look at all areas of your—your time, money, physical health, relationships with others. The concept of ecology is that our lives work as a whole. Ecology in NLP is the study of the impact that any personal change has on the wider system. It is particularly useful to look at this impact in making any change, as it is important to consciously recognize the consequences for self, family, society, and planet.

For example, let's say you want to make more money and expand your client base. You may believe the way to do this is to work more hours. You may also fear this will impact your family life, your leisure time, possibly your health, and your social life. You may not make it home for dinner, or may need to push dinner back by an hour, which will impact when your children go to bed. Now you realize why you may not have been actively pursuing more money and clients: whether consciously or unconsciously, you believed you would have to work more, and that would adversely affect other areas of your life. Once you look at the ecology of your life, you can consciously determine how to go about increasing revenue and client base. You may choose to raise your rates or hire an associate. And if you do decide to work more, you can consciously decide when and where you perform this additional work. In the end, looking at the ecology of your life enables you to become aware of the potential impact a new outcome may have on your life, which in turn enables you to make conscious choices to more effectively create your desired result.

What would you have to give up to obtain your outcome? This could be external (activities, relationships) or internal (beliefs or attitudes). Let's go back to the attorney who wants to hire ten associates. Why hasn't she done so yet? Upon looking at ecology, she may realize she does not want to give up her independence and control. Or she may realize she is scared about her immediate cash flow as she takes this next step. Or she may have some deep-seated beliefs about attorneys with ten associates that she has never explored or even consciously admitted to herself, which prevents her from achieving this outcome. (These beliefs and fears are examples of what she may have to give up internally.) This doesn't mean she cannot move forward toward this goal. On the contrary, this examination will help her move toward her goal, as it will illuminate potential obstacles to achieving it and allow her to consciously work around them.

Cami: Going back to the example of cleaning my office, when I look at ecology, I may see that in order to achieve my goal of having a neat and tidy office, I would need to give up some leisure time or family time to work on the project. Or I might be concerned that I would have to rid myself of old files or books that I no longer need or use, but that I am concerned I may need after I dispose of them. (These are examples of what I may have to give up externally.) Looking at ecology will assist me to either consciously move toward getting what I want or consciously decide, given all the ramifications, I am not going to go after it.

In looking at the ecology of attaining your WFO, answer these questions:

1. What would you have to give up to achieve your outcome?

_____

_____

2. What activities might you have to let go? (External)

_____

_____

3. What relationships might you have to drop or change to have your outcome? (External)

_____

_____

4. What beliefs are in the way of fully achieving your outcome? (Internal)

_____

_____

5. What attitudes do you need to change or let go of? (Internal)

_____

_____

One of the benefits of looking at changes you want to make within the ecology of the system is that you get to be clear on what will be affected. Each part of a system affects all the other parts. Knowing in advance what parts will be affected, and how, will not only give you a clearer picture of what it will be like to actually attain your WFO, but also ideas of how to go about attaining your goal.

8. How will I get it? Action plan

"Be daring, be different, be impractical, be anything that will assert integrity of purpose and imaginative vision against the play-it-safers, the creatures of the commonplace, the slaves of the ordinary."

Sir Cecil Beaton, English photographer and costume designer

Define Your Action Plan

Now that you have fully defined *what* you want and *why* you want it, we will begin discussing *how* you will get your outcome. It is important to note the order in which we have approached this. It is most effective to determine *what* and *why* before asking yourself *how*.

One of the reasons that many projects never get off the ground is because we begin by asking "How am I going to do this?" before we are clear on *what* we want to do and *why* we want to do it. Use this method on any type of undertaking—always ask yourself, "*What* do I want (outcome) and *why* do I want it (purpose)" ***before*** asking "*How* will I get it." Beginning with *how* can lead to a sense of overwhelm and expending time on a project you are not really committed to.

Now we will create a list of what needs to happen and what are your next steps.

a. What resources do I need?

One of the most powerful things people learn through coaching is that they are completely resourceful, lacking nothing. There is an NLP presupposition that states, "People already have all the resources they need. What they lack is access to these resources at appropriate times and places." Recognizing you are completely resourceful is a first step to accessing your resources. The job of a coach is to ask questions that allow you to access your resources—to see them, discover them, remember them, and uncover them. A resource can be internal or external. An internal resource is confidence; an external resource is money. An internal resource is the answer to a question you ask silently within; an external resource is the answer to a question you ask out loud.

The question here is, what resources do you need to achieve your outcome? List all of the resources that you will need to achieve your outcome, both internal and external. Pay particular attention to resources that are dependent on others or which may not be easily attainable. For resources that are not available, find alternatives that will serve your purposes in achieving your outcome.

Obviously, one of your resources is this book. Another may be time. Others may include self-discipline, friends or associates with whom to brainstorm or discuss concepts, and the website (www.mclarencoaching.com/bookdownloads/) we have created to support you in moving through the book. What else do you need?

External resources I need:

1. _____
2. _____
3. _____
4. _____

Internal resources I need:

1. _____
2. _____
3. _____
4. _____

b. What resources do I have?

Now create a list of resources you already have, so you can clearly see what you have now and what you will need to obtain.

External resources I have:

1. _____
2. _____
3. _____
4. _____

Internal resources I have:

1. _____
2. _____
3. _____
4. _____

c. What am I already doing to achieve my outcome?

You are already taking action. Just by reading this book and exploring the concepts and doing the work so far in this chapter, you are taking action. And if the WFO is one you truly desire and have desired for some time, you are likely already taking action toward it, some of which you may even be unaware. In moving consciously toward your goal, it is useful to assess what you are already doing. This has several benefits. It will help you build up speed when you see that you are already moving, it may generate a degree of self-confidence, and it may give you a higher level of energy when you think about creating your outcome. Actions you have already taken if you have been doing the exercises in these chapters include:

- Thinking about it (recognizing that turning your mind toward your desires sets a whole string of consequences into motion)
- Creating a mental plan (beginning to look at next steps)
- Creating a well-formed outcome (things in writing are already in process)
- Reading this book
- Doing the exercises
- What else are you already doing?

Write down all of the actions you have taken toward your WFO:

_____

_____

_____

d. Future Pace

Another way to create a list of steps is to visually imagine yourself at a point in the future having fully achieved your result. Take a moment now and close your eyes. Imagine you are one month, two months, a year down the road. You have completely achieved your outcome. Be in the picture experiencing the result as if you had it now. What do you see, hear, and feel? When you are fully in the experience of having your outcome, look back from that future moment in time and ask, "what did I do to get here?" Write down all the steps your future self can see were taken to get to the outcome.

Cami: For example, when I sit down and imagine my neat and tidy office, seeing what it looks like, feeling how I feel when it is exactly how I want it, I put myself in the future place of having what I want. Imagination is very powerful. When I fully imagine *having* my outcome as if I am experiencing it now, my mind begins to see *how* it can happen in a whole new way. Looking back from the vantage point of my clean office, I realize the steps I took included putting up additional shelving, revamping my filing system so that documents get filed in the appropriate file within twenty-four hours of receipt, purchasing (and using!) a heavy-duty shredder, and instituting a system whereby my desk is clear before I leave in the evening.

Now you try. Imagine your future outcome fully. Put yourself in that future experience. Then ask yourself, what steps did I take to get here? List them.

1. _____
2. _____
3. _____
4. _____

e. What is your first step?

From where you are standing today, what is the first step to take toward your goal? Go back to the lists you have created from the foregoing four sections—What resources do I need? What resources do I have? What am I already doing? and Stepping into the future—and decide what is your immediate next step.

Be sure your steps fit within the SMART goal framework. This framework is used to identify a next step, or goal, that is:

- **S**pecific
- **M**easurable
- **A**ttainable
- **R**isky in some way (a stretch for you)
- **T**ime-Specific

Consider your first step.

Is it specific? For example, "I will make $50,000 more by the end of the year" rather than "I plan to make more money".

Is it measurable? For example, "I will exercise 5 times this week for 30 minutes each time" rather than "I will exercise more".

Is it attainable? This does not mean: Is it easy? It means: Can it be initiated by you? Can it be controlled by you? Is it possible for you to do? It is not useful to create goals you know you probably cannot achieve or that require the actions of others over whom you have no control. But do not mistake this for "risky." While your goal should be attainable, it should also involve an element of stretching yourself.

Is it risky? You will not get what you want if you do not stretch yourself. Nothing can change when you are comfortable. Get outside your comfort zone—make sure you are stretching! How will you know? You may feel nervous, shaky, or scared. Some people call this the "big gulp." It does not have to be on the level of sky-diving, but it should make you uncomfortable. When you stay comfortable, you stay where you are.

Is it time-specific? For example, "I will clean the closets in my bedroom by Friday, November 11, 2011 at midnight PST" rather than "I will begin cleaning clutter in my home."

John's Well-Formed Outcome

1. What do I want?

I want more leisure time to spend exercising or with my family. I want to feel peace and less stress. I want to feel there are enough hours in the day and that I can manage what I have to do for work and still have a life.

2. How will I know when I have what I want?

- What will I see?

I will see the great outdoors as I am running each morning. I will see my kids awake when I get home at night. I will see my wife smiling as she sees me come through the door at a reasonable time.

- What will I hear?

I will hear excitement and love in the voices of my family. I will hear a voice in my head say "This feels better. You can get this done." I will hear silence as I spend time alone meditating or exercising outdoors.

- What will I feel?

I will feel a sense of peacefulness and contentment. I will feel that I can get everything done and there is a feeling of balance and harmony in my life.

3. Context—where, when, and with whom do I want it?

My goal is to have more leisure time. And to feel confidence that I can still get everything done. I will have the feeling at work (that I can manage all of this) and at home (that I have time to myself and to share with my family).

Time wise, I'd like to have this now, but I realize it may take some time to implement so I will choose a date 6 months down the road to have my outcome fully.

As to people, I realize when I am picturing my outcome that it will likely involve many people at my firm and my family as well. There may be others, but this is all I can think of at the moment.

4. Is my outcome a large global outcome or is it of manageable size?

It does feel pretty big—I think because I don't know how I will accomplish it. Maybe I could chunk it down by starting to have conversations with different people and brainstorming. I could talk to my wife and to other attorneys who seem to be able to manage their time better than me. I also feel that ultimately I will need to talk to someone at the firm. I fear it will be the senior partner and that this will not go well, but I am not going to make that plan right now. Maybe there are other people I could talk to at the firm. I will look around for other ideas first and leave this part until later.

John's Well-Formed Outcome (cont.)

5. What is the timeframe for all outcomes?
   - I want a sense of balance by 6 months from now.
   - I will talk to my wife this week.
   - I will begin to think about other people I can talk to this week.
   - I will talk to at least one other attorney within the next two weeks.

6. Why do I want my outcomes?
   - Why?

   I want my outcome because I feel out of balance and I do not feel fulfilled. I am also afraid that this pace of working is not sustainable and that it is having an adverse affect on my health and on my family relationships. I would like my life to feel fulfilling overall. I love my work. And I want to feel there is more to my life than just working. I want to stay in this job and I am afraid I won't be able to if I continuing going like this because I will feel too burned out.
   - What will having this outcome get me?

   I will feel peace. I will have a balanced life. I will continue to love my job and be satisfied in it. I will be more efficient in my job. I will feel more healthy and closer to my family. I will feel my life is working over all.

7. Ecology
   - What would I have to give up to achieve my outcome?
   - What activities might I have to let go? (External)

There might be some work I have to let go of. It might help me to reduce the number of hours I watch TV. I might need to let go of the time I spend on Facebook.
   - What relationships might I have to drop or change to have my outcome? (External)

   I may have to let go of my relationships at work. But I don't know this for sure. In fact, what I know is, it is this fear that has stopped me making changes so far.
   - What beliefs are in the way of having the outcome fully? (Internal)

   I notice several beliefs. I notice a belief that practicing law has to be hard—that it means I am a successful attorney because I leave early in the morning and arrive home late at night. I believe my boss will be mad if I talk to him about this.
   - What attitudes do I need to change or let go of? (Internal)

   I have an attitude that it can't be done—that I cannot be a successful attorney *and* have time for other things in my life.

John's Well-Formed Outcome (cont.)

8. How will I get it? Action Plan:
- External resources I need?
  - My wife's opinion and assistance.
  - Advice from those who have walked this road and seem to have balance in their lives.
  - Perhaps expert advice on how to do this.
  - Perhaps there are books written on this topic.
- Internal resources I need:
  - Being willing to try different things.
  - Commitment to having the result, meaning that I may have to redefine my idea of what is "success" for an attorney.
  - Courage to ultimately talk to people at the firm if that becomes necessary.
- External resources I have:
  - I have my wife.
  - I have a coach.
  - I have an exercise bike in my house.
- Internal resources I have:
  - I am a committed person.
  - I am willing to change my view on what it means to be successful.
  - I am dedicated to have this outcome.
- All of the actions I have taken toward my WFO:

I have hired a coach already. I have written out this WFO. I have spent a lot of time thinking about what I really want. I have started going to the gym once a week and coming home for dinner once a week.

- Future Pace

Imagine your future outcome fully. Put yourself in that future experience. Then ask yourself, what steps did I take to get here? List them.

- I took baby steps—little by little—adding something new I wanted to incorporate into my life every few weeks.
- I was patient.
- I collaborated with others who could help me.
- I never gave up.

John's Well-Formed Outcome (cont.)

- What is my first step?

From where I am standing today, what is the first step for me to take? Go back to the lists I have created from the foregoing four sections—What resources do I need? What resources do I have? What am I already doing? and Stepping into the future—and decide what is my immediate next step.

I think the first thing I will do is (1) talk to my wife and (2) find other attorneys to talk to about this. Regarding the SMART formula, both these steps are *specific*. They are *measurable* if I say that I will take specific action to talk to my wife and other attorneys and ask specific questions, such as how they have created time for themselves or for ideas how they think I could work towards balancing my life. They are *attainable*. They are a *stretch* (risky) for me in that it is a little scary to broach the topic with my wife. I feel nervous that she will complain about how things have been for her. I am also outside my comfort zone in admitting to others how hard this has become for me. I will talk to my wife this week and at least one other attorney within two weeks, so my goal is time-specific.

Homework

1. Congratulations! You have created a WFO for yourself. If you have done the exercises in this chapter as we have gone along, your homework is done! Take a break. If not, go back and do them now.
2. Go back and re-read all your answers and see if there is anything else to fill in.
3. Keep your WFO in a place you can refer to it easily. Refer to it often.
4. Think of another goal you have and apply this process to it.
5. Take this process to your team at work and do the process together for a team or firm goal.

Chapter 3

Accountability—Your Keys to the Kingdom

"Between stimulus and response, there is a space. In that space is our power to choose our response. In our response lies our growth and our freedom."

Viktor E. Frankl

Why Read This Chapter?

1. You feel helpless or powerless to create change in your firm or your practice.
2. You notice yourself increasingly blaming outside factors for the results you have (e.g., I didn't get it done because I was given other work; my secretary was too slow; the judge made us do additional briefing).
3. You want to create sustainable change in your practice and in your life.
4. You want things to be different and you don't see how to change them.
5. You want to feel empowered—that you can change things that aren't working for you.

Introduction

Conscious choice is the key to empowerment. We are *always* choosing. The question is whether we are choosing consciously or unconsciously. The more conscious you are in your choice-making, the more likely you are to get what you want.

Many attorneys experience a sense of futility. Often, "they have lost a sense of their own agency, the sense that their lives are theirs to make of what they will. So people who are among the most gifted and privileged in the world instead live with a sense of drastically constricted possibilities of what they can do with their lives." (Steven Keeva, *Transforming Practices* pp. 195–196 (1999) (ABA Journal book)).

For most people, the real dissatisfaction in their practice and in their lives comes from feeling powerless to get what they want or to change what they have. Most people feel more fulfilled, satisfied, and excited when they realize they have the power to create change in their practices and their lives. When you realize that you have many choices and then start to choose consciously, possibilities are revealed that you never recognized before. The key to seeing your choices and making them consciously is *accountability*.

Without an orientation toward accountability, you cannot create sustainable change. The tools and resources in this book will not be effective and will not create lasting change in any aspect of your life if you are not willing to be accountable for what you have and what you are creating in your life. This includes those things you like and those you don't. If you are going to use this book and its tools effectively, you must take ownership and responsibility for where you are and where you are going. Similarly, the tools won't work if you don't take responsibility for using them.

What is Accountability?

When you hear the word "accountability," what comes to your mind? For most people, it conjures up being criticized or "called on the carpet" or made to explain their mistakes and shortcomings. In the area of law, it often means liability or fault. But that is not how we are using this word.

We invite you to start fresh with this concept. Imagine you have never heard the word "accountable" or "accountability" and that it is a brand-new word with a brand new definition. Erase everything you know about this word and let's start from scratch.

Now, what is Accountability? It is:

- The key to empowerment
- The quickest way to learn from your mistakes and improve your effectiveness
- The ability to take ownership for your choices and your results and to move forward purposefully

Our definition is this: Accountability is the ability to account for the choices you have made and the results that you have. Accounting is a neutral term. When we talk about "the ability to account," think of it as an accountant might, as simple facts and figures. For example: $3 + 2 = 5$. If you consider a ledger or balance sheet, it holds numbers and facts. There is no right/wrong or good/bad. They are just numbers. Think about your choices this way. If you are "accounting for your choices," you are simply stating what is true. For example:

"I chose to wake up at 7:00 this morning."

"I chose not to eat breakfast."

"I chose to take the highway rather than surface streets to come to work."

"I chose to spend __ amount of time with my daughter today."

"I chose not to call you back."

Why do we want to account for our choices? Accountability is how we learn. It enables us to replicate the choices that worked and to make different choices in the future in place of those that didn't work. This is why we call it the "key to empowerment." It is the key to getting what you want.

Accountable vs. Victim

One way to understand accountability is to look at its opposite: victimhood. There is a spectrum, and we are all on it somewhere. The spectrum looks like this:

Accountable   *Victim*

Victimhood is blaming something outside yourself for your choices and results—the weather, your boss, the judge, the traffic, your childhood, your secretary, your spouse, your kids, etc. The opposite is accountability—you account for your choices—meaning you look at *yourself* to see where *you* made choices that work and that do not work. (See glossary for definitions of working and non-working.)

The process is simple: You have a result you don't want, so you look back in time and ask yourself, "What choices did I make such that I now have this result?" You can also do this with results you do like and that you want to replicate in the future. (See, for example, Joan box, page 44.)

It is important to remember to be as neutral and non-judgmental about yourself as possible when looking at your choices and results. Remember, this is a ledger. The results are simply numbers on the ledger. The choice to get up at 7:00 a.m. is not good or bad in and of itself, any more than 5 as a sum of 2 + 3 is good or bad. For some, 7:00 a.m. will be too early, and the result is feeling sluggish and tired all day. For others, it is too late and the result is missing a morning run or not being able to have breakfast with the family. For others it may net the perfect result: enough sleep and enough time to get to work. The trick is to see where your choices lead to results that either work for you or do not work for you, and to see where you can make either the same or different choices to get the results you want.

Before we go into examples of accountability and its opposite, let's explore why human beings generally tend not to be accountable. We live in a culture of blame. We learn early on in life that the best way to avoid trouble is to avoid making mistakes. We consider mistakes to be "bad" or to imply "fault." When a mistake is made, we look around to see who is "at fault." If you are the one who made the mistake, then you are the one at fault.

No one understands this better than an attorney, especially a litigator. The question is always who is at fault. The defendant who is at fault owes money; the plaintiff who has comparative fault sees his award reduced. The goal in litigation is to avoid any blame or fault. So the shift from avoidance of any "fault" to that of taking accountability may very well be a significant paradigm shift for you.

Examples

Tom is late to a meeting with a new client.

- **Victim stand:** "The traffic was awful. There was a terrible accident. I'm so sorry I am late. My kids couldn't find their homework. My spouse turned off my alarm clock. I am sorry. This always happens to me. I guess the gods are against me."
- **Accountable stand:** "I am late for this meeting. I notice as I look back over my morning, at the choices that led me here. I notice that I left at the very last moment. I realize I did not allow time for slow traffic. In fact, that is something I do quite often. I also did not check my alarm last night. I realize I have not set up a process where my kids can get out of the house easily. Starting now, I will leave 5 minutes early for everything and see if that helps. If it doesn't enable me to start being on time, I will make another change until I am easily arriving to my destination early and stress-free."

Notice the distinctions between the two:

1. The victim spends a lot of time apologizing. The victim also spends a lot of time apportioning "blame" and seeking to show he is not responsible for the result.
2. The accountable person realizes where his or her own choices led to the result and where he or she can make changes in the future. This is the true key to empowerment.
3. Of course there are circumstances outside you, such as traffic, that will interfere with your day. *But you cannot control them. Thus, it makes little sense to focus on them and wish they were different.* Empowerment comes from asking "What did I do?" and "What can I change in the future?" even when there were many other factors involved in my result.

The Foundation to Sustainable Change

You can take classes, learn tools, and read books, but the *only* way you can make and sustain the change you want is to take a very honest look at the choices you make and the actions you take. This is the foundation of change. It is similar to the foundation of a house. It is the basis on which all changes must rest. Empowerment is recognizing the power that you have to make change, and then choosing to use it. Victimhood is placing the power in someone or something else.

Always ask yourself: "Where am I placing my power?" If you point to something outside yourself, you will be unable to effect change.

What Are My Choices?

Accountability is about choice. It is the process of looking at the choices you made *and* at the various choices you had. For many people, the first step is to recognize that you *have* choices. Once you begin to recognize this, then you can start to see what your choices are. But you will not be able to see the choices that were and are available to you if, as a basic premise, you cannot see that you *have* choices. People often say, "I had no choice," when faced with a result they do not want. But that is a victim position. (It is also untrue.) The further toward "victim" you are on the above continuum, the less likely you are to see that you always have choices.

An Exercise—Learning to see Choices

As a preliminary step towards accountability, you must begin to see that you *always* have choices. You cannot do accountability work, learn from your mistakes, and make significant change until you see that you always have an *unlimited* number of choices.

In this exercise, we want you to get in the habit of asking yourself, "What are all the choices I have in this situation?" You may want to start with something simple like what you had for breakfast. Notice what you chose to have and notice all the things you chose not to have. Notice you *could* have chosen to eat something in your house, including cake or lunch meat; you could have eaten at a restaurant; you could have gone without breakfast. If your mind says, "No, I cannot eat cake; that is not healthy" or "No, I cannot eat out; I will be late for work," just notice this as the dialogue inside your head that makes you believe you don't have choices. Now say to yourself, "I can choose to have chocolate cake or go out for breakfast. And I am choosing instead to eat cereal at home this morning."

As you begin to think and speak this way, you will begin to see all the other choices you are dismissing without even considering them. It will expand your conscious awareness of *all* the choices you have. This is empowerment. When you realize that you always have choices—including "bad" ones like eating cake for breakfast—you will also start to see other choices that may be more workable, and you will have more and more options to choose from.

Put up a note on your bathroom mirror, in your car, somewhere—everywhere—to remind you to start asking, "What are all the choices I have right now?"

Start simple. When you come to a meeting: "I chose to sit in this chair. There are many other chairs I could have sat in. I could have stood in the corner or sat or lain on the floor or sat on the table or left the room." These are all choices, even if you hold a *belief* that they are not. For example, you may believe it is rude to sit on the table or stand against the wall, or that you cannot leave the meeting because important topics are being discussed or people will think poorly of you or your boss will be mad at you. Because you believe there would be negative consequences to a choice, you see it as *no choice.*

It is vital that you become aware of the choices you have and why you choose to reject some and accept others. When you say, "I choose to deliver the brief to the partner on time," it allows you to also see, "I do not choose to deliver the brief late because I fear I will be fired." This will allow you to examine why you chose to be timely. It allows you to ask, "Would I really be fired? Why do I stay here if I am afraid of being fired? What are other ways to approach this if I really think I might be late?" Acknowledging that in choosing to be on time, you rejected the choice to be late allows you to look at them as *choices*, which will ultimately open your eyes to even more choices.

When you say, "I have no choice but to deliver the brief on time," you cannot see any other options. Your language is a powerful determiner of what your brain believes is possible. When you say "I have no choice," your brain stops looking for other choices. A simple change to, "I choose to be on time," will allow your brain to see more choices. It is quite effective. We often look at life the way an air traffic controller looks at the radar screen. We don't see everything; we see only what is on the screen. As you know, the screen is not the entire picture; it is a very small part of the picture. There is a wide world that is not on the screen. Indeed, within the part of the sky that the radar represents, there are many things that don't appear. For the air traffic controller, what appears is what she is looking for—airplanes. Just because that's all she sees doesn't mean that's all that is there.

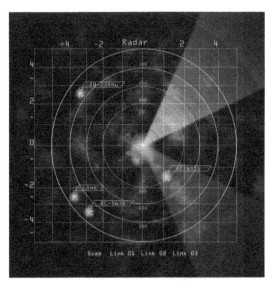

What appears on your screen is limited by what you are looking for and what you are willing to see. If you truly believe that delivering the brief late will get you fired and you don't want to be fired, it may not show up as a choice on your screen. But when your radar is so limited, you cut off your ability to see other, sometimes better, choices. Because you are unwilling to consider the possibility of being late, your radar also does not include the possibility of talking to your boss about asking for an extension, seeking help from another attorney, honestly saying you do not think you will get it done on time, or the myriad—endless—possibilities there are for you to choose from. When you refuse to look at some choices, you begin to close off most, if not all, of your choices. This is why you feel you "have no choice." When you start looking at the choices you don't like, and recognizing that they are in fact choices, you open up to a wider and wider variety of choices. Your radar screen expands. And this will allow many other choices—sometimes wonderful choices you had never thought of—to appear.

Once you have spent time on this exercise and have become adept at seeing that you have choices and asking what they are, you are ready for the next step: the process for learning from your mistakes. You may also use this to learn from your successes. Use this process to intentionally make choices moving forward that support you and generate the results you want.

The Accountability Process

In this process, we look back over our choices to learn from the past. The purpose of this exercise is to learn where you can make different choices in the future in order to generate different results—ultimately the results that you want. The process involves looking at the different choices you could have made in the past and determining how those might have impacted your results. This is a powerful process that will allow you to begin making choices that work better than those you have been making. Using this process will allow you to shift from being reactive (reacting to what happens without thinking), to being intentional (consciously responding to life circumstances).

Neutrality—A Preliminary Piece

Before we get into the process, we must establish a firm understanding of neutrality.

It is not possible to be truly accountable if you are in a blaming mode—if your tendency is to blame things outside yourself for your results. The tendency to blame is so common and prevalent in our culture that it may take some real work, and some real consciousness, in order to shift out of it. As we have said, the position of blaming circumstances and events outside of yourself is a victim position. Similarly, blaming *yourself* is a victim position. It is important you not shift from blaming others to blaming yourself. Indeed, self-blame is largely the reason we do not want to be accountable and learn from our mistakes in the first place. It does not feel good to beat yourself up over the choices you have made. If the choice is between making oneself wrong and making someone or something else wrong, we will likely opt for the latter. The key to learning from your past choices is accepting that there is no "wrong." Your choices and results either "work" or "don't work." Your results are simply feedback on your behavior.

The NLP presupposition is "There is no failure; only feedback." Everything that occurs in your life is feedback for you. Everything you do works or doesn't, and that is your feedback. It is an objective way of viewing the terrain. "Feedback" is like the speedometer in your car, which tells you how fast you are going. It is a way of assessing your speed. If it shows forty-five miles per hour, that is neither good nor bad. Driving forty-five miles per hour on the open highway is too slow. Driving forty-five miles per hour in a school zone is too fast. You decide based on this feedback if you are going too fast or too slow, and adjust accordingly. But the speedometer itself is neutral; it is just information.

Our word for this is *neutrality*. It is a way of looking at your choices without judgment. It is stepping back and taking an objective view and asking yourself, "What can I learn from this?" If you are in a very curious place, as opposed to a "blaming" place, you are more likely to be neutral.

Here are a few tools to generate neutrality. One is to pretend you are a detective looking for clues. You want to discover how you created the result you did. Your job is to ferret out what you did that worked and what you did that did not work. Your job is

not to talk about any outside factor that gave you this result; focus instead on your own choices. You are a detective and this is a mystery.

Another option is to look back as if you were watching a movie of what you did and what you generated. Again, you will be stepping outside of yourself and observing from a very curious vantage point.

Now, remembering neutrality, go through the accountability process.

Accountability Process

Step One—Notice the Result. A result is anything—the state of a relationship, where you are living, the job you currently have, whether you have children, whether you met a particular deadline, whether you kept an agreement, how much you weigh, etc. This may be a result you want or do not want. Just notice the result itself.

Step Two—Own the Result. Looking backward, ask yourself, "What are all the choices I made that landed me here?" The rule in using this tool is that you must identify *your* choices and not the circumstances or what someone else did. Also, you won't get the learning you need if you beat yourself up. In fact, criticizing yourself for choices you made that did not work is still in the realm of victimhood—victimhood to oneself. You are still blaming. To learn, you must be willing simply to look at *what is*, without blaming anyone or anything. Ask what choices you made in a very *curious* fashion, and don't give yourself a hard time about it.

Step Three—Look for Patterns. Ask yourself "Is this behavior a habit or pattern for me?" (See example below.) Use neutral terms in looking at your choices. Use the terms "working" and "non-working" rather than good or bad, right or wrong, smart or stupid.

Step Four—Learn from My Choices. Ask "What can I learn about *myself* in this situation? What are the beliefs, attitudes, and assumptions underlying my behavior? In other words, what beliefs do I hold that generate this particular behavior; what attitudes do I demonstrate about myself, certain people, or certain circumstances; and what assumptions do I make about myself, certain people, or certain circumstances that lead me to make certain choices?" This can be a very powerful step, as we often make choices based upon our subconscious minds. We will delve further into this following the case study below.

Step Five—Act on the Learning. "What will I do differently next time? (Or what can I do again to replicate a working result?)" Decide and **do it**! This is important. You *must* take action to make the change or nothing will change. If you are changing a behavior, put up a reminder so you'll remember it. When you have a habit, your brain is trained to continue it. You *will not* just remember to do something different. To break a non-working habit or start a new habit, you will need something to remind you.

Here is a simple example: I am late for a meeting.

Step One—Notice the Result. My result is that I am late. And I do not want to be late. I believe it affects others' ability to trust me. I want to be known for my word and to be on time to everything I commit to. This is a result I do not want to repeat.

Step Two—Own the Result. Looking back I see a number of choices I made that may have generated this result. I chose to go to bed later than usual last night and I was tired this morning. I chose to hit the snooze button. My daughter was sick and I chose to stay with her later than normal because I did not have a sitter lined up. On the way to the meeting, I chose to stop for gas because I did not believe I had enough to make it to the meeting. (It may sound somewhat artificial to speak this way, but again, the more you speak in "choice" language, the more you will see the choices you have.)

Step Three—Look for Patterns. Are any of these choices characteristic of habits or patterns? I do not have a habit of staying up too late, though I can see it did not work this time to make that choice. It is, however, a pattern for me to not have a sitter lined up for my kids if they are sick on a school day and it is also a pattern for me to let my gas tank get close to empty.

Step Four—Learn from My Choices. What I've learned is that I am not planning ahead enough. First, I don't have a plan for contingencies, such as my children being sick, and I have really just been lucky so far that my spouse is usually available to stay with them. My attitude is that my spouse should be the one taking care of those issues. Second, I tend to leave things to the last minute and then rush a lot. I realize this is based on my belief that things will take less time than they really do. Also, because I am constantly rushing, I believe stopping for gas is a waste of time unless the tank is almost empty. My assumption is that I will have time to stop "later." But that "later" never comes and suddenly I'm on empty. These beliefs and assumptions stifle my own freedom as to when I get gas, as I only fill up when I am about to run out and this often limits my choices.

Step Five—Act on the Learning. I am going to find people who can babysit during school days. I'll create a list so I have choices. I will start filling up my tank when it is half empty. I will put a post-it note in my car to remember this. And I will start leaving five minutes early everywhere I go so I am not rushing. Again, I will need a reminder for this; I'll put a note in my kitchen and in my calendar. I also realize this will require a shift in my own beliefs, attitudes, and assumptions. For instance, I will have to alter my belief that it is a waste of time to fill up the tank when it is still half full. And I will have to change my attitude about my spouse always being available to be with the kids if they are sick. Otherwise, I may have a hard time sticking with my new choices because they will be in conflict with my beliefs, attitudes and assumptions about my life and how the world should work.

Joseph (a result not wanted)

Joseph is a sole practitioner with a wife and two children. One summer, while the kids are out of school, he has a two-week trial. During one of the trial days, Joseph's wife is on an out-of-town retreat. She asks him to pick up the kids from summer camp. He agrees and says he will leave court shortly after trial ends and pick them up. But after trial that day, Joseph's client wants to talk about a witness that gave some surprising testimony. Joseph feels uncomfortable telling the client he has to pick up his kids, so he stays to discuss the matter and is late picking up his children. This not only costs him extra money and the ire of the camp counselor; his family is upset with him. Joseph is feeling like a victim. His traditional response is to complain, "But I had no choice," when asked why he did not pick the kids up on time. Joseph blames his client for needing to talk to him, the witness for creating such a crisis, the traffic for making him late ("I still would have been on time if the traffic hadn't been so bad"), and even the camp for not being more flexible with pick-up times. Joseph looks everywhere but at his own choices.

After engaging a coach and beginning to take an accountable look at his actions, he applies the accountability process as follows:

Step One—Notice the Result. My results: (1) I was late picking up my kids; (2) several people are upset with me; and (3) my family may not trust me as much to do what I say I will do. All of these are results I do not want, particularly #3.

Step Two—Own the Result. What are all the choices I made that landed me here? (1) I did not really think about whether I had the time to pick up the kids. I wanted my wife to be happy so I said yes. (2) I chose to stay and talk to my client because I did not want to experience the discomfort of telling him I needed to go and get my kids.

Step Three—Look for Patterns. Ask yourself, "Is this behavior a habit or pattern for me?" This behavior is definitely a pattern for me. (1) I often say yes to my wife either to make her happy or to move on with my day. I often do not really consider if I can do what she is asking. (2) I also often misjudge how long things will take and often fail to allow for contingencies such as witnesses giving testimony I do not expect and even bad traffic. (3) I notice that staying to talk to my client is similar to the pattern of not wanting to say "no" to my wife. I tend to want to "look good" and also avoid conflict with people (other than adversaries) and this creates difficulties for me.

Step Four—Learn from My Choices. What can I learn about *myself* in this situation? There is a lot of learning for me in step 3, and I will take on new practices in step 5.

Step Five—Act on the Learning. What will I do differently next time? (1) I will stick post-it notes several places in my office and my home that say, "Don't say YES right away. Keep your promises." When I see the note it will remind me to ask myself if I can really commit to what someone is asking of me. I will only make promises I can keep. (2) I will start overestimating the amount of time I think things will take by 50%. For this I will also put up reminders at work and on my calendar, and I will track whether my estimates are getting more accurate.

Joan (a result I would like to replicate)

Joan is a retired attorney. Her days are filled with various activities, such as hiking the 58 national parks in the U.S., writing her first book, becoming certified as a Restorative Exercise Specialist™, teaching Restorative Exercise classes, walking 3–5 miles daily and co-managing the 10-acre ranch on which she lives with her husband. She decided to take on a rigorous new exercise program recommended by her trainer. Joan was somewhat doubtful whether she could complete such a time-intensive physical regime for 30 consecutive days. When she completed it, Joan decided to use the accountability process to capture her learning as to what worked so she could replicate it in the future, and describes it as follows:

Step One—Notice the Result. I committed to, followed through, and completed 50 separate physical exercises, which took me 2 hours 15 minutes, each and every day, for 30 consecutive days.

Step Two—Own the Result. The choices I made that got me here: (1) I asked my trainer to suggest how I might change my exercise routine to address an area of my body that I wanted to improve, and she suggested doing 50 whole body exercises for 30 consecutive days. (2) I made a declaration to do the 50 exercises each day for 30 days. (3) I chose to review my calendar and found a 30-day period that looked somewhat manageable. (4) Each day I chose to look ahead at my schedule for the next day and then adjusted my wake-up time to accommodate the 2 hours and 15 minutes it would take to do the 50 exercises. (5) I chose to do the exercises the first thing upon arising before circumstances could get in the way of accomplishing my goal. (6) I chose to share my goal with my husband and requested his support. I told him I would be exercising first thing each morning. (7) Each morning as I went into my gym, I gave my husband a time when I would emerge and have breakfast with him. (8) After completing the exercises each day, I wrote my accomplishment on a calendar posted where I would see it daily. (9) I chose not to share my goal with anyone other than my husband until I had accomplished it.

Step Three—Look for Patterns. What I can see as I look at my life as a whole is that, from the time I was young, I discovered that if I wanted to accomplish something, I needed to plan ahead and choose a time to do it when I had the least amount of outside interruption. I developed a pattern early in my life of getting up early in the morning so that I could accomplish my goal. I also have a pattern of limiting the number of people with whom I share my goal in order to minimize negative feedback, which I have discovered depletes my energy and gives me doubt. These patterns were evident in law school as I continued working and raising my family while getting my education. And these patterns supported my being able to exercise daily while working full time; and in doing my "morning pages" (90 consecutive days of at least 30 minute morning journaling) recommended in Julia Cameron's *The Artists' Way*; and accomplishing other goals that have been important to me.

> ## Joan (a result I would like to replicate) (cont.)
>
> **Step Four—Learn from My Choices.** I learned a lot about myself, beginning with my initial wondering if I could really do this. I learned (1) I will follow through on a daunting task when it is recommended by someone like my trainer, who I consider credible and an expert in her field. Had this recommendation come from someone whom I did not trust as much, I likely would not have committed to following through. (2) Requesting support and getting an agreement from those, like my husband, who may be affected by my choices, rather than assuming they will just go along with whatever I am doing, supports me in finding and taking the time to follow through. (3) Keeping the goal in front of me and reminding myself why it is important to me also supports me. (4) As I was going through this process, I also realized that my history of success with other difficult and daunting tasks—such as going through law school with 3 young children and a full-time job—helped keep me committed and inspired me to keep going. (5) I learned that calendaring each day what I would do the following day supported me in not giving up because I had created the time the next day. (6) During the process, I also noticed changes in my body, which further motivated me to continue. I realized that this had happened in the past (like in law school when I finally began to understand Real Property). I learned that when I see positive change as a result of my efforts, I am more inspired and trust that if I am persistent, it will pay off.
>
> **Step Five—Act on the Learning.** My husband and I are going to create trails on our 10-acre ranch, which is a daunting task for me. I will take this write-up of accountability, particularly step four, and apply each of my learnings to that task. Applying this learning right away will allow me to internalize it more. The actual process of writing this out was beneficial to me, and I will retain my writing on this learning as reference for my next daunting task.

Using the Process to Replicate Results You Want

As we have said, you can use this process to replicate results that you like. You can use this process, as Joan did, when you undertake a task that you may not have believed you could accomplish (maybe it was going to law school, landing a particular job, having a difficult conversation with someone, winning an important case, or getting a motion filed on time when you were sure you could not). By using the process in this way, you become conscious of your own personal success factors, and you can continue to use them in other challenging situations, as Joan so aptly illustrates.

Looking at Joan's example (box, above), there are a few things to notice.

First, as she states, sitting down and writing out this entire process is immensely useful to capture the learning and be able to replicate in the future. After you get used to doing this in writing, you will likely be able to do it in your head, but practicing this initially in writing is far preferable.

Second, in step three, she looked for working patterns from her life to continue using on a conscious basis.

Third, in step four, she listed new insights about herself and how she was able to successfully complete the challenging task. It is important that she looked for things she did not already know. Had she simply listed the items from step three that she already knew about herself, she would not have accessed this new learning.

Finally, she took two important actions. First, she wrote down the process and all of what she learned: a formula for success that was tailored just to her. Second, and importantly, she took on another project right away that allowed her to internalize her learning.

The Deeper Level of Accountability-Looking for Patterns Based on Beliefs, Attitudes, and Assumptions (Steps Three and Four)

Joseph's example leads us to the deeper level of accountability and illustrates that patterns of behavior often arise from our thoughts and beliefs about a situation. For example, Joseph noticed his repetitive behavior of saying "yes" to people without thinking about whether he really could do what he was promising. When he looked closely, what he realized was this was part of a larger behavior he has of avoiding conflict. He has a belief that saying "no," or "I have to leave now," will create conflict. There seems to be a further attitude that conflict is bad—unless it is in an adversarial setting. Many attorneys do not recognize this mindset of conflict avoidance because they deal with conflict on a daily basis; some even thrive on it. But there is a big difference between saying "no" to opposing counsel's request for a continuance and saying "no" to your spouse's request that you pick up the kids after work.

To generate deeper learning and make more significant changes, it is useful to look closely at the choices we have made and our reasons behind them. In other words, you will be looking for your beliefs, attitudes, and assumptions. Taking Joseph's example, when he asks himself "what was the **belief** at play?" he might notice that he believes life is easier if he goes along with what his wife and clients want. (Note, often people have a hard time identifying a "belief". You might try asking "what was I thinking that had me do that?" A belief is just a thought that we think repeatedly until it becomes truth for us.)

If Joseph asks, "What was my **attitude**?" he might notice an attitude of feeling overwhelmed a lot of the time and sensing that others want a lot from him and that it is hard to balance it all. He might notice this attitude is what causes him to say yes without thinking: he doesn't have time to mull it over or deal with people's reactions if he says no. He may also have an attitude that he *should* be able to do it all, and that he is a bad father and a neglectful husband if he can't.

If he asks what **assumptions** he was making, he may discover he assumes his wife wants him to simply agree to pick the kids up rather than work with her on another solution. He may also assume that either he or his wife needs to retrieve the kids rather than have a third party do it. He may be assuming that his client will not be willing to wait until later in the evening to talk, or that the client will be disdainful of an attorney who needs to go pick up his kids.

An important point to take away from this chapter is that **we are always choosing.** However, we often look back and say, "I didn't choose that." Or, "I don't remember choosing that." This is because so many of our choices are unconscious and are based upon our unconscious beliefs, attitudes and assumptions. The best image we have seen for this model of our minds is the iceberg model. Our model is loosely based on Freud's original model. When you imagine an iceberg, what we know is about 10 percent of the tip is above the surface of the water, while a huge mass (some 90 percent) of the iceberg is under the water. This is like our minds in that about 10 percent of what drives us is conscious, while 90 percent of our motivation comes from "below the waterline." Some 90 percent of our actions are driven by beliefs, attitudes and assumptions of which we are unaware. What does this mean? It explains why you end up with a result you don't think you chose. Accountability work helps to "lower the waterline"—that is, to make more of your beliefs, attitudes, and assumptions conscious. And when they are conscious, then you can change them!

Continuing with Joseph's example, when he looks at his choices account-ably, he recognizes that he tends to avoid conflict. Once he realizes this, he can ask himself, "Why do I avoid conflict?" He may discover a belief that conflict is wrong. Perhaps he believes he should not have conflict with those like his spouse or client who are on "his side." Perhaps he grew up thinking it is simply wrong to disagree with others and that doing so will end up in a "fight." It is not neces-sary for Joseph to go into the psychology of this and ask why he holds this belief or where it came from or look back to his childhood. All he really needs is the discov-ery that he tends to avoid conflict (this is the behavior) because he believes it will result in a fight (this is his belief). All repetitive behavior stems from an underlying belief. The analysis is to look at the behavior and determine the belief, or thought, that drives the behavior. Once you understand that, you can challenge the truth of your belief and its usefulness to you.

Once Joseph sees that the belief driving his behavior is "I am afraid we will wind up in a fight and people who are allies should not fight" he has lowered the waterline of the iceberg and allowed the exposure of a previously unconscious belief. This allows him to make more conscious choice next time. Now, when someone asks him to do something (his wife to get the kids, or his client to stay and talk about the trial), he is in a position to consciously think about what he wants to choose. If he feels like wanting to quickly say yes, he can ask himself why that is. If he is trying to avoid conflict, he can ask himself, "Does saying yes to this right now really support me in getting what I want, or am I just saying yes based on my belief that saying no will cause me a problem? What is the best thing to do right now?" In this way, he has learned to choose from a *conscious* place and not unconsciously say yes as a knee-jerk way to avoid conflict.

Steph

Steph: One area in which I struggle to be accountable is in feeling I have too much to do. I don't like to turn away a paying client or an opportunity to be of assistance to someone who needs my help, and so I often find myself overwhelmed with work.

Step One—Notice the Result. I notice that I am stressed and feeling overwhelmed and not sure how I will accomplish everything I need to accomplish. Being overwhelmed much of the time is a result I would like to avoid in the future.

Step Two—Own the Result. The choices that got me here: (1) I don't like to turn away business, so I took on new cases without considering how I would be able to get all of the work done; (2) I tend to be a bit of a perfectionist, so I choose to spend a lot of time on certain tasks like writing briefs or letters, making them "perfect;" (3) like Joseph above, I tend to choose to say "yes" to requests from my family without thinking if I can really accomplish what is being asked of me.

Step Three—Look for Patterns. Being overwhelmed is definitely a pattern for me. Even as a child, I always kept myself busy. I like to be the "go to" person, the one with all the answers who can get the job done. When someone calls with a legal issue they need to resolve, I go right into hero mode and decide that I will help them, without considering how I will get everything done.

Step Four—Learn From my Choices. My **belief** is that I should help as many people as I can, and that if I turn away business, it is not only hurting the potential client, but I am turning away income. Another **belief** is that I should stay as busy as possible. And I believe that successful attorneys are always busy. My **attitude** is one of the hero or rescuer; I realize I get a lot of my own self-worth from helping others who are unable to help themselves. I also have an **attitude** that unless I am very busy, I am being "lazy" and unproductive. My **assumption** when someone asks for my help, be it a client, a family member, or a friend, is that I am the only one who can help them. I also **assume** that if I turn away business, I am throwing away income. And I always **assume** I can handle whatever comes, and that I can accomplish anything.

Step Five—Act on the Learning. What will I do differently? In the future when I realize I have more than I can comfortably do, I will hire a contract attorney to take on a project. This will enable me not only to help the client but to increase my revenue stream. I have started to turn down cases that seemed destined to require more time than they are likely worth and/or in which I am uncertain if the attorney-client relationship will thrive. In order to do this, I have to be conscious about the cases I take on and be honest with myself about why I am taking a new client. I am also working to change my mindset: to really believe that an attorney does not have to be extremely busy to be successful and to trust that if I turn down certain cases others will come, and my income will remain where I want it to be.

The Power of Language

Accountability is *the ability to account for your choices and your results*. The value of holding yourself accountable at all times is that it gives you the power to make change in order to get what you want. This is true power.

It is sometimes challenging for us to determine if we are being accountable. One way to see if you are being accountable is to notice your language. And one way to be more accountable is to change your language.

The quickest and easiest way to make an overall shift from victimhood to accountability is to listen to, and change, your language.

Examples of Victim Language	Accountable Language
• There is nothing I can do	• What is possible?
• I have/had no choice	• What can I do here/now?
• I hope it will change	• I am responsible. I decide what I am committed to.
• I wish it was different	• How did I create this?
• I can't	• What's working?
• The circumstances (fill in the blank—weather, other people, etc.) caused this to happen	• What's not working?
• I have no control over it	• What action can I take?
• Who's to blame?	• I chose
• I tried!	• I am choosing
• I found myself here	• Active language of ownership—"This was my part in it"; "This was my choice"

- It happened to me

- Passive language such as "It didn't get done."

- This always happens

- If (another person) would only do things differently, this would have turned better

- That would never work

- "I did" or "I didn't"

- I will

- I can

- What is my part in this?

- What do I have control over?
- What can I change?

When you hear victim language come out of your mouth (or even in your head), it gives you valuable information. It tells you where you are feeling powerless.

Example: Your boss says to you, "Are you done with the proposal yet?" You hear yourself say, "I have been trying." Hearing your victim language is a trigger for you to ask yourself what is really true about the situation. You realize you are feeling overwhelmed and a little guilty that you haven't finished the proposal yet. You say you are "trying" in order to point out to him and yourself that you have taken action on it; you have not been just sitting around.

With this insight, you can speak from a place of ownership and also use much clearer language. When he asks if you are done, you can say, "No. I am not done." Realizing you want him to know you have been working on it, you can tell him that. Taking ownership, you may also say, "I did not plan my time to enable me to be done by today. I realize why I have not finished yet. Taking this into consideration, I will make some changes and I can promise you that I will be done by ___."

As you can see, the first purpose in observing your language is to see where you are really coming from—whether you feel you have power in the situation or not. Another way to work with language observation is to change your language to become more accountable, which of course means *empowered* to make change. The language you use affects your feelings, your energy level, and your belief in yourself. Start listening to your victim language, and notice when your speech indicates you are feeling unempowered, like a victim. Then, interrupt that pattern by changing to accountable language. You will be surprised what is possible when you simply change your language.

The Feeling of Power

Try this:

1. Think of a situation about which you feel powerless, in which you hear yourself say things like "I wish," "I hope," or "I have no control." Close your eyes and listen to your language. Really experience your feelings of powerlessness and speak in a fully "victimy" way. This will be even more noticeable if you vocalize how powerless you feel. As you fully express how bad things are for you, notice how you are feeling. When you are done, take a moment and write down all of what you are feeling right now.

2. Open your eyes. Stand up; jump around; shake it off.

3. Next, sit down in a different chair; close your eyes; think again about the situation. As you imagine yourself in the situation, ask yourself questions like, "What else can I do about this situation?" "What is possible here?" "Who are my resources?" "What do I have control over?" "What can I change?" When you come up with some answers, make a statement to yourself that starts with either, "I will..." or "I choose to..." Again, speak what you are thinking out loud. Now notice how you are feeling in your body. Notice any differences in lightness, mood, sense of possibility, sense of power or powerlessness, and sense of hope or hopelessness. Write down your feelings to capture the experience.

Studies have shown we are literally physically stronger when we consider solutions, positivity, and thoughts about how things can work, compared with when we think about how bad things are and that there are no solutions.

As you have now experienced, speaking to yourself and viewing your situation in an accountable way actually makes you *feel* better and makes you more resourceful. Speaking this way will not only improve the quality of your life and its experiences; it will allow you to see what is possible. And that feels much better than arguing about what is not possible.

So when you are wondering if you are in a victim position, one tool is to check and see how you are feeling. You will literally feel weaker, tired, hopeless, when you are in the victim place.

In addition to the language examples above, eliminate the word "try" from your vocabulary. "Try" is a powerless word. When projecting forward ("I will try") it offers very little information or ownership. When referring to the past ("I tried"), it is a victim statement. If someone says to you, "Will you do this for me?" and you begin to say, "I'll try," stop yourself and state what you really mean without the word "try." This requires you look and see what you are really willing to commit to. You might say, "Yes I'll do it, but not until tomorrow." You might say, "I don't know if I will get it done and I am not going to promise right now." (When you choose not to say "try" and instead state that you will not commit right now, you recognize that when someone asks you to do something and you say "yes," you have made a promise.) Or you might say, "No; I will not agree to do that."

The same applies when you make agreements with yourself. Listen to your language. Use accountable language, even—especially—with yourself.

Other language similar to "try" includes the following:

"I need to..."

"I wish..."

"I hope..."

These are not accountable phrases, because they are by their very nature giving power away and refusing to take ownership. "I need to" may be a statement of what is, but it is not a statement of what I will commit to change; rather, it is a statement that something outside of myself over which I have no control has imposed on me. "I wish" and "I hope" are obviously ineffectual statements that very clearly say, "I do not have power over this and that the power lies elsewhere; I am so powerless and ineffectual that the best I can do is hope or wish for something outside of myself to be different." This is not where you want to be. You will never make change from a place of wishing or hoping. It is a victim position.

Exercise

Put up a reminder—perhaps the lists of phrases above—somewhere in your workspace or home environment. Commit to listening for victim language in your speech, and commit to changing it to accountable language. Making this change will take conscious effort and commitment, but you will be amazed what you can accomplish and the results you can attain when you start speaking from a place of ownership and power.

Payoffs and Prices for Accountability

We won't lie to you—this is a powerful tool *and* it takes work. It takes courage, commitment, and dedication to truly be accountable. And it is often uncomfortable, especially in the beginning. It requires a shift—for many people a quantum shift—from how you have always viewed the world and yourself. And in making this shift, there are certain things you will need to give up. Certain of these may be very important in your life.

What You Gain

- **You learn from your mistakes.** In this way, you are less likely to repeat them. For example, when I look at my choices that led to my being late, I can learn from what I did and thus not repeat patterns that don't work.

What You Give Up

- **The illusion that you don't make mistakes.** Sometimes it feels better for us to pretend it is all working, that we don't make mistakes, and if that darned traffic wasn't so bad, I would have been on time. We can't learn like that. Being accountable requires the willingness to admit where you have made a mistake.

What You Gain

- **You become solution-focused, rather than problem-focused.** If I am accountable about my choices that made me late, I look at what do I want to create: the solution. Focusing on the solution, rather than the traffic or whatever you see as the problem, will have a great effect on your attitude. Most people find that it feels better to focus on the solution rather than the problem, and that it gives them more energy and that they are able to find a solution more quickly.

- **You get the results you want.** When I am a victim, I have my story, but I don't have the results I want. You either have your reasons, stories, and excuses, or you have your desired results.

- **Others will trust you more.** You probably know that keeping your agreements builds trust. But being honest when you don't keep your agreements also builds trust. It teaches people that keeping your agreements is important to you. It shows them that when you don't, you are going to figure out what went wrong and you are going to fix it. This builds trust with others.

- **You feel better about yourself/create greater self-esteem.** Not only is accountability empowering, but you will feel better knowing that you are being honest with yourself about your part in events and will find that you have much more control than you thought. Try it for awhile. Be rigorously accountable no matter what and see how you feel.

- **People respect you more**—because you are honest AND you get your results. People also have increased respect for those who have the courage to admit to mistakes and who obviously take on the work to make change.

- **You are in integrity with yourself and this creates higher self trust.** Self trust is important—I know I will do what I say. It is nearly impossible to make sustainable positive change in your life if you do not believe yourself when you say that you will do something.

What You Give Up

- **Avoiding the work of change.** Often it is easier to pretend we cannot affect change than to admit that we can. Once you admit you can make changes, it becomes harder to ignore this. Thus, by being accountable, you may get to give up the complacency of pretending you can't make change, which has allowed you to remain comfortably stuck in the same place.

- **Your stories and excuses.** You always have the choice of pointing to your stories, your reasons, and your circumstances—or of buckling down and creating the results you are after. The two cannot co-exist. You get to choose one or the other. If you opt for accountability, you can no longer rely on your excuses.

- **The "looking good" image.** Often we don't admit to having made non-working choices when we do not keep our agreements based on a fallacy that admitting to our mistakes will break trust with others. So we "try" to build and maintain an image of having it all together. The truth is that honesty and ownership build trust; excuses deflate it.

- **Sympathy.** Sometimes we tell our victim story to get attention and comfort from others. When you stop telling your victim story, you may give up the sympathy. As a side effect, you very well may stop wanting it.

- **Comfort and complacency.** Sometimes this is a big draw. Being accountable involves some risk and requires a certain degree of courage.

- **Staying comfortably where you are.** Let's face it: change can be uncomfortable. Even if you are not getting the results you want, there is some comfort in knowing what to expect—even if we don't like it—and in staying in the same familiar place.

Homework

1. Get in the habit of asking yourself, "What are all the choices I have in this situation?" Really look; do not let yourself off the hook. If you think you have no choice,

then ask yourself, "What would happen if I did _____?" even if that option is not an option you would ever choose. That will allow you to see why you are interpreting it as not a choice. Then say, "I am choosing this. I am not choosing that." Train your brain to seek out and recognize choices.

2. Use the accountability process daily. Use it any time you break an agreement—whether to yourself or to others. This includes anytime you are late for something and anytime you say you will do something and you do not.

3. Listen to your language.

- Ask others to listen to your language and tell you what they hear. When you catch yourself using victim language, find a way to change it to empowering language. It is just a habit that you have developed and been trained to carry out over many years. You can change it. This exercise will enable you to do that.

- Enroll others in your office or family in this game: Have a jar in which anyone who uses the word "try" must put money. When it is full, have a party, go to lunch or dinner, or do something else to celebrate your success.

Chapter 4

Are you Committed? (and If Not Why Not?)

Why Read This Chapter?

1. You've done everything else we recommend and cannot seem to attain the goal you have set.
2. You find yourself making excuses when you fail to accomplish a goal.
3. You are frustrated with your progress on a goal (or goals) and are contemplating "giving up."

Jake

Jake has decided that he is going to bill a minimum of 165 hours each month. The first month he bills only 155. So he prints a big "165" on a sheet of paper and pins it to the wall next to his computer. The next month he does better, but only slightly: 157. When he looks back at his calendar, he notices that on three days he left the office to attend functions at his children's school and he had a lengthy doctor's appointment on another day. Vowing to do better, he hunkers down the next month, but other things keep getting in the way of his billable time and he bills 156 hours. Frustrated, he considers changing his goal. "I tried, but this is too hard," he thinks.

Introduction

In any business venture, goal setting and attainment are key. And in most of these chapters, that is what we have focused on: goal setting and attainment. In the chapter on creating a Well-Formed Outcome (chapter 2), we went through goal setting in detail. The chapter on accountability (chapter 3) is really about learning from your successes and failures in meeting your goals, so as to better attain your goals in the future. Even the chapter on time management (chapter 7) teaches proactive and conscious ways of managing your time and energy so you can ultimately attain your goals.

This chapter takes accountability to the next level. It asks the tougher questions: Why am I not achieving what I say I want? What is it about my own habits and ways of looking at things that is getting in the way of my desired results? Some people are apprehensive about beginning this type of inquiry, afraid of what they might find. But there is a very good reason to look at how YOU prevent yourself from achieving your goals. As you know, all you can really change is you. This is why the question, "What habits of mine are keeping me from what I want?" is really an accountability question.

In this chapter, you will learn the following:

1. How to determine your level of commitment to a goal that you have set; and if you are not fully committed, why not?
2. What are the main obstacles that get in the way of what you want, and how can you move past them?
3. How can you access your own internal resourcefulness in order to manifest what you want?

What is Commitment?

We start by determining your level of commitment to those things you say are important to you. When you say you are "committed," what does that mean? How do you know if you are committed? And if it turns out you really are not as committed as you thought you were, what will you do about it? How will you change that?

Commitment is not necessarily shown by the language you use; it is evidenced by the actions you take. You cannot know for certain if you *are* committed, the *level* of your commitment, or *what* you are committed to, until you have acted—or not. You may say, "I am going to do that no matter what; you have my word; this is the greatest idea ever; I am on it!" But until the time comes for you to take action, you cannot know if you are truly committed to what you say you want. You learn what you are really committed to by looking at the actions you take.

It is through commitment that we generate what we say we want in our practice and our lives. You get what you want by clearly stating what that is, deciding to go get it, and then taking action toward the result. It is in this action that we demonstrate commitment to the result. When we have strong commitment, we create our results *intentionally*. This is different from how we often create results in our lives, which is by default: showing up, doing our best, seeing what happens, and taking what comes. Determining your level of commitment to a project or course of action is an accountable and proactive way of approaching your business that greatly increases the likelihood you will get what you say you want.

The tool we advocate is the Commitment Scale. This is an accountability tool. It allows you to review your behavior to determine how committed you really are to whatever you say you want. And if you find you are less than 100 percent committed, you can figure out why—and determine how to change that.

How to Use this Tool

Let's say you want to increase your business by 50 percent, and you have set this as a goal. But when you examine your progress at the end of the month, you see that you have not generated any more business. The first question to ask yourself is, "What action did I take toward achieving my goal?" If you look back over your month and see that you took no action at all, this demonstrates a low level of commitment. If you took some action, but gave up at some point, you might be around an 8 or 9, on a scale of 0–10. If you barely began, maybe you are at a 6 or 7. By reviewing the actions you took, you can honestly and accountably determine your past month's level of commitment.

Commitment Scale

10   Full intentionality

I am committed to what I say I want; I am fully accountable and always looking for possibilities. I generate the result I say I will, by any means necessary.

9   Fully committed until...

I say I am committed; I appear committed; and I stay committed—until it gets too hard.

8   Taking action, but...

I take action that is easy for me. I don't look for possibilities or take the tougher actions. I have excuses about not producing.

7   Great idea, but...

I can see this is a good idea for other people, but I am not committed to it for myself. I sound more like a cheerleader.

6   Sure, I'll do it

This is something I feel I "have to do" so I agree, but I don't follow through and do the bare minimum to get by. We call this level "compliance."

5   "Whatever"

I do not take any action toward the goal and I don't much care if anyone else does.

4   Slight negativity

I cannot see the value in this idea and it probably won't work anyway.

3   Passive Resistance, Sabotage

I don't believe it will work, so I will not take action.

2   Active Resistance

This goal is not aligned with what I really want; I am committed to something else.

1   Battle

I know this can't work and I will prove it.

0   War

Active conflict. I will do anything I can to make sure this does not happen.

Using our example of generating more business, you can look at the scale and ask how committed you really are to the goal based on the amount of action you took. For example, if you barely began, look at 6 and 7, and ask if you really believe that generating more business is a good idea for you and your life. It may turn out you think it is good for law firms in general to make a certain amount of money or that to be successful you "should" make a certain amount of money, but looking at your actions, and reflecting on them, you realize that you personally do not see it as the best idea for your firm. Maybe you are more interested in representing indigent clients or non-profit organizations. Or you may notice that your partners wanted you to make more money and that you agreed, but your heart was not really in it. When we agree out of compliance, we often do not follow through with meaningful action. Once you have looked honestly at your actions and your level of commitment, based on *the past month*, then today you get to decide again: how committed am I to this *going forward*? It is valuable to know the truth about your commitment level. You cannot get anywhere by pretending to be committed to something for which you objectively demonstrate a lack of commitment.

This scale is also useful to assess the commitment level of others. People can tell you whatever they think you want to hear, but their actions won't lie. If your associate swears to you she will get you the research within forty-eight hours and a week has passed, she was not committed to what she promised. "Not committed" does not mean she did not care. It means looking solely at the result; she did not take the actions necessary to get you the research. She may have been more committed to something else, such as working on a different case she thought was more important or taking care of a sick child or getting more sleep. Rather than judging her or the situation, you can talk to her about her level of commitment. Ask what happened. Learn from it. Help her find ways in the future to keep her promises to you.

Another valuable question to ask—of yourself or someone else—when a goal is not met is, "What was I more committed to?" This can give you even more information. If your associate spent all week on the MSJ and didn't get to your research, she was more committed to getting the MSJ done and did not see any possibility of getting them both done by the end of the week.

Getting back to your goal of increasing your business by 50 percent, if you do not have that result at the end of the first month, you ask "What was I more committed to?" This might reveal that you really don't like to work more than forty hours per week, and you believe it will take working a lot more to increase your business. In that scenario, you are more committed to limiting your hours to forty per week *and* to your belief that you will have to work more to bring in more business. Note that whenever we ask, "What was I more committed to," the answer might be a circumstance or something else you were working on, but it will likely also be a way of seeing the situation—a habitual attitude, viewpoint, or filter. Your associate above was committed to the idea that she could not finish the MSJ *and* the research.

Use the commitment scale and answer the question "What was I more committed to?" whenever you fail to reach a goal you have set. This way, you can determine your level of commitment to that particular goal and if you are not truly committed, why not. Now we look at the main obstacles that get in the way of what you want.

Personal Obstacles

"Personal obstacles" are internal and habitual ways of approaching situations that prevent us from getting what we say we want. The bad news is these obstacles are often unconscious or subconscious reactions to situations. The good news is that because they are internal, they are things we can change! The aim is to realize which obstacle(s) we encounter most often, to recognize them when they arise, and to learn how to move past them.

Personal Obstacles

Rather than achieving the result I say I want, I engage in one of the following:

Disempowerment—I get stuck in an internal feeling state that saps my energy and keeps me from moving forward. Types of disempowerment include cynicism, regret, resignation, and doubt. The danger of this obstacle is that we often lose motivation to take action.

Story-Telling—I have a great explanation of how I tried, but the circumstances were against me. I weave a story designed to convince myself (and others) that I tried but there was no hope of success. The danger of this obstacle is that we convince ourselves and others that circumstances are to blame, and thus fail to see our own ability to change them.

The Analytic Dilemma—I often believe that I do not have enough information. So I feel confused, unfocused, scattered, disorganized. I spin my wheels (often in my head) rather than moving purposefully toward my goal. The danger of this obstacle is that we keep waiting for more information or for the confusion to lift before taking action.

Wasted Energy—Rather than take purposeful action to achieve my stated outcome, I engage in activities, speech, and thoughts that do not move me forward. In this way I fool myself into believing I have taken action toward my goal, by engaging in useless mental activities of worry, hope, and wishful thinking. The danger of this obstacle is because it takes so much energy, we often think we are taking action when we aren't.

Other-Focus—Rather than focus on what I can do to move toward my goal, I judge other people and have their behavior be the excuse for my lack of desired result. The danger of this obstacle is that it shifts our focus from what we can change (ourselves) to what we cannot (other people).

When should you look for your personal obstacles? When you have a goal or an outcome that you want to achieve and you have not been able to meet it. For example, let's say your goal was to go to four networking meetings this month and you only attended two. Ask yourself why you didn't go to all four and listen to the reasons you give yourself. Which obstacles are you noticing?

The Process for Identifying and Moving Past Obstacles

1. What has kept you from achieving this goal? (Identify the obstacle.)
2. Where else do you see this obstacle blocking your progress? In other words, what other goals in your practice (or elsewhere) have you failed to achieve because of this same obstacle?
3. When this obstacle arises for you, how can you tell? Begin to notice the signs that this obstacle is blocking your progress.
4. Decide what to do when the obstacle arises so that it does not get in your way.

Step One—Identify the Obstacle

If you did not attend four networking functions as you had said you would, and you ask yourself why, you might answer, "I did not have the time." You can see that "time" is not one of the personal obstacles. So you will need to keep asking yourself questions and reflecting on your answers until you determine which of the personal obstacles got in your way. As you continue to reflect, you might say, "I can't fit all this in. My secretary was gone this week. She normally signs me up for meetings and I did not have time to do this myself." If you find yourself pointing to your secretary being gone, your obstacle is likely that of "story-telling."

Using our example of having failed to attend four networking events, let's see how each obstacle might present itself:

Disempowerment
Example #1
Sounds like: "I'll never get business this way. Why do I even want to go to a networking meeting? They all just want me to send them business. They're just in it for themselves." (This form of disempowerment is called "cynicism.")

Looks like: When you receive information on a networking meeting, you throw it away, figuring there is probably some "catch." When you look online for information, you find something wrong with each of the meetings—it is in a bad location; you don't think there will be many potential clients; or it costs money—and you decide not to go. Your cynicism about whether networking is even worth it affects your choices to pursue it with commitment.

Example #2
Sounds like: "The last client I represented was mad at me by the end of the case. I need to learn more how to approach this type of law before I start networking." (This form of disempowerment is called "regret.")

Looks like: You think about a networking meeting you attended a few months ago and how you had such a hard time meeting people; you only really talked to one person the whole night, and it was not even a prospective client. You wish you had not decided to go to more networking meetings and start thinking it was a bad idea. Your regret over past events causes you not to take action to generate different results in the future.

Example #3
Sounds like: "Networking doesn't work. What's the point? I should just go into another area of the law." The voice of this obstacle is Eeyore's from Winnie the Pooh—resignation.

Looks like: You wish you were more social, but realize you are just not cut out for these types of events. You start wondering about whether you should even have your own law practice. Obviously you are not going to be able to drum up more business no matter what you do. You do not even bother looking up information on future meetings.

Example #4
Sounds like: "I don't think I will get a good result from networking. I'm not very good at meeting people and talking about my business." (This form of disempowerment is called "doubt.")

Looks like: You talk to others about the lack of success they have had at networking meetings, looking for reasons not to go. When you think about the types of people who go to these meetings, you decide they probably don't have any money to hire you. You decide you would not get very good results even if you did go. Your doubt about yourself stops you from moving forward.

Story-Telling
Example #1
Sounds like: "I have *so much* work to do. I have worked seven days in a row, twelve hours a day. My kids are sick and everything is falling apart."

Looks like: When your secretary tells you about a networking meeting later that evening, you start complaining to her about all of the other things you need to do, telling her about your sick children and how the last time you went to a networking meeting you ended up getting home so late you did not even see your kids before they went to bed, and then you were tired and almost non-functioning the next day.

Example #2
Sounds like: "If my secretary had put the meetings on my calendar, I would have gone." "If the website wasn't so hard to read, I would have found an event to attend." "If my client hadn't called me last minute when I was walking out the door, I would have gone."

Looks like: You feel so put upon by having to make four (four!) meetings, it makes you think about all of the other things that other people have asked you to do recently, and you wonder where the time goes and you think there are just not enough hours in the day and too many people who want things from you and your life should not be this difficult. You find yourself feeling depressed and anxious.

The Analytic Dilemma

Sounds like: "I looked everywhere but I couldn't find the information on networking." Or, "I was doing so many other things this week that I kept forgetting to look for networking events."

Looks like: Confusion often leads to overwhelm, which often leads to a total stoppage of action. Although you look online for a meeting, you get overwhelmed trying to decide which one to attend and you move on to another task. You spend a lot of time trying to figure out where you would park or how long it would take to get to each of the meetings. You print out the information but then are concerned you might have a potential conflict. Ultimately you misplace the information anyway.

Wasted Energy

Example #1

Sounds like: "It might turn out badly if I put myself out there." Or, "I hope I get more clients without going to all these networking meetings." Or, "I hope I have time to go to four networking meetings this month."

Looks like: Because you are "hoping" your schedule will allow you to attend four meetings, you don't put any meetings on your calendar. When you later look for meetings to attend, you realize that you have conflicts on all of the days and times of the meetings. Now you are worried that you won't be able to attend the meetings, but you don't reschedule anything so that you can. You think, "I sure hope that something drops from my calendar or that another networking meeting will make itself available to me." But of course you do not look for one.

Example #2

Sounds like: "I tried to go." "I thought about it and looked for a meeting and told my secretary to find one but we couldn't. I really tried though."

Looks like: The networking meeting is scheduled and on the calendar, but as the time approaches, you "find" yourself on the phone with a client and then "having" to do one more task before you leave, at which time you realize it is too late to make the networking meeting. "Oh well," you think. "I tried."

Other-Focus

Example #1

Sounds like: "All the events that were offered were useless to me. The people who go to those events never refer me business; they're just there for a free lunch. The guy who leads the meeting is annoying."

Looks like: You are in a meeting with your law partners discussing how to bring more business into the firm. Every time one of them proposes a solution, you think, "Wow, that's really a stupid idea." The longer you listen, the more you think, "They really don't know how to do this. I can't believe I work with these people." This voice of judgment will likely cause you to stop listening curiously—that is, to stop seeing if any of their ideas, or a variation on their ideas, might actually work. The obstacle of focusing on others' actions has caused you to stop looking for what you want—to bring more business into the firm.

Example #2
Sounds like: "Networking is a stupid idea and I wish I didn't have to do it. Why don't my clients just refer me more work?"

Looks like: When you think about "having" to go to the networking meeting, it makes you angry and resentful, thinking you should already have all the business you need by now. When you do go to a meeting, you do so begrudgingly, feeling like this is not something you should have to do simply to bring in more business. You find yourself being "short" with clients who you think should be referring business to you when they do not.

Step Two—Where Else do I See this Obstacle Blocking My Progress?

Most people have more than one obstacle that arises for them regularly. Pick the one you think is most problematic right now. (One way you can tell which obstacles you use the most is to notice, as you read the foregoing examples, with which ones you say to yourself, "That's not an obstacle. That just makes sense." For example, if you say to yourself, "of course you can't move forward if you don't have enough facts" there's a chance that The Analytic Dilemma is a personal obstacle for you.)

When you discover a particular obstacle, ask yourself, where else do I ____? For example, where else do I notice myself explaining all the reasons I couldn't do something rather than just doing it? (Story-Telling.) Or, where do I see myself getting confused or overwhelmed about the facts and allowing that to stop me? (The Analytic Dilemma.) In what situations do I simply say "I tried" rather than looking for the real reason I did not produce the result? (Wasted Energy.) How often do I blame the way others have acted for a result I do not want? (Other-Focus.) Begin to notice the types of situations in which each obstacle arises.

You might notice for example, that when your boss asks if you have the research she wanted done by Friday, rather than saying, "No I don't," and working with her on a solution to the problem, you give her a long story. You tell her about all the other things you've been doing and how you didn't think this was a "hard" deadline and other people aren't working as many hours as you are. Later when your spouse notes that you are late for dinner, rather than work on a solution, you tell her the whole story of your day. Then, you explain that most of your colleagues work much later than you do and you point out that you did not work at all the entire previous weekend. Then, when your child asks if you brought home the magazines she wanted from your office, rather than being straight-forward and honest that you forgot, and figuring out how you can remember the next day, you launch into your explanation. You tell her there were other papers you needed to bring home, and you tell her she has homework tonight anyway and that she really has plenty of magazines. All of these involve the obstacle of Story-Telling. We each have a few obstacles we use the most. When you look, you will likely see them everywhere in your life and your practice.

Step Three—How do I Recognize this Obstacle?

You want to be able to recognize the obstacle when it arises. What are the "red flags" you see when this obstacle is getting in your way? How can you tell that you are **story-telling** rather than producing, or being **analytic** or **other-focused** or **wasting energy**, and thus stopping yourself from reaching your result?

This will require that you observe yourself when these obstacles arise. When you fail to achieve a goal, what do you hear in your head? What are the "whys" you tell your-self and others? What are your excuses or reasons? You might learn that when you don't reach a goal you spend so much time beating yourself up and feeling regret that you stop moving forward (disempowerment). So from now on when you hear a voice in your head offering self-criticism, you know you are in beat-up mode and can step out of it and say "oh; this is the disempowerment barrier."

When you hear yourself giving excuses, you say, "This is the story-telling obstacle." In this manner, you learn what to listen for and instead of believing the stories that come from the obstacles, you can simply say, "This is an obstacle. Now what?"

Based on the above examples of what each obstacle looks and sounds like (under step #1), start figuring out how to tell when your dominant obstacle(s) arise. Then, notice that you are under the influence of one of your obstacles.

Step Four—A Strategy for When the Obstacle Arises

Once you have figured out which obstacles are most likely to get in your way and you are able to identify them when they arise, you need to develop a strategy for moving past them. For most people, a big part of the strategy is simply in identifying the obstacle. Here are some further steps you can take once you have done so.

Decide in advance what you will do when the obstacle arises. For instance, if you hear yourself explaining rather than acknowledging the result and working on a solution, or if you hear yourself using the word "try," or if you realize you feel like just giving up, you might interrupt yourself (for example, just say "stop") and then ask "What do I really want here?"

With many of these obstacles, it can help to simply ban yourself from using certain words and phrases. You might decide to stop using the word "try" or "hope" (for the wasted energy obstacle), "it's no use" or something similar (for the disempowerment obstacle), or the victim language from the accountability chapter (chapter 3) for the story-telling obstacle. Ask others to support you by listening for, and pointing out, the language you want to get rid of. Have a coin jar where you deposit a quarter every time you use one of the words or phrases you have excised from your vocabulary.

For the Analytic Dilemma, if it is hard for you to move forward when you don't feel you have enough information, give yourself a deadline; say "I will take action by ___ date even if I don't have all the facts." Stretch your comfort zone and take action without having all the facts. Begin to experience what this is like. For the barrier of disempowerment, you might realize you are focusing on the past and feeling resentment or regret. When you see this, perhaps your strategy will be to take pen and paper and answer the question, "What can I do about this *now*?" For the other-focus obstacle, you might ask yourself "What can *I* do here?" shifting the focus from others and back onto you.

Note that a strategy is most useful when it has an action element. It is less useful to just ask yourself questions inside your own head; it is more useful and effective to actually DO something. So you may want to answer your internal questions *in writing*. Perhaps have a pad of paper or a notebook dedicated to answering these types of questions when you get stuck. Then add a further action step. After answering the question, make a promise to yourself to do something based on your learning. For example, if I am judging my secretary as incompetent and I blame her for not getting my work done on time (other-focus), the strategy is to ask "What can *I* do here?" Then write down the answer; *and promise yourself* that you will take that action *by Tuesday*.

Develop your own strategy for moving past your particular obstacles once you have identified them. Everyone has obstacles. And you will never get rid of them, so you will want to know when they arise and how to move forward in spite of them.

Resourcefulness

With anything that you want to accomplish, it is important to be resourceful. What does it mean to be "resourceful" or "non-resourceful"?

When you are **resourceful**, you have access to your *internal* resources, which gives you a greater ability to see the extent of your *external* resources. **Internal resources** are your inherent attributes; they include things like confidence, trust, commitment, creativity—qualities or attitudes that inspire you to move forward and do what you need to do.

External resources are outside of you, such as money, people, books—things you can use to work toward your goals. If you were building a house from scratch, internal resources might include creativity, confidence, and knowledge of how to build a house. External resources would be wood, tools, nails, and people to help you.

The word **"resourceful"** as defined in Webster's Dictionary, literally means, "able to use the means at one's disposal to meet situations effectively." Note that this definition has nothing to do with how many external resources you *have*. It is the ability to *recognize and utilize* your resources.

By comparison, when we are non-resourceful, we are not able to see all that is available to us. This can very often be the difference between success and failure—whether we see our resources or not.

Being MacGyver

Many of you will recall the television show MacGyver, about a man who was truly resourceful. He could enter any situation—typically dire or dangerous— and see solutions where it seemed there were none. He could find or make tools out of whatever he had available. He always saw possibility. He never whined. He never said, "This is too hard." He always said, "Of course this will work— there's some chewing gum and a piece of twine; I will make a bomb!"

Another resourceful fellow is Les Stroud, the star of "Survivorman." Mr. Stroud would get dropped off in far-reaching, remote places and have to survive for several days, sometimes even find his way back. He would use his vast knowledge of plant and animal life to make himself a shelter and feed himself. He was honest about getting discouraged, cold, and hungry at times, but he was always optimistic. And he was always resourceful.

Resourcefulness is an attitude. It consists largely of a belief that there are unlimited external resources available and the game is for you to find them and figure out how to use them. The main difference between resourcefulness and non-resourcefulness is **belief** and **attitude**. If we believe we are doomed, we are. If our attitude is doubtful or pessimistic, we cannot see our resources. We are wired with a desire to be right about the things we believe. So when we believe there is no possibility, we cannot see resources that are right in front of us. When we believe there are possibilities available to us, we *look for them* and therefore, we see them.

Nearly all of the tools Cami teaches are designed to help her clients access their resources. One particular tool is accountability (chapter 3). When you learn about choice, and stop blaming things outside of yourself, you become resourceful—able to see your external resources. The resourceful person says, "I know there's another choice I can make, another way of doing things that can work better. Let me discover what that is." This is like MacGyver saying, "There's some chewing gum and a piece of twine; I will make a bomb!" That's the game!

Ways of Being Resourceful

1. Don't reinvent the wheel

Look for a solution that someone else has already created. It might be a book, a software program, or someone's existing checklist or procedures. You can learn almost anything from books or on the Internet. For example, if there is something you need your computer to do, you know that someone has probably already written software to address it. You can find many elegant solutions by researching your problem and finding something that already exists.

For example, in the area of starting and running a law practice, Cami's clients have used the books The *E-Myth Attorney*, by Michael Gerber; and *How to Start and Run a Law Practice*, by Jay Foonberg. For networking, there is *The Little Black Book of Connections* by Jeffrey Gitomer. There is a book or blog on just about everything.

2. Leverage your network

Build and maintain a network of people you can call on with questions and for support, and make sure you make yourself available to these same people when they need help from you. People from various backgrounds, fields, industries, and even age groups can provide tremendous objective insights. Be willing and eager to call and ask for help. Contrary to popular belief, people like to be able to help you. Think about how honored you feel when someone you care about or respect asks you for help. Also, be willing and eager to give help to others. We all have a tremendous network. We often do not use it. This is a *huge* element of resourcefulness—who can you ask for information or for assistance?

Cami: I have a friend who is a doctor. I call her with my symptoms before deciding whether to go see my primary care physician. I have a friend who is a property manager. Anytime I need a plumber or handyman for one of my properties, I call her. She always has a name. I have someone who maintains my website and a Virtual Assistant to do administrative tasks for me. This includes tasks I could do, but which are not the most efficient use of my time, as well as those I do not know how to do and for which learning is not the best use of my time.

Start to make a list of people who are resources for you.
Who can help you with marketing?

_____

_____

Who can help you with networking?

_____

_____

Who can you call when you need to brainstorm about your business?

_____

_____

Which people would drop everything to help you out?

_____

_____

Who are the most important people in your circle of influence?

_____

_____

Who else do you know who you would consider a "resource" not yet listed here?

_____

_____

3. Learn everything you can about how to find information
Learn how to search online, in the library, and everywhere else. In this day and age, an incredible amount of information is literally at our fingertips. There are numerous websites devoted to the distribution of specific and general information on a variety of topics.

4. Teach resourceful habits
If your staff wants certain information, teach them how to find it themselves. When your team members come to a meeting with a problem, make it part of your company culture for them to also show up with a proposed solution. Make sure to encourage initiative. When your staff asks you a question, have your first response be, "What do you think?"

Resourcefulness means empowerment instead of dependency. In the long run, teaching others to be resourceful will free you up to do your own work more effectively. Empowerment is knowing you can find your own answers. Dependency is always relying on others for the answers. Note this distinction: _relying_ on others for the answers is unresourceful; using your relationships with others to _find_ the answers is resourceful. An added benefit is that people who are empowered to do their jobs themselves have more ownership and investment in their jobs and are often more effective, engaged, and happy in their work.

Resourcefulness Self-Reflections

Earlier we talked about MacGyver and Stroud. Take a moment now and reflect on the following questions:

Where/when are you often non-resourceful (ex: when I am hungry, feeling defeated, tired, sick)?

_____

_____

_____

Where (in what types of situations) have you been resourceful recently?

_____

_____

_____

Think of a time when you believed there was no way to get what you wanted, and yet out of your commitment and determination, you did it anyway. How were you able to do this?

_____

_____

_____

Non-Resourceful and Resourceful States

Non-Resourceful and Resourceful States

A **Non-Resourceful state** is one in which our internal resources are such that we cannot see all of our external resources. (For example, when we are tired, hungry, run down, or depressed.) Human beings have all the resources they need. The challenge is to be able to *access* those resources. It is the nature of coaching to assist people in recognizing their resources.

Resourceful [Webster's Dictionary]: "Able to use the means at one's disposal to meet situations effectively." This is the ability to recognize and utilize external resources.

How to Access Resources

When you have a goal, you may want to start with an intentional checklist of your resources. In chapter 2, on creating a goal—what we call a Well-Formed Outcome—one of the questions you ask yourself in fully defining your goal is "What resources do I need?" In that chapter, we state, "One of the most powerful things people learn through coaching is that they are completely resourceful, lacking nothing. There is an NLP presupposition that states, "People already have all the resources they need. What they lack is access to these resources at appropriate times and places." Recognizing you are completely resourceful is a first step to accessing your resources. The job of a coach is to ask questions that allow you to access your resources—to see them, discover them, remember them, and uncover them."

Below are questions a coach might ask in order to get you more in touch with your internal and external resources. This might be at the initial goal-formation stage, or when you feel stuck and are having a hard time moving forward. (Tip: These questions are often even more effective if you go through them orally with a partner or a group of people in a brainstorming session.)

Thinking about your goal, answer the following questions:

1. What is another way to get what I want? This is something you haven't tried or haven't thought of. (Many people say, "Well, if I knew what it was I would have thought of it by now." That is not necessarily true. Our minds don't see everything at any given time. These questions are designed to help you see things you have not seen before.)

_____

_____

_____

2. Who else has information that might help me? Again, your job is to look for resources where you have not looked before.

_____

_____

_____

3. What is something very similar to what I need that might also work? Think of other solutions to other similar problems and how those solutions might apply, in some altered form, to this problem. For example, one time Steph was getting ready to go hiking and her shoelace had broken. She found a bag with a drawstring that was similar to a bootlace and used that as a shoelace. Had she been fixated on finding an actual shoelace, she would not have been open to using the drawstring.

_____

_____

_____

4. Who is the expert in this area? Write down names of all the people who could help you get what you are after.

_____

_____

_____

5. What is one more thing I can try? This is where you think creatively and come up with options even if they seem silly or unworkable.

_____

_____

_____

6. **What am I not seeing?** Again, this is designed to have you look deeper or approach the solution in a different way

_____

_____

_____

7. **What would someone I admire do in this same situation?** (WWMD—What Would MacGyver Do?) It is powerful to put yourself in the shoes of someone you respect and admire and ask what they would do. You will be amazed at the ideas you can access in this way. Who do you know (or know of) who would handle this situation well? What would they do?

_____

_____

_____

8. **What are all the resources I have?** This includes both internal and external.

_____

_____

_____

9. **How can I make this work?** Again, consider even silly or foolish ideas; it will help you access other, more workable ones.

_____

_____

_____

_____

_____

Homework

Commitment

1. Review all of your business goals. For each one, assess your level of commitment—from 0 to 10—based on the *actions* you have taken. Do not assess based on what you are thinking about doing or would like to do. Do not assess based on how committed you wish you were. Look only at what you *have done.*

2. After completing number 1 above, for any goal in which your commitment level is less than a 10, ask yourself, "What am I more committed to than this goal?" You will find the answer by looking at your actions and what you have chosen to do

that has kept you from being at a level 10 commitment to your goal. Be sure to look for internal attitudes and beliefs that you might be more committed to than to reaching your goal.

Personal Obstacles

1. For any goal you have not yet reached, go through the process in this chapter on obstacles and identify your obstacles and create a strategy to move past them when they arise.

2. Make a list of those obstacles that seem to arise most frequently. At the end of each day or week, review your progress toward a particular goal or goals, and write down how you allowed those obstacles to stop you from fully achieving what you want. Also, track how you moved past the obstacle(s).

Resourcefulness

1. Write down all of the resources you have, and which you are already using, for various issues that arise. For instance, you may make a list of your business contacts, your referral lists, the skills of your staff and family members and books or other reference materials. Keep this list where you can easily access it.

2. Form a small group—your family members, co-workers, or colleagues—and after each of you completes Exercise 5 above, compare each other's resources, and see where you can "pool" them.

Chapter 5

Values-Based Living

"It's not hard to make decisions when you know what your values are."

Roy E. Disney

Why Read This Chapter?

1. Your life feels out of balance and you need a way to balance it.
2. You are dissatisfied with your position at your firm and are not sure why.
3. You want to find a way to choose a firm that fits your needs.
4. As managing partner, you want to find ways to hire associates and staff who will fit in with the firm.

Sam

Sam was very excited to be offered a position at Smith & Smith, a small litigation firm with a reputation for winning difficult cases. At first he loved his job; the cases were interesting and Sam was immediately in the thick of things. But after a while Sam began to dread going to work each day. At first, he could not figure out why. But then he realized that in his excitement, he overlooked certain aspects of the firm that made him uneasy. For instance, one of the married partners is having an affair with his secretary. And almost every Friday after work, all of the attorneys gather in the conference room and discuss the week's events, typically over wine or beer. Sam is married and has a baby on the way, so attending these Friday meetings is

Sam (cont.)

uncomfortable for him, as he would prefer to be home. They are also uncomfortable because the meetings often devolve into gossip about clients and even staff members at the firm. Sam sometimes finds himself joining in the banter, which makes him feel awful, especially when he encounters on Monday the staff member he was talking about on Friday. And he finds these meetings a waste of time—time he could be spending at home. He has made peace with the long hours during the week, but did not envision having to spend his leisure time at the office as well.

Sam has considered leaving the firm but when he thinks about it rationally, he cannot justify leaving. After all, he is paid a competitive salary; he is working on interesting cases; and he and his work appear to be valued. He tells himself he cannot ask for more. And yet he cannot shake his feeling of discomfort and dissatisfaction. Why does he feel so uncomfortable in a job that seems to suit him so well?

Judy

Judy is a young associate at a probate firm. When she applied for the job, she understood the firm did a lot of litigation, but now she finds herself in the estate-planning department, drafting wills and trusts, and performing legal research on various tax issues. When she asks to help with some of the litigation, she is told that she is more needed in the estate-planning department. When she makes other suggestions, such as how to handle certain clients, or proposes lectures that she or others in the firm could give at local events, or even regarding how she approaches her own workload, she is repeatedly—in her mind—"shot down." The firm has a certain way of doing things, and it is up to her to conform. She finds herself bored and seeking more challenge. Her job is tedious and she does not feel valued. Why does she feel so dissatisfied?

Part I—Personal Values

How Values Affect Life Balance

It is often with some surprise that young lawyers, fresh from law school, step into their first jobs and discover the amount of time required to be successful practicing law. Whether it is because she works for a firm that requires minimum billable hours or because he is starting his own practice, the new lawyer quickly realizes that practicing law requires a huge time commitment. Different attorneys deal with this time commitment in different ways, but the vast majority typically take time from other, more personal and satisfying pursuits, such as family, exercise, entertainment, relaxation, and sleep.

When combined with the inevitable pressures that seem to define the job (billable hours, client demands, partner or employer demands and the hallmark conflict that is the nature of the business) many attorneys find themselves feeling dissatisfied and typically out of balance. One can only deprive oneself of companionship, entertainment, exercise and sleep for so long before feeling like something has to "give."

Some attorneys deal with these challenges by ignoring them or hoping they will just go away until they begin to wonder if they have made the right career choice. Others self medicate with alcohol or recreational drugs. Statistically, attorneys have twice the incidence of alcoholism than the general population. (Debra Cassens Weiss, *Lawyer Depression Comes out of the Closet*, ABA Journal (2007).) And according to a 2006 study of NALP (National Association for Law Placement), 78 percent of new associates leave their firms by the end of their 5th year (up from 60 percent in 2000). Some attorneys cope by doing nothing until something in their personal life demands attention; for example, a neglected spouse threatens to leave the relationship or a child starts to act out.

In this chapter, we will discuss what we call "life balance." A few words about this term. Some people use the phrase "work-life balance." We don't like that term because it implies there are two facets to your existence: "work" and "life." We believe there is only life, and that fragmentation and compartmentalization of "work" and "personal life" do not serve you. It is far more useful to have your life function well as a whole. We believe every area of your life affects the whole of your being.

Also, let's be clear about the term "balance." We do not suggest that you should devote an equal amount of time to all areas of your life. That would be unworkable. The term "balance" as we use it refers to a situation in which you feel satisfied with the level of time and attention you are paying the different areas of your life, that you are honoring those areas you find important, and that you are conscious of where you spend your time and make choices that honor all your values.

Having said this, there are many ways to introduce more balance into your life. And it is most useful to do this *before* you feel the effects of being out of balance. In this chapter, we will offer one fundamental way to start making choices that balance your life: identifying and beginning to live your **values**.

Most people do not give a lot of thought to the concept of "values." But you have values that are uniquely yours even if you have never thought about them. You live your values every day, even if you do not realize it. They are guiding you right now. But when you honor certain values and ignore others, you will feel "out of balance." This is often a feeling that something is not quite right, that no matter how hard you work things will never be how you want them to be. Being out of balance can also manifest through sickness and other bodily ailments or a lack of energy and enthusiasm or a breakdown in your relationships.

Your values are more than simply what you like or want; they are principles you need to honor in order to be who you truly are and to feel fulfilled in your life. If you take the time to discover your values, you will become conscious of what is important to you. By making conscious choices that honor all of your values, you will create a sense of balance in your life. Ignoring any of your values will cause stress, dis-ease, and frustration. As you discover what is truly important to you and begin to make choices based on what you value, you will experience a greater sense of well-being and fulfillment. So let's see what your values are!

What are Values?

Values are the consciously-chosen guiding principles that actively encompass every area of your life.

Values align with who you truly are.

Values are greater than your likes and dislikes.

Values, once declared and owned, require action.

Values, unlike beliefs, encompass every area of your life.

Values, once embraced, do not change, although your definition and understanding of them may expand through the years.

Values define your "stand" in life.

Values, because they define your "stand" in life, require certain behaviors, decisions, and choices.

Values, because they define your "stand" in life, create the boundaries and standards by which you live.

Values, which define your way of "being," flow into and define your behavior, your way of "doing."

Values are not prioritized; every value you embrace is equally important.

Values-based choices are simple, though not always easy to make.

Values-based choices, while not always easy to make, are clear.

Values-based choices, while clear, may be difficult to act on.

Values-based choices, while difficult to act on, are simple.

Thank you to Premier Educational Systems, Focus material, 6-13-05

Discovering Your Values

There are several ways to determine your values. We will give you three exercises. We suggest you do all three. This will allow you to clearly determine *your* values.

A few examples of values:			
Creativity	Integrity	Honesty	Respect
Productivity	Self-expression	Service	Kindness
Spontaneity	Spirituality	Individuality	Team-work
Partnership	Courage	Education	Commitment
Humor	Diversity	Accountability	Vulnerability
Acknowledgement	Fairness/justice	Health	Connection w/others
Abundance	Peace	Collaboration	Diligence
Loyalty	Gratitude	Growth	Risk-taking

Note: There are websites where you can find hundreds of examples of values. Sample values are given here only for the sake of example because we believe it is more effective for you to name your values yourself.

Exercise No. 1: Honoring your values

1. Set aside an hour or so.
2. Bring to mind three different times in your life when you were very happy, truly fulfilled, and felt energized and alive. Answer these questions for each experience, and write the answers down in detail:
   - What was I doing?
   - Where was I?
   - Who was I with?
   - What made this a fulfilling experience?
3. As you reflect on these experiences, ask yourself, "What value was I living and honoring at that time in each experience?" Whenever we feel happy, fulfilled or at peace we are living our values.

Determining what value or values you were honoring in each experience will be a very personal undertaking. For example, if the time you recall being most fulfilled, you were skydiving, perhaps you value RISK, COURAGE or ADVENTURE. If your fulfilling time was being on vacation in Yellowstone National Park, you might value BEAUTY, CONNECTION with nature, SOLITUDE, PEACE, SPIRITUALITY or something else that time evoked for you. The point is that your value will represent whatever was important about the situation *to you*.

If you need help identifying your values, see the insert above. The main question is this: what is important to you at your core? Do not simply pick values from the list. Look into *your* life and uncover the values that are already there. This requires real life examination, not an intellectual process. Make the distinction between something outside yourself that you *place value on* (such as your home, your family, or nature) and *internal qualities*, unique to you that *cause you* to place value on certain experiences or possessions. For example, "family" is not a value, but if family is important to you, then "connection with others" or "being in service" as a parent may be the value that having a family honors. Always ask what is the *internal* value that makes a particular experience important to you?

Once you have created a list of five to ten values you recall living, move on to the next exercise.

Exercise No. 2: Ignoring your values
This second exercise is the flip side of the first.

1. Set aside some time to reflect.
2. Think of three different times in your life when you were dissatisfied—angry, frustrated, or upset. Answer these questions for each experience, and write down the answers in detail:
   • Where was I?
   • Who was there?
   • What was happening?
   • What choices did I make?
   • What made this a dissatisfying experience?
3. After describing the experiences, ask yourself what values you were neglecting at that time. For example, if you remember a time when you were experiencing chaos in your family and people were not getting along with each other, what is the fundamental value you were not honoring? Was it PEACE, CONNECTION, LOVE, RESPECT or something else? Perhaps during your unhappy time you were indoors a lot. Perhaps you were ill or had a desk job under fluorescent lights. The value you were neglecting may have been HEALTH, PHYSICAL ACTIVITY, or perhaps even CONNECTION with others. The value not being honored will be different for different people. The question is, for *you*, what was missing; what fundamental piece of your makeup did you ignore at that time? The values you discover in this exercise may be the same as the five to ten identified in Exercise No. 1, or you may discover additional values.

In the case studies at the beginning of this chapter, it may be that Sam values LOYALTY and RESPECT, and that he did not feel those values were being honored by his firm. The firm may have had other values—like CONNECTION WITH OTHERS and SELF-EXPRES-SION—which it believed it was honoring by holding Friday night meetings and turning a blind eye to the partner's affair. Judy may value CREATIVITY and RISK-TAKING, and it may be those values are not shared by her firm. That firm may have been honoring other values, such as PRODUCTIVITY and DILIGENCE. There is nothing inherently right or wrong about any particular values. The question is how they are expressed—individually and at a firm level—and whether those values held by others, such as clients, co-workers, or the law firm itself, are similar to or clash with ours.

Exercise No. 3: The pie of life

To bring your life into balance, you must find a way to honor all of your values. This requires you to look at where you spend your time. The benefit of determining your values by observing your activities is that it reveals what you value, based not on who you would *like* to be or who you think you *should* be, but based upon who you *are*—what you are honoring in your life today. This exercise will also help you determine what values you may be ignoring to the extent you feel out of balance.

In this exercise, spend one week writing down *everything* you do—work, sleep, talking with family, chores, working out, watching television, socializing, gardening, etc. At the end of the week, add up the number of hours you spent on each activity (there are 168 hours in a week) and then create a pie chart. (For a tool to create a pie chart, go to our website, www.mclarencoaching.com/bookdownloads/.) Divide the pie into sections that describe where you spend your time. For instance, if you spent fifty hours sleeping this week, then somewhat less than one-third of the pie would be devoted to sleep. From the list of values you developed in the first two exercises, label each daily action by the value or values you are honoring in performing that activity. Or you may discover new values in this exercise. Label the values in a way that resonates for you. For example, for one person, exercising may represent the value of HEALTH; for another it may represent PEACE; for another RESPECT of self; for another, FUN. Or it may be several of these. Each pie wedge will represent the percentage of the total amount of time (out of 168 hours) you spent living each particular value. Your chart of activities may look like this:

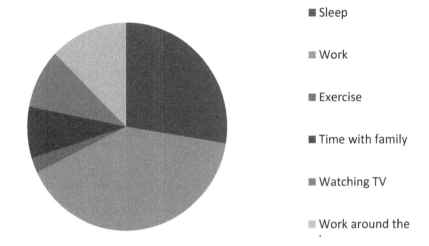

When you translate your activities into your values, your chart may look like this:

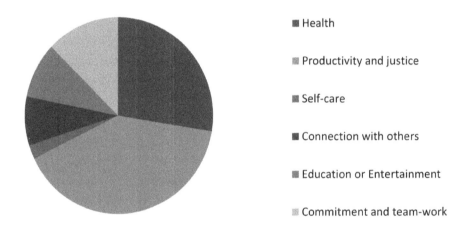

Define Your Values

When you have completed each of the foregoing three exercises, create a list of your top ten values. These may include a value that surfaced only once during the exercises but that really resonates for you, as well as those that repeatedly appeared in each exercise. However you choose your values will work for you.

The next step is to define your values. List your top ten values, then create a definition for each one. Do not refer to the dictionary or any other outside source, at least initially. Rather, define what each value means to you, using the definitions they represent for you. You will know how to define your values by looking at the prior three exercises and the experiences you recalled which brought these values to light. For example, perhaps in Exercise No. 2, you remember a time in your life when you did not feel well because you were not eating well and you thus articulated a value called HEALTH. Perhaps in the Pie of Life, you identified time you spent sleeping as HEALTH and the time you were meditating was also called HEALTH. Looking at all three exercises, therefore, you may define HEALTH as a body-mind connection that honors the strength of your body and the peace in your mind.

Another person may have labeled HEALTH as the value honored during activities such as rock-climbing, running marathons, taking vitamins and drinking sufficient water. This person's definition of HEALTH may be different from yours. Perhaps this person defines HEALTH as "pushing my body to the limits of endurance and physical challenge while maintaining the internal reserves to allow me to function at a high level." The definition of HEALTH will be different for everyone. Defining values is an intensely personal experience.

The foregoing are examples of how to use the three exercises above to craft definitions for your values. The definitions are important because they allow you to set a framework of values from which to live your life and practice your profession.

Finally, display your values. Take some time, tap into your inner artist, and create a document for all to see. We know attorneys who frame their values and hang them proudly on the walls of their office. Clients see what is important to the attorney. It sets the attorney apart from others in the profession. We know one attorney who is a single parent of two young boys; she had meetings with her children in order to establish their family values, and then had the values stenciled around the top of the kitchen wall in her home. She is displaying the family values proudly for the children to learn and remember, and for visitors to see what is important to her.

Values are the guiding principles in your life and represent who you are and the stand you take. There is no need to deny or hide them. It is useful to have them out for all to see. Being bold and articulate about your values will make you a model for balance and intentional living.

Living in Balance

Once you complete these exercises and have written and defined your top ten values, the next step is to see where you are out of balance. As to each of your values, rate yourself on a scale of 1 to 10 as to how satisfied you are with how you currently "live" each value.

You may wish to look back at your Pie of Life to determine your ratings. The Pie of Life gives you an honest assessment as to how you are living right now. It is important to begin by honestly observing your behavior as it really is, rather than as you wish it were. If you discover that SELF-CARE is one of your values but your Pie of Life shows that you barely sleep six hours a night and spend no time exercising or socializing with friends, this is important information in rating your level of satisfaction with the value you call SELF-CARE[1]

Once you have established your values and the extent to which you live each one, you can begin to make changes in your life that will allow you to live all of them consciously and more consistently. Begin small; create an action step you can take this week that will allow you to live one of your values that you are not fully recognizing. For example, if your fulfillment of your HEALTH value is low, this week commit to exercising three days, or eating more vegetables and/or taking vitamins—whatever works for you. See how it feels to put these practices in place. You will feel better when you honor your values more consistently. The following week, increase your time with another value. If you are neglecting your PEACE value, perhaps you will go on a solitary walk for ten minutes a day or meditate for five minutes. (See chapter 6, The Case for Self-Maintenance, for how to meditate and the benefits of meditation.)

When you consciously choose where to spend your time, it is much easier to balance the various areas of your life. As stated above, "balance" is different for everyone. Balance is often identified as a feeling. When your life is in balance, you bring more energy to your work and to everything you do. As a result, you feel more centered, fulfilled and satisfied.

Making Decisions Based on Your Values

Not only is it beneficial to know your values so you can create a sense of ease and balance in your life; knowing your values is useful as a decision-making tool. We often find ourselves unsure of what to do, what job offer to take, whether to accept a particular client, or which litigation tactic to employ. Making those decisions is easier and results in fewer regrets when based on one's values.

Steph: After completing these exercises I identified certain of my values as PEACE, RESPECT and COMPASSION. I vowed not to become antagonistic or needlessly confrontational in my practice. One day, I received a rather scathing letter from opposing counsel, accusing me of being unethical. The letter contained factual inaccuracies about some of my actions and blew the significance of others out of proportion. I immediately felt defensive and my first instinct was to fight back. But then I remembered my values. When I focused more on my values and less on my ego, I realized that such a reaction would not only be counter to my values of PEACE, RESPECT and COMPASSION—values I had decided to uphold in my life and my practice—but could jeopardize my client's case by needlessly antagonizing opposing counsel. Once I focused on my values, I was

---

1.   You can also go to our website, www.mclarencoaching.com/bookdownloads/, and find a "spider graph" to use in creating a visual representation of your life balance. The "spider graph" is a wheel with your top eight values. When you assess your level of satisfaction with each value, the wheel is re-shaped based on the different levels. The closer you are to having the same level of satisfaction in each area, the smoother the wheel will turn. The wheel illustrates that life balance is not about achieving maximum satisfaction in any one area, but about improving satisfaction in the areas you have neglected.

able to craft a response that was neither defensive nor submissive, but that acknowledged how opposing counsel might have misconstrued or misunderstood my actions (COM-PASSION), urged him to call me on the telephone if he had concerns about certain of my actions (RESPECT), and stated my intention to litigate the case professionally and urged him to do the same (PEACE). This letter took a lot of unbilled time to write, and admit-tedly, my early drafts included back-handed insults (it can be challenging to let go of this attorney "drift"). But in the end, it was not only a letter of which I was proud; it enabled me and opposing counsel to litigate more peacefully. Had I not been in touch with my own values before responding to the letter, I might have quickly found myself out of bal-ance with my PEACE value!

As this example illustrates, the benefit of knowing your values is that it allows you to become conscious in making choices. Notice how Steph's initial reaction to fight back did not consciously honor her values. This situation is a good example of how values define our "stand" in life. Remember in chapter 1 we discussed that the attorney "drift" is often to be confrontational and disrespectful. As we described, a "drift" is an unconscious, habitual way of reacting to a situation. Here you are learning to respond to situations *consciously*. Steph's work in defining her values and her commitment to make choices based on her values, allowed her to take a stand for those values and thereby improve the quality of her life and practice.

Let's look at another example of values-based decision-making:

Bill is at that point many attorneys reach in their careers where they ask themselves, "Do I want to go out on my own or work for a firm?" To assist Bill in discovering his best path, a coach would suggest he look to the values he determined from the exercises above. Let's assume his top five values are: CREATIVITY, AUTHENTICITY, DIVERSITY, INTEGRITY, and CONNECTION WITH OTHERS. How might Bill decide whether to start his own practice or join a firm?

This is a very personal decision that will be based largely on the definition of the val-ues Bill has identified. What does it mean to be CREATIVE? How does being creative affect his professional life? What is AUTHENTICITY to him? Can he honor this value and still work in a firm? Does his choice depend on characteristics of the firm? He will want to ask himself if he is more likely to honor his DIVERSITY value at a firm or on his own He will consider if his value of CONNECTION WITH OTHERS means he wants to work with others on a daily basis and might feel lonely on his own. Bill will look at his values and the definitions he has given to them and then ask these types of questions. In this way he guides himself to his answer.

If Bill ultimately decides he is better suited to working in a firm based on his values, he should also check his values in determining *which* firm, or which type of firm he wants to work for. He will ask many questions similar to those above. For example, using these same five values of CREATIVITY, AUTHENTICITY, DIVERSITY, INTEGRITY and

CONNECTION WITH OTHERS, Bill will ask (1) Will this firm allow me to be creative as I have defined this value? (2) Will I be able to be my authentic self at the firm? (3) How diverse does this firm seem to be, and how diverse are the clients? (4) What do I know about the firm's integrity, or lack thereof, as I have defined this value? (5) How open are members of the firm to having personal connections with others? And of course, (6) What can I do to help me determine the values of this firm?

Part II—Determining Firm Values

We started this chapter with basics on how individuals may determine their own values. Whatever you are doing in your career, we highly recommend going through these exercises and identifying your values and beginning to live them. At the end of this chapter, there are exercises you can do to help you become accustomed to living in this manner, deciding in this manner, determining whether your values are in alignment with your actions at any given time, and developing new habits in keeping with your values.

Now we will discuss applying values to a broader group of people: the law firm. In this section you will learn the benefit of creating, and how to create, a Values Statement for your firm. We will also discuss the benefit of addressing, and how to address, the idea of values in your firm. This may well be a novel concept for your firm.

Note: As you go through this section, all of these ideas and procedures can be applied to other groups and organizations, including the family unit. Much good will come of sitting down with your family and talking about values, particularly with children. Consider where you were in relation to talking and thinking about values when you started this chapter and what you have since learned. If you have children, imagine the possibilities if they grow up talking about values and learning about family values, what they are, what they mean and how to use them. This can provide a place for families to come together and create a foundation for behavior and expectations in your household. It will provide guidance to your children as they encounter challenges throughout their lives. If you don't have children, try talking to your spouse, siblings, or parents.

1. Why Do you Want to Articulate Your Firm's Values?

These days many companies have a Mission Statement and/or a Values Statement. What is the benefit of a company Values Statement? Consider the following:

- As with personal decisions, firm decisions are easier to make when based on articulated values.
- Values provide a measure of consistency and alignment within the firm.

- A company Values Statement allows individual attorneys and staff to determine if their values align with firm values.
- The people who come together to create the firm's Values Statement will have a greater level of ownership for firm activities, policies, procedures, management and actions.

a. As with personal decisions, firm decisions are easier to make when based on articulated values.

As described earlier in this chapter, when people learn to make decisions based on values, decisions become easier to make. When firm members are solidly grounded in firm values and what they mean, those members can use them to guide their choices. Rather than feeling "at sea" when a new or unexpected situation arises, members of the firm, from managing partners to secretaries and law clerks, will have a solid basis on which to make decisions and take actions.

b. Values provide a measure of consistency within the firm.

When all firm members make decisions based on the firm's values, you can be confident the firm is acting consistently. This not only creates a sense of stability and consistency within the firm, but it enables members to know what to expect from one another and what is expected of themselves.

Later, we will offer you an exercise to determine your firm's values. For now, let's look at another example:

Pam's law firm has done the work outlined below and her firm's values include HONESTY, CONTRIBUTION, INDIVIDUALITY, and ABUNDANCE. (Part of the exercise below is to define what these terms mean.) In defining these terms, Pam's firm decides the following: HONESTY means integrity, open communication within the firm, and telling the truth to clients, judges, and opposing counsel. CONTRIBUTION means all are in service to members of the community, and all provide value to the clients and to one another. INDIVIDUALITY means firm members value the opinion of each person at the firm; attorneys are allowed to guide their cases with oversight, but without micro-management; and there is a belief in the capabilities of each person at the firm. ABUNDANCE means the firm's intention is to make money for all involved in the firm in a way that honors each person's contribution.

Now a client comes to Pam's firm, and Pam does the intake for this client. Pam discovers this client is lying about pertinent facts and that part of her firm's representation of the client would require the firm to conceal those facts. This client is offering to pay a large sum of money for the firm's representation. Without a set of firmly articulated values, this might be a difficult decision for Pam to make, and may result in second-guessing by other members of the firm. But since Pam's firm has clearly-articulated values, which she understands and has been trained to examine in making the decision, then whatever

Pam decides—whether it is to reject the case, explain to the client that the firm is unwilling to conceal facts, or some other action—that decision will be consistent with her firm's values. No matter what the ultimate decision, it will be the "right" one for the firm, as it will honor the firm's values of HONESTY and ABUNDANCE, regardless of the outcome.

Having clearly-articulated values helps guide all members of the firm in their decision-making process. For instance, your legal secretaries will be more likely to bring something to your attention that seems dishonest. Junior associates will be less likely to take actions that may be problematic for the firm. Managing partners will know what example they are setting. This is because all members will be clear as to what is expected of them. In this way, all members of the firm will be working on the same team.

c. A firm Values Statement allows individual attorneys and staff to determine if their values align with firm values.

An old episode of "The Practice" illustrates the problems that can arise when a firm does not have a set of clearly articulated values. In this episode, associate attorneys Eleanor and Lyndsey face a situation in which one of the jurors in the criminal case they have just finished trying sees Lyndsey and tells her the client has "nothing to worry about." Young, idealistic Lyndsey tells Eleanor about the conversation and insists they inform the judge. Eleanor explains that they don't have to, as the evidence is in and the trial is over, and Lyndsey did not initiate contact with the juror or even speak to him. Although Lyndsey is convinced they need to tell the judge, she eventually agrees with Eleanor. The plot thickens when the District Attorney offers the client a good deal, which the client decides to take. At that point, Eleanor tells the client about the juror's comment, and the client decides to reject the deal. But when the jury comes back with a guilty verdict, Eleanor tells the judge that the client would have taken a much better deal, but for the juror's comment to Lyndsey, thus prompting the judge to decide they should both be disbarred.

What follows is the essence of why a firm needs specific articulated values. When managing partner Bobby Donnell is informed of these matters, he becomes enraged and tells Eleanor and Lyndsey that they have disgraced not only themselves but also the firm. Not so fast, Eleanor retorts. She explains that her decision not to tell the judge is precisely in keeping with the firm's "culture," and that she was acting consistently with what Bobby has made it clear the firm stands for, which is to win at all costs; bend the rules; integrity be damned. After learning what his associates think of his firm, and of him, Bobby does some soul-searching. He calls a meeting of all the attorneys to discuss the purpose and vision of the firm. This opens the door for Bobby's staff to explain how they see him and the firm. And it gives them an opportunity to determine whether their own personal values align with the firm.

Obviously this is television, and not real life. But it provides a perfect example of what can happen when attorneys "think" they understand the firm's values and the managing partner has never made it clear—or perhaps has never even thought about—what those values are. And it certainly highlights the problems that can arise when the managing partner thinks the firm has one set of values, while his actions demonstrate another. The truth is a law firm, like an individual, has a set of values that guides its collective behavior, even if not articulated.

It should not take a potential State Bar complaint from a judge to goad a firm into identifying and describing its values. This will not only provide your employees with a set of guiding principles from which to make decisions, but it will allow them to determine whether their own values align with the firm's.

d. The people who come together to create the firm's Values Statement will have a greater level of ownership for firm activities, policies, procedures, management, and actions.

It has been said that parties to a lawsuit are more likely to comply with a settlement to which they have agreed and in which they had input, than they are with a judgment that is handed to them from the court. Why is that? It is likely due to a concept called "ownership." When we create a plan ourselves, as opposed to having someone else impose it upon us, we are more likely to follow it. Similarly, involving all members of the firm in determining the firm's values gives those individuals a sense of ownership and alignment with those values.

The process of the firm coming together as a team and going through the exercises in this chapter will create an alliance among participants, with each feeling a part of the process, rather than having the concepts thrust upon them and being forced to comply with an agenda they had no hand in creating. This process makes it far more likely they will act in accordance with the values. It will also give them a sense of ownership within the firm. They will feel it is "their" firm, in which they play an integral part. It is a way to demonstrate true respect for all members of the firm and each person's contribution.

2. How to Discover and Articulate Your Firm's Values

(1) **Ideally, you will bring together all members of your firm for this process.** This includes not only the attorneys, but the secretaries and other legal staff. In addition to promoting alliance and ownership, having everyone's input (managing partners, associates, legal secretaries, paralegals, and even your receptionist) is useful because it gives you everyone's perspective, which may be very different. You may be surprised what you learn. This is partly because in determining firm values, you will not be asking what you *wish* the firm stood for, but asking what it actually does stand for. You will be seeking a realistic assessment of what the firm actually *demonstrates* as its values.

(2) **Find a time you can all be together for an uninterrupted period in a relaxed environment.** Turn off all phones and discourage interruptions.

(3) **Consider using a neutral and uninvolved facilitator or coach to run the meeting.** If not, be sure your facilitator is not attached to the outcome. This could be done by having the facilitator either agree not to offer opinions on the values or to only do so anonymously.

(4) **Explain the concept of "values" to participants.** (You may wish to have them read part I of this chapter.) You may even want to present this concept in writing, either in a Power Point, or as part of a handout. As we noted above, your firm values already exist. Articulation of values will *not* be a list of what sounds good to you. It *will* be based on *evidence* of behaviors and decisions currently being made and observed at your firm. If you are a partner, it may take some courage to ask these questions. As in "The Practice," values are the principles that show up in actions and decisions and are modeled by the partners, associates and staff. Be willing to ask people what they are seeing.

(5) **Break into manageable-sized groups for discussion.** Have each group discuss the questions listed below, identifying specific evidence to support their answers. Do not rely on feelings, but on concrete evidence that shows up in decisions and actions. If you say this firm values "respect," you will need to support that statement, perhaps by citing evidence that last week you saw Sally upset about something and Frank discretely called her into his office to discuss the situation. You may say this is evidence of respect. Or perhaps the firm values "teamwork," as evidenced by the fact that all of the secretaries and attorneys stayed late to finish Vicki's motion for summary judgment—even though it was not their own case. None of the questions listed below is meant to imply a particular answer or that there is a right answer or that your firm should be different than it is. This is simply an inquiry to enable you to notice what actually occurs in your firm in the context of values determination. This is not a place for blame-laying or finger-pointing. Indeed, it will be important for members to approach this inquiry neutrally and objectively, being very curious about what goes on at the firm. For example, one of the questions asks about the number of men, women and minorities at your firm. This question is not meant to imply that if all the attorneys are white men, you are lacking in respect. But it may have implications as to presence or absence of a diversity value. On the other hand, you may notice diversity elsewhere, or that diversity is not a value for your firm. This is not a judgment, but a chance to simply notice, objectively, how values are honored in the firm through actions and decisions. You will want to look at all of the questions to decide.

- What do people celebrate in this firm?
- What do people disparage at this firm?
- What kinds of language do you use in the firm? Is it respectful? What is your tone?
- What do people talk about?
- What happens when someone needs help?
- Where do firm members spend most of their time during work hours?
- Where do firm members spend most of their time during non-work hours?

- What does the physical environment look like?
- Do most employees work alone or in teams?
- What is the level of acknowledgement for individual efforts?
- What is the attitude towards money?
- What is the attitude towards productivity?
- How do people feel about overtime?
- Who works overtime, how often, and why?
- What is the relationship between attorneys and support staff?
- What do you notice with regard to integrity and honesty?
- Where does your firm fall on the continuum between risk-taking and safe-playing?
- How many women, men, people of color, or gay people work at your firm?
- What is the sense of humor in your firm?
- What pro bono work do you do? How much? What is the attitude toward it?
- What is the reaction when one person expresses a view not held by the firm, particularly if that person is support staff?
- To what extent do people take responsibility for their own actions?
- Are there people at the firm you find intimidating? Why do they intimidate you?
- Who are your typical clients?
- Add other questions you think are helpful.

Note, the questions are meant to elicit members' ideas about firm values. They are meant to open a discussion about what different people observe at the firm.

(6) **After the foregoing discussion, distribute a 3x5 card to each participant.** On the card, have each person individually list the top five values he or she believes exist in the firm. Collect the cards and list the top ten values on an easel (top values are determined by counting how many people chose the same value).

(7) As a group, create definitions for at least the top five values.

3. Now That you Have Them, What Will you do With Them?

With regard to your firm's individual values, we recommend that you have them printed and framed and posted conspicuously in your office. Spare no expense. Make this document beautiful and elegant and display it proudly. You may wish to have all participants sign it.

Begin engaging in activities that solidify firm values. See the end of this chapter for exercises to solidify firm values.

Use values in your hiring process. Talk to potential employees about your firm values and ask what they think about these values. Although certain laws may prevent you from delving too deeply into the potential employees' own values, their reactions to the description of the firm's values can be very telling. This may help you avoid making a costly investment in an employee whose personal values may not align with the firm's.

4. What if Your Firm Does not Want to Talk About Values?

We have examined a process that will allow the firm to work together in identifying values. But what if other partners in your firm are not open to this type of process? Or what if you are an associate and are not comfortable bringing this to the firm's attention? Do you still want to discover your firm's values on your own? What would be the benefit?

The main reason to discover your firm values is to see if there is a "fit" between the values of your firm and your own personal values. It is a good idea to do this regardless of how you feel about your firm. If you are feeling uncomfortable at your firm, we definitely recommend you do this, as discomfort is often indicative of values being out of alignment. But even if you feel comfortable, values determination will give you insight as to how well you fit with the firm's values, allowing you to make an informed decision about your future.

You will recall that values already exist. As such, you can begin to determine firm values simply by looking at the behavior you see inside the firm. Our recommendation is you look at the list of questions posed above in the section on determining firm values and that you answer those questions yourself. A word of caution: since you will be deciding your firm values alone, your perception may be skewed. Be sure to look at all of the *evidence* you can find. If you feel there are people in the firm with whom you can discuss this, ask for their input in answering the questions. Perform this exercise when you are feeling neutral and not emotional about something that is bothering you at the firm.

Once you have answered the questions, create a list of firm values. Then, take your own values, and compare the two. Because values are deep-seated and are your guiding principles, your own satisfaction in the firm will be based on the level of alignment between your values and the firm's. Note: You cannot change your values to fit with the firm's, and trying to do so will likely cause unease. If the firm values homogeneity and you value diversity; if it values safety and you value risk-taking, you will likely feel a mismatch in this environment. You may decide this environment is not best for you. You may wish to find a firm that aligns more with your values.

Homework

For Individuals

1. **For two weeks, every day note how you are *feeling*.** Do this at three different times during the day. You may want to set an alarm to remind you to do this at different times. If you feel good, notice what values you are honoring. If you feel bad, notice what values you are not honoring.
2. **For the next two weeks, every day make a decision that is consciously based on your**

values.[2] Even if it is where to go to dinner, stop and ask which choice will honor a value or values. In this way, you will get in the habit of consciously choosing from your values.

3. **Talk to people about values.** Talk to your spouse and family about values and what they mean to you and to others. Be very curious with them, knowing this may be a concept they have not considered in the past. Be open to values that may differ from your own.

For the Firm

The sky's the limit here. You will truly be limited only by your own imagination. Because you are dealing with a team, the possibilities are endless. Here are a few suggestions.

1. **Talk about values.** At your meetings, bring out your values statement. Relate your activities (the cases you take, the clients you represent, your employee policies) to specific values. Make sure all employees have their own copy of the firm's values. Encourage them to keep a copy at their desk or on their office wall. Foster an open dialogue on firm values.

2. **Set up a meeting at least once a month to discuss the values and how the firm is aligning with them.** Ask for examples of where the firm is aligning with its stated values and where it is not. Do this in a non-judgmental and neutral conversation in which everything comes out on the table and suggestions are made for how to align with whatever values are not being honored. Be very curious about when and where and which values members of the firm are and are not exhibiting.

3. **Have a copy expensively printed and framed and placed on your firm wall in a common area, where everyone can see it, including clients.** Values are important to articulate and display. They let people know where you stand. Posting them makes a statement—this is what we stand for and we are proud of it. This makes your firm more attractive to clients and employees who share the same set of values.

---

2.   As set out above, we are always choosing based on our values. The objective of this exercise is to begin to *consciously* choose based on *particular* values.

Chapter 6

The Case for Self-Maintenance

"[The] most productive lives are characterised by the ability to fully engage in the challenge at hand, but also to disengage periodically and seek renewal."

Loehr and Schwartz, *The Power of Full Engagement: Managing Energy, Not Time, Is the Key to High Performance and Personal Renewal*

Why Read this Chapter?

1. You are tired, stressed or sick a lot.
2. You feel like there are not enough hours in the day to take care of yourself.
3. You feel overworked.
4. You are having a hard time getting all your work done.
5. You discovered in the prior [values] chapter that you have a value regarding "self-care" and do not know how to define or honor it.
6. You are feeling "out of balance."
7. Unless you are feeling relaxed and focused most of the time, there is really no reason *not* to read this chapter if you are a practicing attorney.

Introduction

There is nothing more important in balancing life, practice and one's entire existence, than self-maintenance.

One of our favorite metaphors for personal maintenance is that of the oxygen mask on the plane. After you get on the plane and sit down to read, the flight attendants tell you that should there be a loss in cabin pressure, oxygen masks will drop out of the overhead compartment. They state that if you are traveling with small children you must put on your oxygen mask first before assisting your children.

Here is the problem: most parents are unlikely to put the oxygen mask on themselves **before** helping their kids. But what will happen in this type of situation if you do not take care of yourself first? You have a minute or two before you pass out. You go with your instinct to save this person you love—and in the process you lose consciousness. But if you put the mask on yourself first, then you maintain consciousness and are thus able to help your child—and other people.

Why do we have to be told this? Because frequently we do not, as a natural response, take care of ourselves first. We often see taking care of ourselves as selfish. What we do not seem to fully appreciate is that we are of little use to anyone else if we have not taken care of ourselves first. We may appreciate it logically, but we often do not really believe it in a way that affects our behavior.

As we express repeatedly in this book, the key to making significant change in our lives is to learn not to be "reactive," but to be "responsive." A *response* is a conscious assessment of the situation and a conscious and deliberate action. It reflects an awareness of the situation. A *reaction* (which is a reflexive action) is unthinking, unconscious and knee-jerk in nature. If you are conscious of the ramifications of working to get an oxygen mask on one child (or more), you will realize you *must* take care of yourself first.

The late Stephen Covey called this "the pause button." This is the space between stimulus and response. It is the difference between reacting from an impulse and responding from conscious choice. And it is *key* to making the choices that work for us as opposed to the choices we unthinkingly make, that often do not work as well.

Steph: I remember a story I heard about a doctor in a war-torn third-world country. Sick and injured people were arriving at the hospital faster than the medical staff could care for them. Doctors and nurses were rushing around at a break-neck pace. Suddenly one of the doctors stopped, sat down, and began eating a sandwich. A woman whose child had just been brought to the hospital saw this and yelled at him to get back to work or her son would die. The doctor looked up at her and calmly said, "That may be true. But if I don't get something to eat, many more will die."

The challenge is to see the connection between your well-being (physical and otherwise) and your ability to do your job well and help other people. It may feel like everything is urgent and life-threatening, but that is a reaction and not a response. In this chapter our intention is you learn to consciously assess the need to take care of yourself, and do it even when it seems inconvenient or pointless.

This chapter follows the values chapter because the chances are good that you have a value you call SELF-CARE or HEALTH or something along those lines. If you did not discover it in the values chapter work, you may have called it something else. Another reason this chapter follows the values chapter is because honoring all of your values is a great way to engage in self-maintenance.

This chapter precedes the time management chapter because the oxygen mask metaphor is counterintuitive to most people and it is similar to certain of the time management techniques that we will teach you. In that chapter, among other things, you will be coached to take more personal time for yourself as a way to work *smarter* and not harder, and thus more efficiently.

There are many terms for the concept of self-maintenance. You might call it self-care, health, self-preservation, regeneration, or rejuvenation. In his book, *The Seven Habits of Highly Effective People*, Stephen Covey calls it "sharpening the saw." He uses this term because it is part of a metaphor he describes in which two men are sawing down a tree. One man saws consistently and without pause. The other regularly stops and sharpens the blade of his saw before resuming. It is the second man who fells the tree first, and with less total effort than the first.

For most attorneys, it takes either a high degree of trust and faith or an experience of "hitting bottom" to become truly committed to self-care. You may opt for the former and begin to make changes based on faith or even just to "try it out." On the other hand, many attorneys (and others) must face a health scare or other crisis before they realize they must make a change. This is partly because of the drift we described in chapter 1. Attorneys believe hard work and sacrifice are the paramount virtues of law practice. Indeed most achievement-oriented people in other lines of work believe the same thing, though few are as ensconced in this drift as the attorney. Part of the "hard work and sacrifice" mindset is "I don't need to take care of myself; when I get this task done, I'll feel much better; I feel fine now, so I don't need to do anything for myself; I've done this for years and I'm still here...."

Susan

Susan is the head of litigation in a small well-respected firm. Her specialty is defending medical malpractice claims. She is an excellent trial attorney. Thus, her clients, most of whom are doctors and hospitals, insist that she, and not one of the other partners or associates, try their cases. Consequently, she is always either in trial or preparing for trial. Given the nature of medical-malpractice cases, she is always either working or thinking about work.

Her rare vacations come unexpectedly and sporadically—typically only as the result of a case suddenly settling—and during those rare vacations, Susan usually finds herself drinking too much, staying up late, and returning even more tired than when she left. Susan has done her best to make peace with the fact that this is her life; she is a highly sought-after attorney who makes a fine living and is respected by her peers. But one day, while preparing for the plaintiff's deposition, having stayed up most of the night poring over medical records, having foregone breakfast, and having spent the entire morning at her desk without even a bathroom break, she suffers a breakdown. Her vision gets blurry, she feels sick to her stomach, her heart beats furiously, and she fears she is going to die. Her first thought is that if she dies, she cannot take the deposition.

Fortunately, Susan's secretary has the foresight not only to continue the deposition, but to convince Susan to hire a coach. (As one might imagine, being Susan's secretary under these conditions has had its own stresses.) Susan's coach talks to Susan about her practice, her life, and her goals. What becomes apparent is that Susan really needs to take care of herself. "Are you kidding?" she says. "I can barely take care of everything here. I don't have the time to take care of myself."

"Hear me now and believe me later..."

Saturday Night Live's Hans & Frans' quote seems to apply here. (Check out old episodes of SNL if you've never seen this skit.) How many times have you heard that you "should" take care of yourself? Unfortunately, for too many people like Susan, it takes having heart palpitations, fainting, or going to the hospital before they realize that in taking care of their cases and clients and business, they have forgotten to take care of themselves. They have neglected self-maintenance. Practicing in this manner, as Cami's mother used to say, is "self-limiting." You may practice for a while like this, and in the short-term you may be effective, but it will limit your long-term effectiveness. Even if you don't end up in the hospital or ill, you are highly likely to burn out on the practice of law. Or you might turn into someone you (or your family) don't like very much. People who ask a lot of themselves but give nothing back in return usually have low levels of satisfaction in their lives.

The now-famous Dr. Oz, in his book *YOU Staying Young*, talks about the effects of stress on aging. While stress can be a good thing, because it heightens our senses and allows us to react quickly and appropriately in emergencies, it is only meant to last for a brief, limited amount of time. In the practice of law, stress tends to be an ongoing state, which causes a great deal of physical problems as a result of heightened chemical reactions in the body, lowered immune system, and lack of sleep, all leading to premature aging, disease, and death.

Often the lawyer with a family comes to realize, sometimes too late, that when she spends more time at the office and less time at home, she is less able to relate to her spouse and children. As she feels less and less appreciated at home and less able to connect with the people she lives with, the office looks more and more attractive. This is a place she can truly make a difference. Thus she spends even more time at the office, which makes it all the harder to maintain her relationships at home. It's a vicious cycle. As a result, she feels not only increasingly estranged from her family, but increasingly out of touch with herself.

Why is it that a California study found a majority of lawyers, if they had the chance, would not choose this career again, and well over half said they would not recommend law as a career to their own children?

Why is it that 15–18 percent of the nation's lawyers abuse alcohol or drugs, compared to 10 percent in the population at large?

Why is substance abuse a factor in up to 75 percent of disciplinary complaints involving lawyers?

Why do lawyers top the list of professions with individuals suffering from depression?[1]

Many of these problems are due to a serious lack of self-maintenance within the profession and the pervasive attitude among practitioners that they simply do not need to take care of themselves.

What is Self-Maintenance?

Much as an airplane or automobile needs to be maintained in order to continue to work effectively, your mind and body also need to be maintained for maximum efficiency. Most of us would never let our car run out of gas or go for 15,000 miles without an oil change or drive around with the tires under-inflated, but we are perfectly willing to do the same with our bodies and minds. What would you think of an airline that boasted, "We fly to more destinations every day because we have dispensed with time-consuming maintenance"?

Like maintenance of a car, airplane, or any machine, self-maintenance involves ensuring

---

1.   These statistics are compiled Steven Keeva's TRANSFORMING PRACTICES 4–5 (1999) (an ABA Journal Book), which we highly recommend as a source for learning to practice law in a more holistic and satisfying manner.

that our bodies and minds are able to work at their peak performance. Maintaining a state of peak performance is the key concept that relates self-care to time management. When we do not care for ourselves in a way that provides for peak performance, we function at less than optimal capacity. Things take longer to do, are less enjoyable, and are less precise. We make mistakes. Thus, work actually takes longer when you run yourself ragged than when you do your work in a strategic fashion that allows you to care for yourself as you would any machine.

There are essentially two areas of self-maintenance: the physical and the mental/emotional. The challenge here is that, unlike a machine, which typically requires a set amount and type of maintenance, each person will have his or her own need for particular types of renewal. You will not maintain yourself in precisely the same way others do. Our advice is that you start noticing what makes you feel good, rested, and balanced, and what assists you in working at your peak level. We will give you a lot of suggestions, but this is a personal question; what works for you may not work for others.

For now, reflect on these questions:

1. What activities make you feel the best?

_____

_____

_____

2. What activities make you feel the worst?

_____

_____

_____

3. When do you feel the most rested? What do you do that makes you feel rested?

_____

_____

_____

As a starting point, look back to the values you identified in the prior chapter. You may have a health value, a creativity value, a mental-stimulation value, a spirituality value. Rejuvenation and self-maintenance dovetails with the concept of honoring all of your values. In fact, much of your self-maintenance will involve honoring your values.

For example, from a physical perspective, you may maintain your human machine by eating well, drinking enough water, getting enough sleep, exercising, and limiting your exposure to toxins.

Self-maintenance may also involve regular spiritual pursuits such as, meditating, praying, reading inspirational books, going to church, knowing your own personal values, and living by them.

Personal self-maintenance might involve a social aspect, perhaps building friendships, spending time with loved ones, and being of service to others. And it may well involve self-growth that involves constantly educating yourself academically, professionally, or personally. This could include reading or attending classes on new and different ideas and beliefs or simply cultivating a new awareness of yourself and how you operate and learning more about yourself. This includes determining what type of self-maintenance works best for you, as in the end it is truly a very personal question.

The Lawyer—An Owner's Manual

Hopefully, at this point, you are convinced (or at least curious about the possibility) that your body/mind/self needs maintenance, like any machine, in order to function at optimum capacity. At this point we will offer you an owner's manual of sorts. This manual first lists different methods of maintaining the physical and the mental/emotional machine. "Maintenance" is a proactive and preventative way of operating. We do it without any signs of a problem. We do it so problems don't arise, like getting the oil changed before your car breaks down and getting gas before the car stops. Unfortunately, this is why many people don't engage in regular self-maintenance: because often we neglect ourselves *until* there are signs of a problem.

We spend a lot of time here on practices to enhance mental/emotional self-maintenance, because while both mental/emotional wellness and physical wellness are important, the former is often more neglected. Sometimes problems from a lack of mental/emotional maintenance are not so readily apparent as those from a lack of physical maintenance. Often, lawyers believe we need to "tough it out" when we start recognizing signs that this type of maintenance could be helpful. For a variety of reasons, our mental and emotional well-being is often overlooked. And so we will spend considerable time on it here.

Note that sometimes neglected physical maintenance leads to mental/emotional deficiencies and vice-versa. That is why it is so important to take care of both aspects of your apparatus. If you are getting regular exercise and eating well but not maintaining your mental or emotional life, you will not feel well. Likewise, if you are meditating, renewing your spiritual life, and spending meaningful time with friends but get very little sleep and regularly eat fast food, you will not feel well. Health in one area will very often affect the level of health in the other.

Signs that you are Overdue for Physical Maintenance

- You are often tired.
- You are gaining or losing weight and don't know why.
- You have unexplained aches and pains.
- You are winded going up a flight of stairs.
- You have a hard time sleeping at night or getting up in the morning.

Signs that you are Overdue for Emotional/Mental Maintenance

- You are working too much.
- You are spending most, if not all, waking hours in intellectual pursuits.
- You are neglecting your physical body and ignoring the importance of physical well-being.
- You experience mood swings.
- You make play into work -- taking leisure activities too seriously or becoming overcompetitive.
- You are neglecting friends and family.
- You fail to have any time alone.
- You spend too much time thinking about the past or the future and too little time being aware of the present moment.
- You eat unconsciously, without concern for whether you are really hungry or how your food tastes.
- You eat too much or too little.
- You sleep too much or too little.
- You engage in "escape" activities such as excessive drinking, watching television, "surfing" the internet, or other behaviors to an excessive degree.
- You frequently feel restless or irritable.
- You have difficulty getting up in the morning and/or going to sleep at night.
- You frequently go to bed at night feeling your day was incomplete.
- You wake with a sense of dread.

The following are guidelines and suggestions for self-maintenance. Many of the segments will have an exercise or two that you can employ to put the idea into practice.

1. Take Care of Your Physical Body

The need for maintenance of the physical body is more obvious for most people than the need for maintenance of the emotional/mental body. Here is a list of what you may wish to consider in maintaining this physical machine:

- Five to seven servings of fruits/veggies per day.
- Regular exercise (3–5 times a week for at least 30 min.).
- Seven to eight hours of sleep a night.
- Take vitamins (ask your doctor which are best for you).
- Yoga or another stretching program.

- Drink enough water. (Go online to research the proper amount for your body weight.)[2]
- Limit your intake of caffeine, alcohol, sugar, and processed foods.

For many of these, you may wish to consult a resource or two—your doctor or a book.

Steph: I believe my regular running routine, along with other exercise such as swimming and hiking, allows me to maintain a fairly strenuous law practice and still maintain a sense of balance and a healthy outlook on life. Eating fresh fruits and vegetables and limiting processed or sugary foods also contributes to a steady supply of energy throughout the day.

Experiment with eating well and exercising regularly and notice the changes that occur in your mood and energy level.

2. Take "Vacations"

"Every now and then go away, have a little relaxation, for when you come back to your work your judgment will be surer; since to remain constantly at work will cause you to lose power of judgment . . ."

Leonardo da Vinci

When was the last vacation you took? What was the value of leaving it all behind, getting on a plane, boat, train, or car and getting away for a while? How was your emotional and mental well-being when you returned? Vacations make you smarter. When we let go of something mentally, we are refreshed, more productive, and more enthusiastic about it when we return. As such, we do better quality work in a shorter period of time.

In this section, we will advocate not only those longer, more traditional vacations, but also taking daily "vacations," commonly known as "breaks." We focus on how you can use these breaks, along with longer vacations, to not only avoid burnout and reduce stress, but actually increase productivity and efficiency in your work, as well as enhance your life and the lives of those around you. If in a one-year period of time, a one-week break makes you more efficient and productive, think about the effect tiny "vacations" in a one-week, or even a one-day, period might have.

Taking Regular Breaks

*Continuous work over time without breaks is **less effective** than work that is consciously broken up in a purposeful way.* Constant use or work by any tool or instrument (including our brains!) ultimately leads to inefficiencies and a lower level of productivity than does work over the same amount of time when interspersed with breaks. We are more

---

2.   In our Neuro-Linguistics Programming training, we were repeatedly told to drink water and reminded of the close link between water and brain functioning. Drinking enough water supports your energy levels and brain functioning/clear thinking. Joshua Gowin, *Why Your Brain Needs Water*, PSYCHOLOGY TODAY (Oct. 15, 2010), http://www.psychologytoday.com/blog/you-illuminated/201010/why-your-brain-needs-water.

efficient and productive when we take breaks. Remember Covey's "sharpening the saw" metaphor. This has also been called "strategic pauses."[3]

The most elite long distance runners know that in order to run a 50-mile or a 100-mile race successfully, they must take breaks. It is impossible to run such a long race by just gunning the engine the entire time. Instead, every 3 to 10 miles or so (depending on the weather and the terrain), the runner will stop running, have something to eat or drink, maybe even stretch or change shoes, and then head off down the trail. Those few minutes are not wasted. They may feel wasted when at mile 20 you are still feeling fresh and strong and not in need of a break. But they are some of the most important minutes of the race. They are the minutes the runner's body calls upon at miles 45, 75, and 92 that enable her to continue strong into the finish.

The same is true with your law practice. Many of us only stop when our bodies scream out to us: when we suddenly get sick and cannot even drag ourselves off to work, or when we are so overwhelmed we suffer a panic attack. That is like deciding to put fuel in the car after it runs out of gas in the middle of the road. None of us would actually drive our cars after the gas gauge reads "empty," thinking "Well, the car is still going; I guess I don't really need fuel after all." But this is what we do with our bodies and our minds when we fail to take breaks. Taking one or two week-long vacations a year but no other breaks is like fueling up in Los Angeles and expecting to drive to Chicago because you have "a lot" of fuel. It doesn't work.

What we are advocating is a paradigm shift.[4] The old paradigm says "Work harder, more and faster. There's too much to do, not enough time. If I just put in one more hour, sleep less, skip lunch, maybe I will get it done." The new paradigm says work smarter, consciously choosing what supports you overall. It is a paradigm that says when you stop to sharpen your saw—even many times—you still finish ahead of time.

What Types of Breaks and How Long?

The breaks we advocate are consciously-chosen. This is different from the unconsciously-chosen break, and is a very important distinction. As we have said, the key to transforming

---

3.   Robert Cooper, The Other 90%, Reaching Your Full Potential (2002).
4.   A paradigm is a world view that controls the way we understand the world in which we live. A paradigm shift occurs when the dominant paradigm is replaced by a new paradigm.

your practice and your life is to learn to make *conscious* choices. This includes consciously choosing your breaks.

What is the unconsciously-chosen break? Many of Cami's clients report that after working hard for long periods of time, they later "find themselves" on Facebook for two hours, or mindlessly overeating, or watching TV until 1:00 a.m. These are unconsciously-chosen breaks. They are what happens when your paradigm includes the belief "I have too much to do and I have to work nonstop to finish it." When this is your paradigm, you push yourself as hard as you can. When you believe you cannot take breaks, then the breaks take you. One way or another, you will eventually take a break. Once you recognize that you have a real need for breaks, or self-maintenance of any kind, then you can consciously choose when to take them and you will less frequently "find yourself" surfing the 'net for two hours!

Consciously-chosen breaks probably will not include taking the day off right before a big trial or canceling a deposition to go to the movies. However, each of these may have merit for the lawyer who is literally on the verge of a nervous breakdown. But the goal is to avoid finding yourself on the verge of a nervous breakdown. The goal is to consciously take time when you can so that trials can be handled and depositions taken without requiring hospitalization.

We all know the lawyer who likes to "work hard and play hard" where "playing" means drinking excessively, staying up all night, and possibly making poor choices that will require attention during the working hours of the next week. That is not the type of break we are suggesting. That is merely substituting the breakneck pace of work with the breakneck pace of partying. It hampers, rather than enhances, productivity. Again, the idea is to consciously choose your breaks, rather than unconsciously falling into them.

Remember Susan? After talking with her coach, Susan realized the pattern of her work days: in a typical day, she would get up early, drive like a maniac to the office, work through breakfast and lunch, and continue moving as quickly as she could for the entire day, until her husband called, wondering when she was going to be home. By that time, her son was often already in bed.

As she began talking to her coach and observing her routine, she realized that by about 10:00 a.m., when she was feeling the ill effects of having ingested nothing but coffee all morning, her work slowed and she sometimes had trouble focusing. But she would push through, have another cup of coffee and maybe a doughnut or two, until lunch. Then she would eat at her desk, neither tasting nor chewing her food very well, and then often felt lousy in the afternoon, when she would "recharge" with more caffeine and urge herself to keep going. She also realized that by evening, after most of the staff had gone home, she would find herself looking at her e-mails every five minutes, and then chastise herself for doing so, and then do it again. Ultimately, she realized that the last three hours at the office probably only yielded her about one to two hours of productive work, but she was reluctant to leave, afraid she would not be able to get everything done.

Susan's coach introduced her to the concept of conscious breaks. Susan realized that the way she usually held her body while she worked on her computer was causing tension in her neck and back and, like many people, she was starting to suffer pain as a result. So once every thirty to sixty minutes, Susan would consciously choose to stand up, stretch her arms high over her head, take a few deep breaths, and reach down to touch her toes, where she would just hang her body for a few seconds. Then she would rush back to her desk and resume working. This took about thirty seconds, and thus constituted several minutes of precious work time in the day, but Susan found she felt more energized throughout the entire day as a result. During the first month or so of this new practice, Susan had to set an alarm on her computer to remember to take the breaks. And even so, sometimes she worked through the alarm. This, her coach said, is normal. But it is important to have a reminder in place to break such a long-standing and insidious habit as never taking a break from work.

Susan also forced herself to take at least fifteen minutes to eat lunch in her office kitchen without work in front of her. During this time, she would speak with some of her colleagues, read the newspaper, or just stare out the window. This enabled her to focus on and enjoy her food. As a result, she felt refreshed and recharged and ready to work in the afternoon. After several weeks, Susan decided to start taking brief afternoon walks outside—no more than ten minutes—if the weather was nice. After taking these breaks for a few days, Susan realized she was less likely to want to check her e-mail constantly at the end of the day. She also decided to leave work earlier at least three days a week. This not only allowed her to enjoy her family more, but it gave her more energy for the next day.

Robert K. Cooper, the author of *The Other 90%, Reaching Your Full Potential*, recommends that we take strategic pauses of up to thirty seconds in length every half hour of our working day, and that at least twice a day we take a two–three minute break. During these pauses and breaks, he recommends deepening and relaxing your breathing; refocusing your eyes; rebalancing your posture; and/or sipping ice water. He also suggests enjoying some humor or inspiration, such as looking at a cartoon or an inspirational quote or photo on your desk.

What to do During Your Breaks

Daily Breaks

Stand up. Just the act of standing after sitting for so long gets the blood flowing to all parts of your body—including your brain. During this time, focus on your breathing. Check in with your body and see if you are stiff anywhere.

Stretch. Raise your hands above your head and stretch, then reach down and touch your toes. Hang there for a few moments. Inversion exercises allow blood to flow to your head, which makes you more alert and clear-headed. Do this a few times.

Move around. One beneficial exercise is called the cross crawl: Stand tall; then bend your elbows and slowly raise your left leg and lower your right elbow to that knee until they touch, then repeat with the other leg and arm. Do this about ten or twelve times. This gets the blood flowing to all organs—including the brain—and it integrates the right and left side of your body which again makes you more alert and helps with logical processing. You may want to shut your door so no one can see you. Or you may want to include others in this. Tell them what you are doing. Be a stand in the office drift.

Breathe. Stop and close your eyes and breathe deeply for three breaths, focusing on your breath.

Steph's practice is to take at least one break of maybe ten to fifteen minutes at or around noon to eat lunch or take a walk outside. She might go to the bank, return some books to the library, or even do a bit of shopping, as long as it is relaxing. Rushing to the bank and spending the entire time in line tapping your foot wondering furiously why the tellers are taking so darn long is not the type of strategic break we are talking about. We are talking about a leisurely or even a brisk walk, but one that allows you to enjoy the journey and not be so focused on the destination. The purpose is to stretch your body (physical) and give your brain a rest and shift your focus (mental) so when you return to work you are refreshed physically and mentally. It takes a surprisingly short amount of time to refresh yourself.

One of Steph's favorite things to do during these jaunts is to buy small presents for the people she loves, or even window shop and think about things she might like to have. In this way she also has an emotional experience, connecting with her feelings for others and her desires for the future.

Weekly Breaks

In addition to taking breaks throughout the day, it is important to have "down time" on a weekly basis where you take time for yourself. Many people claim this is what weekends are for. Most lawyers believe differently. But the weekly strategic breaks need not even be during the weekend. There is nothing wrong with taking off Wednesday afternoon to see a movie or even go out of town for a few days. Pay attention to your body and your productivity and your sense of well-being. If you are ready for a break mid-week and the tradeoff is to work on Saturday, give it a try. New practices require experimentation.

One note here: Many of Cami's clients, after taking a week-long vacation, or even taking off both days on the weekend, come back and say, "That's not worth it. Now I have more work to do." Be warned of this mindset. It is common to have this reaction. This type of thinking is the paradigm from which you have been operating your entire career. It will take a leap of faith for many of you to start taking breaks of any length. Trust us and trust Covey, Cooper, and other experts and try this for a while. Committing to experi-mentation with the ideas we suggest is the only way that you can change the paradigm.

Self-Observation

It is important to know what types of breaks will revitalize you most effectively. This is a very personal question.

The breaks that enhance productivity can take many forms, and you will want to determine what works best for you. This is a two-pronged approach. First, experiment with many different practices. Second, be very conscious: observe how you feel with each practice and the effect it has on you. For example, Steph enjoys running. She includes as part of her weekend running in the woodsy trails with friends, long runs by the river by herself, and even short runs with the dog or one of the children. She used to believe that running a fifty-mile race or even a marathon "revitalized" her. By paying attention to how she felt during and after running such a race, she discovered that those types of runs are more akin to work. She often needs a break after she enjoys such a run.

What revitalizes you? Think about times you feel the most energized. What were you doing?

_____

_____

_____

_____

Introvert or extrovert?

Whether you are an "introvert" or an "extrovert" will also have some bearing on what revitalizes you. The concepts of introvert and extrovert were first identified by Carl Jung. Most current personality theories include some form of this idea. Believe it or not, the main difference between introverts and extroverts is that the former gain their energy by being alone, while the latter gain energy from being around people. This means that introverts may also love to be with people and extroverts may enjoy being alone. It is simply an indication of what will rejuvenate you.

It is generally believed that introversion and extroversion exist on a continuum, meaning most people are not one or the other, but do **tend** more toward introversion or extrover-sion. If you are unsure as to whether you tend toward introversion or extroversion, there are quizzes you can take online. Neither one is "better," but it is helpful to know your-self because it helps you know what types of strategic breaks to take and whether they involve seeking out the company of others—including other attorneys in the building on your lunch break—or whether they involve quiet, solitary time when no one is around.

Cami: Being on the introverted end of the spectrum, I need to revitalize by doing something by myself that does not include anyone else. I love to read, take solo walks, or just stare out the window. This is especially true if I have been in a situation in which

I have been immersed with other people. Some of my favorite things to do are putting on workshops, group coaching, teaching, and being with my family. What I learned after many years, though, is that these activities do not provide me with lasting energy. I am energized while I am in the activity, but I tend to experience a drop in energy right after the event. From this observation, I have learned to schedule time alone after workshops and classes to re-energize myself.

Steph: I am more of an extrovert. If I am solitary for long periods of time, I need to be revitalized by being around other people.

Why does it matter? When you make choices in your life that are congruent with your own nature, you are able to access your vast stores of energy. On the other hand, when you spend time battling your temperament—the extrovert who spends hours in front of the computer, the introvert who spends most of her time in meetings—you deplete yourself. There is nothing wrong with a job where an extrovert spends time on the computer or where a more introverted person spends a lot of time teaching. It simply means that these people must also know what is needed to rejuvenate themselves, and then do it.

Exercise: Commit to taking a certain number of breaks per workday. Start small if you are nervous about it. They can be thirty seconds to fifteen minutes long. But promise yourself to do this and provide yourself with reminders—a note by the computer or a device that beeps every thirty minutes to an hour. Try different activities during your breaks. Observe yourself. What is working and not working?

3. Acknowledge Yourself

The dictionary definition of the word "acknowledge" means "1.a. To confess, avow, or admit the existence, reality, or truth of. b. To recognize the validity, force, or power of. 2.a. To express recognition of <*acknowledged* our presence> b. To express gratitude for."

As a coach, when Cami uses the word "acknowledge," she means both "admit the existence, reality, or truth of" as well as "recognize the validity, force, or power of"; and also "express gratitude for." As human beings, we are typically quite willing to acknowledge all the things we do that we think are "bad" or don't work. But for whatever reason, we are far less likely to acknowledge when what we do is "good" or works for us.

Acknowledgement in the context we use it here means to look for, notice, and shine a light upon (1) What I have done that I am proud of; (2) What was challenging, yet I completed; and (3) What I have simply completed. It is a process to do at the end of something—the end of a project, the end of a day, the end of a week, the end of anything that is closed down for you. It allows you to feel good and, importantly, to move on.

Psychologically, acknowledging yourself increases your energy. Going from one task to another without stopping to congratulate yourself can make a worthwhile, fulfilling job seem like drudgery.

Cami reports many of her clients have an initial resistance to acknowledging themselves. Attorneys have a drift that includes thoughts such as the following:

- I am "soft" if I say "good job" to myself.
- I won't try as hard next time if I stop and congratulate myself.
- I haven't done anything "big enough" to acknowledge myself for.
- This is my job; why should I acknowledge myself for something I am supposed to be doing?

To get the most out of this book, you will need to trust the coaching, at least enough to try out what we are suggesting. And the fact is that the thought processes listed above are very nearly the opposite of what is true. When we do not stop and acknowledge ourselves for what we have completed, we end up feeling beat up; we feel a lot is expected of us and there is very little reward; we check things off the list, but are not truly present to what we are doing; and we lose energy for the next task. This is why acknowledgement is a self-maintenance practice. Analogous to not getting enough sleep, the lack of acknowledgement will ultimately drag you down.

It is also important *how* you acknowledge yourself. It is not as useful to tell yourself "good job" as it is to state precisely what you are acknowledging yourself for. For example,

- I got the brief in ahead of time, even though I thought I would need an extension.
- I came to work today even though I didn't feel well.
- I did not snap at my secretary even though she made a dumb mistake that caused me extra time to fix.
- I ate healthy food today.
- I exercised three times this week.

The idea is to be specific about what you have accomplished, so you recognize all of what you get done in a day. This allows you to shift from an energy-draining focus on feeling behind, not doing enough, and not being done to an energy-increasing focus on completion and productivity. The facts do not change, but how you view them does. There will always be more to do and it is likely you will often feel behind. As Richard Carlson said, your inbox will always be full.[5] It is not useful to tell yourself that you will acknowledge yourself when "it is all done." That will never happen. The value in acknowledging your completions (even when small) is that it creates an energy that allows you to move on to

---

5.   A wonderful little book for stress management is Richard Carlson, DON'T SWEAT THE SMALL STUFF, AND IT'S ALL SMALL STUFF (1997).

the next thing with far more enthusiasm. Acknowledging what you have accomplished will also improve your overall satisfaction with your job and your life.

Exercise: For at least thirty days, every night, sit down with a notebook and, looking back over your day, list at least five things for which you acknowledge yourself. It is important that you write them down in freehand and not just think them in your head. We have a different mental experience when we write with pen and paper than we do when we intellectually state something in our heads, or even when we type it. Acknowledgement is a muscle. Many people come back after promising to do this assignment and say, "I did not do anything big enough to acknowledge." This is like saying I could not lift the fifty-pound weight, so I gave up. Start with the five-pound weight. Acknowledge that you got up and went to work. Acknowledge that you ate breakfast, that you were on time, that you smiled at a stranger. If this is a challenge for you, then this exercise is even more important, as your acknowledgement muscle needs work. As you begin to create this habit, you will notice more and more things that you can acknowledge yourself for.

4. Practice Gratitude

As with acknowledgement, gratitude shifts your focus. The facts and circumstances of your life are what they are. We choose what to focus on. And what we choose to focus on affects our experience of our lives and our practice. When you experience your practice as negative, hard, and heavy, it affects your ability to do the work and to get fulfillment from your job. This obviously affects overall life satisfaction.

From a law-of-attraction standpoint, you will attract more of what you focus upon. This was written about extensively in 1937 in the well-known and ground-breaking work of Napolean Hill, *Think and Grow Rich*.[6] Learning the tool of gratitude has many benefits. It will shift your focus from that which you do not want to that which you do want. As such, gratitude allows you to (1) acknowledge that you have more in your life than you thought you did, which will allow you to appreciate things you have been overlooking; (2) improve the quality of your life by improving your emotional experience; and (3) attain more of what you want by focusing on what you have that you appreciate.[7]

We think gratitude is one of the most powerful self-maintenance practices you can engage in. It will strongly affect your experience of yourself and your life. Without changing any of the actual circumstances of your life, your life experience will change in a whole new way. Try it.

Exercise: For thirty days, every morning or evening, write down five things you are grateful for. Again, be sure you do this in freehand and not in your head or on the computer.

---

6.   "What the mind of man can believe and conceive, he can achieve" is another famous quote from Hill supporting a similar concept that what you focus upon is what you ultimately attain.

7.   Much has been written on this topic. For example, in THE PASSION TEST, Janet and Chris Atwood also note that the best and quickest way to get what you want is to acknowledge what you have on a regular basis.

Experiment with morning vs. evening. Which has the best effect on you? During this thirty day period, do not repeat anything. Stretch yourself to see all of what you appreciate in your life: your spouse, kids, that good parking spot, the weather, the tree outside your window, getting the extension, the ruling in your favor, someone brought doughnuts to the office, you have a job, a home, your health. The list is truly endless. This exercise will build this muscle, as with the acknowledgement muscle.

5. Celebrate Even Small Accomplishments

When do we celebrate? In our culture, celebrations occur on major accomplishments or milestones, such as weddings, graduation, a certain birthday, or the completion of a large project. Celebrations often represent a transition—the completion of one facet of life so that the next can occur. For example, the completion of single life and beginning of married life; or the completion of law school and beginning of a law practice. Typically celebrations are reserved for something *big*. But look at the effect celebrating has on us: we acknowledge that we are proud and we acknowledge the closing of one thing and the beginning of another. Celebration gives us energy and constitutes acknowledgement of our efforts.

Cami recommends her clients engage in regular celebration, even for (especially for) small things. It allows you to relish and enjoy your accomplishments and keeps you looking forward to more success. Finished that appellate brief? Tell your family and go out for pizza or ice cream. Got a new client? Go out for a drink or take the family to the movies. Even something as mundane as taking a walk with your family, doing a word puzzle, or sitting on the porch swing for a short while can be celebratory. The main factor is your intention. If you are intending to celebrate yourself and your accomplishments, then virtually anything can be a celebration for you.

The purpose of this exercise is to remind yourself that you have accomplished something. Too often, once we accomplish something, we go right on to the next thing, without ever acknowledging ourselves for our accomplishment. This can lead to burnout. The problem with going from one thing to another is that it takes some of the "fun" out of the accomplishment. We forget why we do what we do when we go from one thing to another, just checking tasks off the list. Finishing an important brief is not just one of many mindless tasks you have to do each day; it is an accomplishment; it is a relief; it is why you are here. Think about why you became an attorney. When we quickly go from one thing to another with no stop for celebration, then we begin to see what we do as rote, mundane, fast-paced drudgery. One of Cami's clients said, "The reason I come to work on Saturday is to remember why I practice law. I do not feel rushed and so I take my time and I really enjoy what I am doing. Sadly, Monday through Friday do not feel that way."

You can stop and take a five-minute celebration after each completion. Or you might celebrate at the end of each day with a bowl of ice cream. There is more to celebrate than accomplishment and completion. Think about your birthday celebration—you are celebrating your life. Each day you might have a mini-celebration of your day: looking back at what you accomplished, and also looking back and being grateful for all you have. This will make a big difference in your attitude, which will affect your enjoyment of your practice.

One caveat on daily celebration: make sure your celebration is not a substitute for escape. For example, you may have a glass of wine at the end of the day to celebrate your accomplishments for that day. Or you might have three glasses in order to escape the feelings you have about your life. The former is celebratory. The latter is not; the latter is an escape. And the difference is not solely the amount of wine you drank. The difference is the motivation: celebration or escape? This is a question you will need to ask yourself. Needing to escape from whatever is going on in your life is a great indicator that you are not taking enough strategic breaks, or that your self-maintenance is lacking. You will need to determine where and remedy it. So be honest with yourself - is this celebration or escape? If it is escape, do not do it. If you feel the need to escape, do take significant action to employ some of the other exercises in this chapter.

Celebration Ideas

Here are some of the things Cami's clients do to celebrate small (or large) accomplishments:

1. Go out for ice cream.
2. Go to a movie.
3. Take a long walk.
4. Take a day off.
5. Spend time doing absolutely nothing.
6. Do a jigsaw or crossword puzzle.
7. Go out to dinner.
8. Eat strawberries and whipped cream by the pool.
9. Go to the beach.

Exercise: For thirty days, at the end of each day, do one small act that constitutes celebration of your day. Each day, as you embark on the act, mentally consider what you are celebrating. Include others in your celebration some of the days. Tell them what you are doing. A party is often more fun and meaningful when others are there to share. But you can and should also celebrate by yourself. There is much to be learned by celebrating with one's self.

6. Spend Meaningful Time Alone

Most attorneys do not spend much time alone without working. We are often in court, in the office, or talking with clients. Obviously, when we are by ourselves performing research or writing briefs, we are not spending quality time alone. As stated earlier, people typically lean toward either extroversion or introversion. In our simple definition, extroverts get energy from being with others while introverts get it from being alone. We believe that all people need an amount of time alone. If you are more extroverted, you may need less. If you are more introverted, you likely need more. Experiment with time alone and see how it affects you. Though it may seem obvious, time alone working does not qualify as meaningful time alone for purposes of self-maintenance!

Note the effect on your attitude if you take a walk, read a book, putter around the house, or watch television. Be very observant when you choose activities that distract you from the experience of being alone, such as watching TV. These activities are fine, as long as you choose them consciously, and not as an escape. As with all coaching exercises, you must experiment to find what works for you. This requires you to try different things and be very aware of your experiences to decide if they are valuable to you.

1. What activities do you like doing alone?

_____

_____

_____

_____

2. When do you crave alone time? What do you do when you feel this craving?

_____

_____

_____

_____

3. How often do you feel a need to be alone?

_____

_____

_____

_____

Exercise: Spend time alone every day this week—five minutes to an hour. Note how you feel during this time. Note how the rest of your day goes. Notice if you feel better or worse in different lone activities. As with other self-maintenance activities, you may feel better immediately or the activities may have a more cumulative effect on your life and practice. In other words, you may not feel refreshed immediately after spending time alone for ten minutes, but after regularly engaging in this practice, you may begin to feel more relaxed overall.

7. Meditate

Similar to spending meaningful time alone is the practice of meditation. Meditation has value to all people, but we think it is particularly valuable for attorneys. We spend a great deal of time using our brains. It is a thinking job. We think about how to win our cases; we think about writing a great brief; we think on our feet in court; we even think about our cases and strategies and our work when we are with our families or in the shower. We have a problem-solving/argument-oriented mindset. We can be challenging as spouses and as parents if we do not choose to turn that off. And often that choice is difficult to make, unless we are conscious that we need to make it.

One of the purposes of meditation is to quiet the mind. This can be a great experience for lawyers, as it is a break from thinking. And yet it can be difficult, even uncomfortable at first. In the end, meditation is a *practice* and many people get discouraged before they spend enough time practicing to see the benefits. Meditation improves mind focus, which is very important for attorneys. Mind focus is built through meditation by practice. It is similar to building a muscle. It has been described as leading a bull by a nose ring back to the focus of your attention—over and over again.

We recommend starting with a simple breathing meditation. In this exercise, you will designate an amount of time, during which you will sit and focus on your breath (see box below). When your thoughts take you away—and they will do so regularly—you bring your attention back to your breath. In this way you are training your mind to focus on what you want it to focus on. You are learning to be more conscious and purposeful. Think about the times you lie in bed at night thinking about a case when all you really want to do is sleep. This is a result of your mind wandering and you not having control over where it goes. The practice of meditation enables you to exert some control over where and when your mind focuses on a given subject.

There are a wide range of other benefits that have been studied and reported as a result of regular meditation. For example, Jon Kabat-Zinn, Ph.D., of the University of Massachusetts Medical School, recorded the brain waves of stressed-out employees of a high-tech firm in Madison, Wisconsin. The subjects were split randomly into two groups. Twenty-five people were asked to learn meditation over eight weeks, and the remaining sixteen were left alone as a control group. All participants had their brain waves scanned three times during the study: once at the beginning of the experiment, another when meditation lessons were completed eight weeks later, and again four months after that. The researchers found that the meditators showed a pronounced shift in activity to the left frontal lobe. In other words, they were calmer and happier than before.

Benefits of Meditation

Meditation has various health benefits. Apart from its physiological benefits, it can also improve your psychological and spiritual well-being. In recent years, the various health benefits of meditation have become more and more acknowledged by the scientific community as well as the public. While initial research focused more on the physiological benefits of meditation, there have recently been an increasing number of studies on the various psychological benefits as well. In addition to the pioneers of meditation research, such as Harvard University's Dr. Herbert Benson ("The Relaxation Response") and Jon Kabat-Zinn, there are now scientists such as Richard Davidson (Director, Lab for Affective Neuroscience, University of Wisconsin) and Sara Lazar (Director, Lazar Lab for Meditation and Yoga, Massachusetts General Hospital) using the tools of modern brain research to explore the effects of meditation on the mind and health.

Physiological Benefits of Meditation

Meditation has been found to have the following physiological health benefits:

- Meditation decreases the metabolic rate and lowers the heart rate, thus indicating a state of deep rest and regeneration.
- Meditation reduces stress, as indicated by lower levels of stress hormones such as cortisol.
- Meditation reduces high blood pressure.
- Meditation has been found to help asthma patients, making breathing easier for them.

Psychological Benefits of Meditation

On the psychological level, studies have shown the following benefits:

- Meditation increases the coherence of brain wave patterns, which suggests it improves creativity and learning and actually changes the way the brain works.
- Meditation helps to decrease anxiety, depression, irritability and moodiness.
- Meditation improves memory.
- Meditation increases the subjective feelings of happiness and contentment.
- Meditation increases emotional stability.

Spiritual Benefits of Meditation

In many Eastern cultures, meditation has traditionally been used as a tool for spiritual realization and fulfillment. While in the Western Hemisphere we have mainly focused on the physiological and psychological benefits, modern brain science helps us to understand and explore the spiritual aspects of meditation.

- Studies show that people who meditate are likely to report a shift in their outlook and goals in life away from materialism and towards personal growth and spiritual fulfillment.
- Brain research shows that meditation can train the higher capacities of the mind, such as perception, awareness and compassion. The progress of brain research opens up

ways of getting a clear, scientific understanding and evidence of the spiritual dimension of meditation.

The benefits of meditation have been written and lectured about extensively. If you are in doubt as to the benefits or wish to learn more, Jon Kabat-Zinn has written extensively on the subject. And of course, the internet is a wonderful resource and will direct you to a plethora of reading material.

Exercise: Commit to meditating for at least thirty days, every day. The benefits of this experiment may not become apparent until you have practiced for a while. Many people quit prematurely because it is "not working." If you sit for ten or more minutes a day and focus on your breath, it *is working*—no matter how many times you get distracted, follow your wandering mind, or lose track of your breath. So commit to a period of time, keep sitting, keep bringing your focus back. This is meditation and it is working.

A Simple Breathing Meditation

The first stage of meditation is to stop distractions and make your mind clearer and more lucid. This can be accomplished by practicing a simple breathing meditation. Choose a quiet place and sit in a comfortable position. Sit in the traditional cross-legged posture or in any other position that is comfortable. If you wish, sit in a chair or on a cushion. Find a posture in which you can easily sit erect without being rigid. The most important thing is to keep your back straight to prevent your mind from becoming sluggish or sleepy.

Let your body be firmly planted on the ground, floor or chair, your hands resting easily, your eyes closed gently. Consciously soften any obvious tension. Let go of any habitual thoughts or plans. Bring your attention to the sensations of your breathing. Take a few deep breaths to sense where you can feel the breath most easily, such as coolness or tingling in the nostrils or throat, as movement of the chest, or rise and fall of the belly. Then let your breath be natural. Feel the sensations of your natural breathing very carefully, relaxing into each breath as you feel it, noticing how the soft sensations of breathing come and go with the changing breath.

A Simple Breathing Meditation (cont.)

Breathe naturally, preferably through the nostrils, without attempting to control your breath, and become aware of the sensation of the breath as it enters and leaves the nostrils. This sensation is the object of meditation for this exercise. You could choose another focus as well. Any regular sensation of the breath will work—the feeling of the belly rising and falling; the quality of the breath; or the movement of the chest. Concentrate on it to the exclusion of everything else.

At first, your mind will be very busy, and you might even feel that the meditation is making your mind busier; but *in reality you are just becoming more aware of how busy your mind actually is.* There will be a great temptation to follow the different thoughts as they arise. Do your best to remain focused single-pointedly on the sensation of the breath. If you discover that your mind has wandered and is following your thoughts, simply return it to the breath. Repeat this as many times as necessary until the mind settles on the breath.

Like training a puppy, gently bring yourself back a thousand times. Over the weeks and months of this practice you will gradually learn to calm and center yourself using the breath. There will be many cycles in this process; stormy days alternating with clear days. Just stay with it. As you do, listening deeply, you will find the breath helping to connect and quiet your whole body and mind.

If you practice patiently in this way, gradually your distracting thoughts will subside, and you will experience a sense of inner peace and relaxation. Your mind will feel lucid and spacious and you will feel refreshed. When the sea is rough, sediment is churned up and the water becomes murky, but when the wind dies down, the mud gradually settles and the water becomes clear. In a similar way, when the otherwise incessant flow of our distracting thoughts is calmed through concentrating on the breath, our mind becomes unusually lucid and clear.

8. Try Journaling

Journaling is a practice in which you simply write about anything and everything that comes to mind. Why would you want to journal? Some benefits include:

- Releasing emotion
- Problem-solving
- Learning about yourself
- Letting go of the experiences of your day
- Putting your circumstances into perspective
- Gaining clarity

The very process of getting your thoughts out of your head and putting them down on paper allows you to gain insights you would otherwise never see.

When you feel intense emotions, journaling is a good way to release them. Write freely and uncensored as quickly as you can. Daily journaling, even for a few minutes a day, is a great way to check in with yourself—to determine how you feel and what you may need—thereby raising your level of awareness of the need for various types of self-maintenance.

Attorneys typically spend a lot of time writing briefs, motions, memos, and letters. Journaling is a completely different type of writing; it is writing for its own sake, without worrying about grammar, punctuation, or even if it makes sense. It is freeing and cathartic.

Steph finds that keeping a journal is valuable because the very act of writing allows her to see her emotions and situations in a new perspective. It also allows her to look back on how she has dealt with problems and situations in the past, and even to learn how far she has come in dealing with them into the future.

Exercise: Every day for one month, write in a notebook about anything that comes to mind. Set aside a period of time—perhaps ten minutes—and simply write. As with other self-maintenance activities, you may not see a direct cause-and-effect relationship between writing and feeling better. Or you may. But you will likely notice an overall change in how you feel and approach your day, your practices, your challenges, and your family. As with the other exercises, commit to a period of time and notice how it affects you.

9. Read Inspiring Books

This practice will raise your level of inspiration and fulfillment. If you choose books that are suited to you, reading even a few minutes a day can improve your overall well-being. Check out our reading list at the back of this book. You may also want to *stop* reading certain things, such as books, magazines, and even the newspaper, that bring you down. This is another area in which you should experiment with how what you do affects your feelings. As a general rule, if doing something gives you a bad feeling, there is a good chance it is not good for you. Like with machinery, part of self-maintenance involves looking for indications of a problem. Begin to become aware of how you feel and of what you may be doing that causes those feelings.

Exercise: Begin a practice of daily morning reading. Find books that interest you or inspire you. Note how you feel during the day after taking on this exercise. Commit to it for at least twenty-one days.

10. Change the Way You Think

Your thoughts affect your emotional state. Your emotional state affects how well you work.

As we pointed out above in the sections on acknowledgement and gratitude, your life will be enhanced when you focus on what is working in your life. Many of us do not realize the power we have to choose our thoughts.

A tool you may try is one we call "interruption." To use this tool, you must first recognize that you have certain thought processes that are not supporting you in getting what you want and in feeling how you would like to feel. In order to identify these thoughts, you must listen to the thoughts that go through your head and identify those that do not work for you or that make you feel bad. This may be a new concept for you: the idea that *your thoughts are not you and that you have control over them*. If you do not learn to control your thoughts, they will control you.

To start identifying your insidious and non-supportive thoughts, here are examples of thoughts that may pass through your head that you will want to interrupt. These were contributed to us by colleagues and clients:

- That was stupid.
- I can't believe I could be so careless.
- I know [that person] does not like me and/or is mad at me.
- I bet this will never work.
- I could just kick myself right now.
- A jury is not going to like me because I am not attractive enough. Maybe someone else should try this case.
- Even if I ask for help, I probably won't understand the answer.
- If I don't understand what someone says and have to ask for clarification, they will probably think I'm stupid or that I wasn't listening.

What are your typical non-supportive thoughts? Likely they will be habitual thoughts—that is, thoughts that recur in many different situations.

_____

_____

_____

Now that you have learned to identify thoughts that you don't want to focus on, in order to use the tool of "interruption," once you hear a thought or a stream of thoughts that does not support you, literally tell yourself "Stop." Say it out loud and forcefully and then move your attention to something else. It is a simple process. If you commit to it and do it regularly, you will begin to train your mind to focus on the thoughts that really are helpful to you.

Another resource for learning the power of your thoughts is *The Astonishing Power of Emotions*, by Jerry and Esther Hicks, which describes a way to use your feelings and emotions to determine where your thoughts are not supporting you.

Exercise: Post notes at different places in your office and home that say something like "STOP non-productive thinking." Then, practice interrupting your non-productive thoughts as described above. You must commit to doing this regularly because it is a challenging habit to break.

Or try this: Wear a bracelet and change it to the other arm each time you hear a negative thought come through your mind. As you change the bracelet to the other wrist, say "Stop" and interrupt the thought. The bracelet will become a physical anchor for you to interrupt non-productive thoughts.

11. Yoga

According to Jon Kabat-Zinn, yoga is a form of meditation. Whereas meditation involves focus on one's breathing, yoga requires specific focus on particular parts of the body as the pose is held and continuous focus on the breath as well. As such, it creates benefits for the mind as well as the body. The mind-focus benefit is in addition to the physical benefits, which are many, as yogic poses increase strength and flexibility.

Benefits of Yoga

As with meditation, much has been written and lectured about the benefits of yoga. Below are some of the common benefits espoused by practitioners and participants:

- **Flexibility**—Yoga stretches not only the muscles, but the soft tissues as well.
- **Strength**—When practiced correctly, nearly all poses build core strength in the deep abdominal muscles.
- **Posture**—With increased flexibility and strength comes better posture. This is a huge benefit for attorneys, who often spend much of their days hunched over their desks and may even walk somewhat stooped with the weight of their briefcases (and the weight of the world) on their shoulders!
- **Increased Body Awareness**—Those who practice regularly are more able to notice when they are slouching or slumping and can adjust their posture.
- **Breathing**—Because of the deep, mindful breathing that yoga involves, lung capacity often improves. This in turn can improve sports performance and endurance. Most forms of yoga emphasize deepening and lengthening your breath. This stimulates the relaxation response, which is the opposite of the fight-or-flight adrenaline boost of the stress response, and is of perhaps the greatest value to attorneys.
- **Less Stress, More Calm**—Even beginners tend to feel less stressed and more relaxed after their first class. Some yoga styles use specific meditation techniques to quiet the constant "mind chatter" that often underlies stress. Other yoga styles use deep breathing techniques to focus the mind on the breath. Either way, your mind will begin to still.
- **Concentration and Mood**—Concentration and the ability to focus mentally are common benefits voiced by yoga students. The same is true with mood. Nearly every yoga student will tell you they feel happier and more content after class.
- **The Heart**—Perhaps one of the most studied areas of the health benefits of yoga is its effect on heart disease. Yoga has long been known to lower blood pressure and

slow the heart rate. A slower heart rate can benefit people with high blood pressure, heart disease, and stroke.

- **Other Benefits**—Some studies have suggested that yoga may also have a positive effect on learning and memory. Other researchers have been studying whether yoga can slow the aging process, increase a person's sense of self-acceptance, and improve energy levels.

Some potential benefits of yoga may be hard to study scientifically. For instance, yoga has been said to increase spiritual awareness. Nevertheless, there are many anecdotal claims for what yoga can do. Go to any yoga studio and listen to students after class. Some will even tell you that yoga can help improve marriages and relationships at work.[8] The only way to find out what yoga can do for you is to try it for yourself.

Exercise: Try yoga once or twice a week for a month. Go to a class or get a DVD. Whatever makes you most likely to do it.

12. Do Something for Yourself Morning and Night

What you do upon waking in the morning has a big effect on the course of your day. For example, if the first thing you do is check your e-mail, you immediately put your attention in the hands of someone else rather than deciding yourself what to focus upon. If, instead, you do something uplifting, inspiring, or peaceful, this action will set the tone for a more peaceful day.

Similarly, what you do in the last few minutes before you go to sleep at night will affect the quality of your sleep. If you fall asleep reading a brief or thinking about a case, or even watching something stimulating or violent on television, you are setting the tone for your sleep to be less peaceful. And of course restless sleep affects your following day.

Exercises: Experiment with your mornings and evenings. In the morning, try any or all of the exercises listed in this chapter (i.e., yoga, physical exercise, meditating) and see how they affect you and your days. Likewise, in the evening, engage in some of the exercises that help you feel calm, such as journaling, acknowledgement, or reading a book, before going to sleep. Practice one or two of these exercises—or even try something else—every day for at least a week. Observe how it affects your day and your sleep. Observe how your days change when you choose to focus on something meaningful in the morning and when you get a better quality of sleep at night. Note: It is important you work with each

---

8.   For more in depth discussion of the benefits of yoga and meditation on stress and disease, check out Jon Kabat-Zinn's book FULL-CATASTROPHE LIVING. Kabat-Zinn began the Stress Reduction Clinic at the University of Massachusetts Medical Center and has had overwhelming success with using mindfulness meditation and yoga to help medical patients with chronic pain and stress. Kabat-Zinn's book is styled in a way that anyone can use it to make changes in their own lives toward reduced stress and greater peace and well-being.

practice every day for at least a week, as many of the positive effects of such practices are not immediately apparent but take effect over time.

13. Laugh

The health benefits of laughter are far-ranging. Studies have shown that laughter can help relieve pain, bring greater overall happiness, and even increase immunity. We have heard that healthy children may laugh as many as 400 times per day, but adults tend to laugh only 15 times per day, if that.

Benefits of Laughter

- **Stress:** Laughter reduces your stress level.
- **Physical Release:** Laughter provides a physical and emotional release.
- **Internal Workout:** A good belly laugh exercises the diaphragm, contracts the abdominal muscles, and even works out the shoulders, leaving muscles more relaxed afterward.
- **Distraction:** Laughter takes your focus off of anger, guilt, stress and negative emotions in a more beneficial way than other mere distractions do. Laughter dissolves distressing emotions. You can't feel anxious, angry, or sad when you're laughing.
- **Perspective:** Studies show that our response to stressful events can be altered by whether we view something as a threat or a challenge. Humor can give us a more lighthearted perspective and help us view events as "challenges" rather than "problems," thus making them less threatening and more positive. Humor shifts perspective, allowing you to see situations in a more realistic, less threatening light. A humorous perspective creates psychological distance, which can help you avoid feeling overwhelmed.
- **Social Benefits of Laughter:** Laughter connects us with others. Laughter is contagious. By bringing more laughter into your life, you can bring it to those around you, allowing them to realize these benefits as well. By elevating the mood of others around you, you can reduce their stress levels, and perhaps improve the quality of your social interactions with them, reducing your stress level even more.
- **Laughter relaxes the whole body.** A good, hearty laugh relieves physical tension and stress, leaving your muscles relaxed for up to forty-five minutes afterward.
- Laughter and humor help you stay emotionally healthy. **Laughter makes you feel good. And the good feeling you get when you laugh remains with you even after the laughter subsides. Humor helps you keep a positive, optimistic outlook through difficult situations, disappointments, and loss.**
- **Laughter helps you relax and recharge.** It reduces stress and increases energy, enabling you to stay focused and accomplish more.

Did you hear about the dyslexic, agnostic insomniac? He lays awake at night wondering if there really is a dog.

Creating Opportunities to Laugh

- Watch a funny movie or TV show.
- Go to a comedy club.
- Read the funny pages.
- Seek out funny people.
- Share a good joke or a funny story.
- Check out your bookstore's humor section.
- Host game night with friends.
- Play with a pet.
- Go to a "laughter yoga" class.
- Goof around with children.
- Do something silly.
- Make time for fun activities (e.g. bowling, miniature golfing, karaoke).
- When you hear laughter, move toward it.
- Spend time with fun, playful people.

The Benefits of Laughter

Physical Health Benefits:
- Boosts immunity
- Lowers stress hormones
- Decreases pain
- Relaxes your muscles
- Prevents heart disease

Mental Health Benefits:
- Adds joy and zest to life
- Eases anxiety and fear
- Relieves stress
- Improves mood
- Enhances resilience

Social Benefits:
- Strengthens relationships
- Attracts others to us.
- Enhances teamwork.
- Helps defuse conflict.
- Promotes group bonding.

Exercise: This week, find something to laugh about every day. Make this your number one goal. You might need to prepare for your week of laughter by doing some research: find something funny to read, watch, and experience. Be committed to laughing every day. Also, find the humor in everyday events—especially ones that might otherwise cause you to be angry or irritated.

14. Be in Service

A great tool for rejuvenation and stress-relief is serving others. This can take several forms, but typically involves helping those who are in need or less fortunate than you. Serving others, in whatever way you choose, puts your attention outside of yourself and onto others who need your generosity. The benefits of service are far-reaching. It has been said that being in service to others can alleviate depression. It can assist in a sense of fulfillment and higher purpose. Often, people experience a spiritual component when serving others. Certainly being in service can contribute to your sense of gratitude for what you have. It will get you outside of the world you live in and offer you some perspective. And that can be very valuable for attorneys.

Ways to be in service:

- Do pro bono work for a group or a client.
- Find a charity whose cause you believe in.
- Volunteer at a school or church.
- Give food to the homeless.
- Work with children who are underprivileged.
- Go to the SPCA and walk dogs.
- Think about what is important to you: this is the most significant factor regarding **where** you go to be in service.

A final note on giving: It is far more satisfying to give time than money. This is ironic because attorneys tend to have more money than time. However, it is the **act** of service that typically resonates for people, much more than simply writing a check. And for attorneys or other busy professionals, giving something you have so little of is part of what makes this true *giving*.

Exercise: Find a place to give that resonates with your values.

15. Stretch Your Comfort Zone

What is a "comfort zone?" It is a physical, mental, and/or emotional "place" where we typically hang out. For the shy person, the comfort zone may be standing back in a group gathering. For the outgoing person, the comfort zone may be excessively talking to others in a group gathering. For the hurried and harried person, the comfort zone may be in being late, rushing around, possibly even barking orders to others. For the cautious, fearful person, the comfort zone may be in avoiding strangers, keeping the doors locked, and staying away from certain parts of town, even during the day.

We all have an area that feels familiar and thus "comfortable," and we will do just about anything to stay in that place. A comfort zone is not necessarily where you feel happy and relaxed; rather, it is where you stay when you are not challenging your beliefs, attitudes and assumptions. For example, many attorneys believe they must work long hours to succeed, and that they must work long hours just to get everything done. For these people, working long hours without taking a break is their comfort zone. It may not be literally **comfortable**, but it is what is known and familiar; therefore it is where we return over and over, rather than trying something new and different—perhaps a little scary—and in this sense uncomfortable.

Leave your comfort zone as often as possible. Nothing can change when you are comfortable and are doing what you always do. Change requires doing something different.

It is easy to determine the boundaries of your comfort zone. Just look at what you do on a day-to-day basis. Most of us live in our comfort zone and are very attached to being there. So look at your life and see what patterns you engage in regularly. What is the same from day to day?

For many overworked attorneys, any exercise on this self-maintenance list will represent a "stretch" outside your comfort zone. For many attorneys, taking a five-minute break in the middle of the day is scarier than navigating Class 4 rapids. But nothing in your life will change unless you are willing to step outside of your comfort zone.

So stretch: Choose something on this list that is scary to you. And stretch for the sake of stretching. If it is scary to ride the rapids, do it. Does riding a roller coaster sound ridiculous? Do it. Does having a difficult conversation with your spouse make you feel queasy? Do it. Stretching in and of itself is a valuable tool; it will help you feel more satisfied in your life and will make you feel you are truly *living*. Staying comfortable is nice, but it will not give you the experience of living your life to the fullest.

Exercise: Observe yourself on a daily basis. Notice what you avoid and why. Carry a small notebook and note the things you avoid, whether it be a conversation with a particular client; taking a break for lunch; confronting someone on a particular topic; speaking up in a specific group; exercising or going to the gym; or speaking at an event. This will help you become aware of the walls of your comfort zone. *As you gain self-awareness, your next step is to **do those things you avoid**.* Your comfort zone will expand when you stretch yourself. When your comfort zone expands, there is more of life for you to experience and more choices available to you.

16. Leave your Work at Work

In the chapter on time management, there is a section on completion. This section will teach you how to be "complete" at the end of each day. Use this process to leave your work at work. This will greatly reduce your stress level, improve your relationships at home and improve your sleep. It will allow you to be more focused on work at work and on your family at home. (See page 168 in chapter 7, Managing your Time and Energy.)

Exercise: For a period of two to four weeks, every day fill out the completion worksheet before you go home at night. (Found on the website, www.mclarencoaching.com/bookdownloads/.) See what changes.

17. Keep a Dream Book

We all have wishes and dreams. Many attorneys call them "goals," but the term "dream" is different from a goal. A dream is usually bigger, bolder and more exciting than a goal. It tends to be uncensored and as such, often something we don't necessarily believe we can do. Dreaming is more a right brain activity than goal-setting, which tends to be a left brain cognitive endeavor. Often we do not vocalize or express our dreams. And yet achieving our dreams typically starts with knowing what they are. The "dream book" is a journal or notebook in which you jot down all those things you want in your life, from the tangible ("a Ferrari") to the intangible ("to feel confident in federal court"), no matter how crazy; in fact, the crazier, the better.

There are great benefits to this exercise. First, focusing on what you want in life will raise your spirits. It feels good to focus on what we want—especially big and exciting things. Second, from a neurological perspective, your brain is wired to look for what you say you want. So an added benefit to listing your wishes and dreams is that you are much more likely to achieve them than if you don't really think about them, or worse, disregard them.

Exercise: Buy a beautiful journal. Every day write down things you want. Do not censor at all. Include drawings and pictures. Let yourself go wild imagining.

18. Be More Social

Time with friends can be extremely rejuvenating and can assist in not only gaining perspective, but in dealing with the daily stresses of life. Do something that is fun and social: join a book club, meet a friend after work, have some neighbors over for a barbecue. Don't turn down those invitations because you have to work. Friends help to make life special and fun. Being with friends reduces stress and can lead to more laughter. Cultivate friendships wherever possible.

Exercise: Commit to doing something with someone outside your family once a week.

19. Cultivate your Spiritual Life

When many people hear "spiritual," they think of religion or church. If you have a religion or belong to a church, then you know how being a part of that community rejuvenates you. But you do not need to go to church to cultivate your spiritual life. In fact, many of the exercises and tools described above, such as yoga, meditation, reading from inspirational books, and even journaling, have significant spiritual aspects. The goal is to get in touch with your spirit. However you do that, do it.

Exercise: Experiment with "spiritual" activities. This can be anything from walking in nature to going to church. Do something once a week for a specific amount of time. Notice what changes for you in your life overall.

20. Cultivate Self-Growth

What do we mean by self-growth? We mean getting in touch with who you really are, improving upon yourself mentally and emotionally. Many of our above suggestions do, in fact, cultivate self-growth. Other ways to cultivate self-growth are to attend seminars and classes that have nothing to do with the law. Your local community college likely has dozens of classes and activities from ballroom dancing to origami to making sushi. Buy or rent CDs that you can listen to in your car; this will make your commute not only more relaxing and pleasant, but a learning experience for you. If you are a parent, explore activities that your children enjoy. Go to plays, museums, and craft fairs. Broaden your horizons. It will not only give you a new perspective; it will open your mind and your world. And who knows, you may even pick up some new clients!

Exercise: For one month, try something new that educates or enlivens you in some way. Do this every day, every other day, or at least once a week.

21. Manage your Stress

As stated above, ongoing levels of stress are not good for the human body. The above self-maintenance strategies will help a great deal in reducing stress. Below is a list of other activities in which you might engage when you realize you are feeling stressed. They vary in length, but many you can do quickly once you start feeling stressed or anxious:

- Garden
- Play music
- Cook/bake
- Make something with your hands
- Paint
- Play with a pet
- Get a massage
- Smile
- Look up[9]
- Eat a piece of fruit
- Take a walk
- Exercise
- Jump on a trampoline
- Jump in a swimming pool
- Get/use an inversion table
- Read or listen to something inspirational, even for a few minutes
- Play your favorite song
- Sing
- Dance
- Hug someone[10]
- Pray, meditate, or just close your eyes and breathe
- Get a facial, manicure or pedicure
- Engage in a favorite hobby
- Take pictures of silly things
- Watch cartoons

---

9.   Smiling and looking upward have a neurological affect on the mood. Try it out.
10.   Close physical contact releases oxytocin into the blood stream, which improves mood and decreases stress.

One of Steph's favorite things to do in the summer after she comes home from work is to jump in the swimming pool. This creates a huge physical shift in her body that necessarily creates a shift in her mood. It is difficult to feel stressed when you are floating in the water.

Exercise: (1) Try a stress-relieving activity each day regardless of how you feel. (2) Be aware when you are feeling stress and choose a stress-relieving activity. (3) Consciously choose to interrupt feelings of stress.

Trouble-Shooting—What Could Get in Your Way?

If you are not engaging in regular self-maintenance, there are likely other matters "getting in the way." These are your barriers, and they are typically part of your "drift." In addition to simply deciding to engage in self-maintenance, you should also explore what might get in your way. And once you have determined what those barriers are, think of ways to overcome them. This is similar to figuring out what your opposing counsel's arguments might be and then finding the authority and the facts to oppose them: it gives you the best chance of success. Confronting your barriers will allow you to make the changes that enhance and improve your practice and your life.

There are a myriad of barriers (you may even seek to rationalize them by calling them "reasons") in the way of engaging in regular self-maintenance. The most common barriers we see in attorneys include:

- I don't have the time.
- This is just one more in a host of obligations.
- My firm will not support these new practices.
- These practices probably won't be helpful.
- I just don't feel like it.

There is also the likelihood, as we have discussed earlier, that you may resist these changes because they are outside your comfort zone, even if that zone is not literally comfortable for you.

It is therefore important to articulate beforehand how you will overcome your barriers. For instance, one way to combat the barrier of "not enough time" is to actually calendar your self-maintenance activities so they are not crowded out by other commitments.

One way to deal with a firm that is not supportive is to talk to other members of the firm and explain why this is important to you—and to your level of productivity—and brainstorm ways that you can take small amounts of time to yourself. Indeed, if you can make the case, you may enroll them in firm-wide self-maintenance, which would have far-reaching benefits that may change the "drift" of your firm and likely support you even more in what you want to achieve.

One way to overcome the barrier of feeling obligated by self-maintenance is to choose those that seem more "fun" to you and maybe have a "celebration" following your success.

One way to combat the drift of simply not wanting to engage in self-maintenance or thinking it will not be helpful is to enroll a friend, co-worker, or family member in some of these activities and simply try some of them out for a week or two.

These are just some of the many ways you might overcome your barriers and engage in regular self-maintenance. In the end, you must be able to see the value of regular self-maintenance for yourself and you must commit to it in a way that you will not allow yourself to be derailed.

What barriers do you foresee to engaging in self-maintenance? That is, when you think about starting any of these activities, what objections arise in your mind?

_____

_____

_____

How will you overcome them?

_____

_____

_____

Homework

1. Practice a different strategic break every day and observe how it affects you. Journal/keep track of your experience. After doing this for a few weeks, you will have an idea of what works best for you.
2. Track where you spend your time, looking for clues on how much self-maintenance you already do and how much more you need. You may want, as you track your time, to also track how you feel during certain activities and at certain times of the day.
3. Do the exercises listed throughout this chapter.
4. Practice a different technique each week.
5. Find someone in your firm or family to practice these exercises with you.

Chapter 7

Managing Your Time and Energy—A Different Way to Practice

Why Read this Chapter?

1. You feel that things are falling through the cracks.
2. There are too many things to do and not enough hours in the day to do them.
3. You want to feel more focused and grounded and less scattered.
4. You want a model of time management to use for yourself, and to teach to your staff.

Introduction

In coaching lawyers, no topic arises more frequently or foundationally than "time management." Indeed, many lawyers hire Cami, but then are too busy to even meet with her. The first workshop Cami created was one in which she taught time-management tools to attorneys.

Over the years of teaching and coaching in this area, Cami has come to call this "the management of your time, your energy and yourself." She believes *time* is not the problem. Time is a reality. There are twenty-four hours in a day. You cannot change that. What you can change is (1) the way you view and approach your time and tasks and your attitude toward them, and (2) your energy level, which has a huge effect on your ability to get things done in a timely fashion.

Changing your relationship to time, how you deal with time—and particularly how you manage your energy—require a paradigm shift. Because your energy definitely is something you can manage.

Part I—Foundational Pieces

Like Everything, We Start with Accountability

If you have read the chapter on accountability, you know that accountability means accounting for the choices you have made and will make in the future. Accountability is foundational to our ability to make change in our lives and in our practices. At the heart of accountability is the concept of *choice*. We are always choosing—whether consciously or unconsciously. Accountability requires consciousness. When you decide to do something different, even if it is a little bit scary, that is a conscious choice that will lead to other conscious choices. It is by consciously choosing your actions and responses that you will make important changes in your life. **Choice is power.**

There are two basic categories of circumstances and events:

1. Things that are entirely out of your control;
2. Things that are in your control.

In a lawyer's life, there are many things outside of your control. This includes what mood your judge is in, the weather, the court's docket, and your client's finances. And yet there are many things we *think* are out of our control, but over which we actually have some control. We can stop ourselves from interrupting the judge; we can dress appropriately and allow sufficient travel time during bad weather; we can bring additional work with us in case our matter is not called until late in the calendar; and we can require adequate retainers and send regular billing statements to our clients. A funny thing about human nature is that we tend to focus on what we cannot control and ignore what we can control. This is a frustrating and powerless approach.

It is important to start by distinguishing between things you can control and those you cannot. Stop focusing on those things you cannot control and begin to ask what you *can* control.

Assume you are late with interrogatory responses because your client did not get you the information in time. If you get angry and complain about how annoying and unreliable the client is and blame the client for being late, you are focusing on something you cannot control. And you are ignoring what you can control. You can control what you choose to tell people—whether you blame the client or take responsibility for being late. You can control your future actions; for example, you may begin to tell clients that responses are due two weeks before the actual deadline. You are even in control of whether to get angry at your client or not.

Imagine if rather than blaming your client, you were to ask, "Now what? What can I do to improve the situation? What can I learn from this? What is my next best option?" Now you are focusing on what is in your control. This is somewhat different from how most people approach this type of situation. And yet focusing on what you can control is the only way to make effective changes in your life.

NLP (neuro-linguistics programming) presuppositions are instructive:

> We are all responsible for creating our own experience. Even in the face of challenging events that we cannot control, we are responsible for our response to these events. Typically, however, we have much more control than we think we have. Another way of stating this presupposition is that "We consistently create our own environment through our beliefs, filters, capabilities and behaviors."

Another example: if you get stuck in traffic and are late for a meeting, you could say this experience ruined your day or "made" you late. It may seem that you have no control over your experience with regard to the traffic. But you CAN control your response. You can decide whether to get mad and allow it to ruin your day. Or you can look at whatever part you played in being late, learn from what occurred, and perhaps arrange your schedule so you are not driving when traffic is heaviest or leave time to allow for heavy traffic.

Most lawyers are stressed and under pressure. And yet **some** lawyers seem to manage their time very effectively; they are relaxed, have time for their kids, and even play a sport. What is the difference between the harried attorney and the calm attorney? Choice and accountability.

Ultimately, two questions that will change your relationship to time and the other results in your life, including your energy, are, (1) "What choice can I make right now?" and (2) "What choices have I made up to this point?" These two questions will help you determine (1) where you are spending time that is not serving you; and (2) where you can make change.

But you must first commit to focusing on what you can change as you read this chapter and do the exercises. Make a promise to yourself that you will not blame your circumstances for how busy you are or for not having enough hours in the day or for being low on energy.

I promise I will read this chapter, looking for what I can improve and change. I will be curious about identifying behaviors and habits that are not working for me and I will isolate and change those non-working behaviors. I further promise that whenever I catch myself blaming my circumstances for my lack of energy or time, I will put $1 in a jar, and at the end of one month, I will

❑   Give the money to _____ charity.

❑   Take myself out for free time to _____.

❑   _____

Agreed? If so, sign the contract below:

_____

Okay, now let's begin.

Human Beings (Even Attorneys) Can Only do One Thing at a Time

Is this you?

If you are like most people—and especially like most attorneys—you may have a reaction to the statement "You can only do one thing at a time." You may say yes, but I am reading this book and watching television at the same time. So perhaps it is more accurate to say you can only do one thing at a time and do it *well*. That is because you cannot fully focus on more than one thing at a time. If you are reading this book and watching TV, you are not fully focusing on one or the other. Instead, you are shifting your attention from the book to the TV and back to the book and so on. The problem with this approach is that because our brains only focus on one thing at a time and it takes time to shift your focus from one thing to another, doing so actually wastes time.

And there are other problems with this approach:

- You are not getting all the information from either source
- You are causing your brain, and likely your body, to feel stressed
- You are far more likely to make a mistake

Be Present

The underlying premise of effective time management is **be present in what you are doing.**
This means two things:

1. **Do** one thing at a time;
2. **Focus** on one thing at a time.

Our brains are very intelligent and effective processors and analyzers when they are focused.
They are more efficient than we often realize. You may not know this because most of
the time you are doing one thing *and* simultaneously doing or thinking about something
else as well. This takes attention from the task at hand, which makes you slower and less
efficient. You work more slowly because you are not bringing the considerable power of
all your brain to bear on the project. And you tend to make mistakes, which costs more
time in the long run.

When we are fully present with what we are doing, we are more focused and effective.
This means we will finish more quickly and will do a better job, thereby saving time in
the long run.

We know it may be challenging for you to believe that it actually takes *more* time to
simultaneously dictate a letter, write a brief, and look at e-mail than it does to do them
consecutively. But try it. Separate out your multi-tasks, being fully present to each one.
You will find you are quicker, less stressed, and more accurate.

Could this be you?

Another benefit to being present in
the moment is that it helps you respond
to situations when they arise rather than
reacting to them after they have become
emergencies. As we will discuss in detail
in this chapter, one of the greatest imped-
iments to ease and productivity for
attorneys is that most attorneys spend
a lot of time *reacting* to emergencies. The
goal is to move from a reactive mindset
to a responsive mindset. The more present we are to what is happening in the
moment, the more we can *respond* to it
by consciously choosing the best way to
proceed. In this way, we take back control of our time and energy.

Part II—Introducing a New Paradigm for Time Management

The Old Paradigm

What is the old paradigm of attorney time management? In our experience, attorneys have a strongly-held belief that if we are getting behind and we need to get caught up, we must work faster, do more things at once, work into the night, skip the gym, eat lunch at our desks, and (once again) miss dinner with the family. In the old paradigm, we focus on *time*—how much time we have, how much time we spend, how much we can get done in a particular amount of time. We try to "squeeze things in." We work faster, more and harder. Yet we still feel behind.

This old paradigm does not work very well for most attorneys. It is what has resulted in so much of the burnout and dissatisfaction with the practice. In this old paradigm, we may get "caught up" in the short run—the brief is filed on time—but in the long run we are never caught up, leading to repeated late nights at the office and more frustration.

A New Paradigm

What is the new paradigm? For starters, it is not one in which you work faster, but where you make better and smarter choices. You will look at where you spend your time in a whole new way. Let's illustrate with a common example. If you are like many attorneys, you stop every twenty to thirty minutes (or every four to five minutes) to check your email. You can do this all day long and still not get that inbox cleaned out. We suggest you check your email *less frequently*. For most people, this sounds absurd. How can I catch up if I check it *less* frequently? But Cami's clients use this time-management tool with great success. Calendar a certain amount of time—say thirty to forty-five minutes—in the morning and in the afternoon to check and respond to your email. Maybe you want to check it three times per day. Experiment with the frequency. What is important is that you have specific times and an amount of time that you devote to your email, and for the rest of the day you ignore it. Surprisingly, this frees up a lot of time. Why? First, when you check your email at a specific time, that is all you are doing; your brain is not distracted, but is focused solely on your email. By the same token, during other parts of the day, you are not distracted by your email and are more efficient at each task. Second, you are not wasting precious minutes throughout the day constantly transitioning from one thing to another.

As in many chapters of this book, we are encouraging you to switch from the unconscious to the conscious. The way you currently manage your time is probably mainly unconscious. We tend to manage our time based on patterns and habits we developed when we were younger—in school or in our first job, by observing our parents or our first bosses—and we never consciously thought much about it. Now is the time to change all that.

Starting with Self-Observation

As with many of the tools throughout this book, this one begins with conscious self-observation. As a starting point, think back over the last seven days and consider the five things on which you spent most of your time. For purposes of this exercise, do not count time sleeping. And for each work activity, write the specific activity on which you were spending time, for example, a particular brief; client communication; time in court; marketing; etc. At the end of this chapter, we will suggest you do a more in-depth review of where you spend your time. For now, this quick assessment gives us a place to start.

1. _____

_____

2. _____

_____

3. _____

_____

4. _____

_____

5. _____

_____

Looking back at your answers, what do you notice that is working in the way you spend your time (remember "working" means producing the desired results)?

_____

_____

_____

What is not working (producing non-desired results)? What is missing?

_____

_____

_____

Overview of the New Paradigm

Because so many attorneys spend their time "putting out fires," in explaining the New Paradigm, we use the metaphor of the firefighter. In this paradigm, we do the following:

1. Move away from "fire fighting."
2. Spend more time "fireproofing."
3. Seek to eliminate "stray sparks" by reducing and eliminating distractions and interruptions
4. Employ the "controlled burn" method of reducing and eliminating time-wasters.

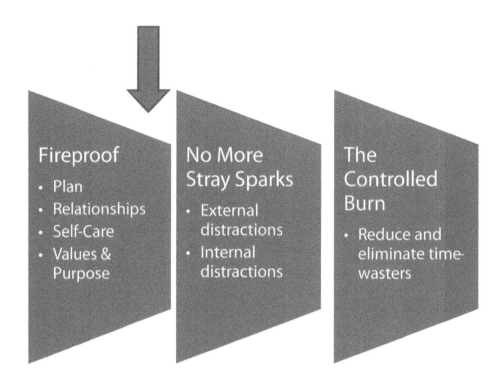

1. Being a Fire Fighter—Where Many Attorneys Start

If you are like most attorneys, you will have noticed some "firefighting" in the above exercise. Most attorneys spend a great deal of time "putting out fires," rushing, hurrying and dealing with emergencies. Most attorneys operate at a high level of stress. When we are highly stressed, we cannot see anything other than what is right in front of us. So when you get an emergency deadline—one you must spend all your time on for fear you won't meet it—you focus all of your time and energy on that one thing. And yet there are many other important tasks that need your attention, which have not yet become emergencies, that you are ignoring while you are fighting that fire. And when you have met that deadline and the smoke has cleared, you find other items that have become emergencies onto which you now have to put all your attention, to the exclusion of still other important tasks that have not yet become emergencies. And so on. Such is the life of the firefighter. What you may notice is that these tasks become emergencies largely because of where you place your attention, energy and focus, and what you consequently ignore.

Jake

Jake is a young associate who works for three partners to whom he answers, all of whom give him work from time to time. He works from 6 a.m. to 7 p.m. most days. When he began as a new associate, he was eager to please and took all the work given to him. He had no guidance as to how to manage or prioritize his work. But he had done well in law school and other non-legal jobs, so he assumed he would know how to get everything done here as well.

When Jake began his associate practice, he prioritized tasks as he had in school: he looked at the due dates and worked on whatever project was due first. For the first week, this worked. On week two however, one of the partners gave him a rush job: a motion to draft in two days. This became Jake's priority and he went to work on it right away, letting go of other tasks. When he finished and turned his attention back to the brief he had been working on, he now had one day to finish it. This became the emergency assignment. He stayed at work that night until 1:00 a.m. and finished the brief.

In the morning, he looked at his "to do" list and realized all the other tasks he had ignored for three days were now much closer to being due. He chose the one that was due the soonest and worked on that. He began to panic, worrying he would not finish in time. A partner then gave Jake another "rush." Jake stayed late until it was finished. Then he returned to the prior project. And so on.

Jake is constantly in an "emergency" mindset. If you look closely, you will see that most of Jake's emergencies have not arisen because of short time frames. The majority of the emergencies are created by Jake and the culture at the firm. First, Jake does not tell his partners when he has too much to do. When they give him work, he takes it. He feels he has "no choice." Second, Jake believes staying late as often as necessary is a useful and workable method of time management. After all, the other attorneys do it. Third, when Jake works on something deemed an emergency, he ignores everything else, which makes those tasks become emergencies as well. Finally, the partners do not talk to each other or Jake about whether associates have too much to do, and they are in the habit of giving "rush" jobs without asking about the consequences to the associate's work load.

Another side effect of this practice is that if Jake keeps working this way, he becomes addicted to the motivation of time deadlines. The looming due date becomes both the carrot and the stick. Like many attorneys, he is operating under fear and high adrenaline, both of which are powerful motivators. But attorneys who typically work in this mindset find that once a deadline is met, if the next project is not yet an emergency, he is unmotivated to work on it. This creates a cycle in which we are driven by our adrenaline rushes and urgency mindset. But the body simply is not designed to be in constant adrenaline rush. (Look at the self-maintenance chapter for the dangers of operating in this manner over time.) This adrenaline rush produces a high level of physical and mental stress, dissatisfaction, and often feelings of anger and hopelessness. Most of Cami's clients report feeling defeated when they look at the next task on their list and cannot motivate themselves to work because it is not due right away.

This is a result of the "emergency" mindset prevalent for most attorneys. It is a *reactive* cycle with little consideration as to appropriate *response*. It is a circular problem. Once it starts, it is very difficult to interrupt.

The Emergency Cycle

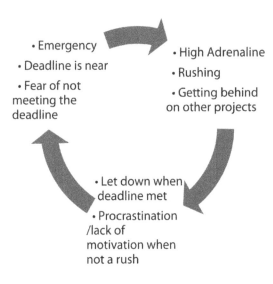

- Emergency
- Deadline is near
- Fear of not meeting the deadline

- High Adrenaline
- Rushing
- Getting behind on other projects

- Let down when deadline met
- Procrastination /lack of motivation when not a rush

The emergency cycle is largely reactive and short-term in nature. When we work only on emergencies, we focus only on what is right in front of us. We do not see how this work connects to our larger mission; we usually see only how doing this work will keep us from getting in trouble. Attorneys who operate this way do not believe they can effectuate change; they rarely, if ever, feel their heads are above water. And they often become addicted to the adrenaline rush of the emergency. As such they find themselves more and more in "emergency" mode. These attorneys tend to "crash" after a big project is completed and find no way to motivate themselves to the next project.

2. Fireproofing—A Better Way to Spend Your Time
"[T]he degree to which urgency is dominant is the degree to which importance is not."

Stephen Covey, *First Things First*, **at 42**

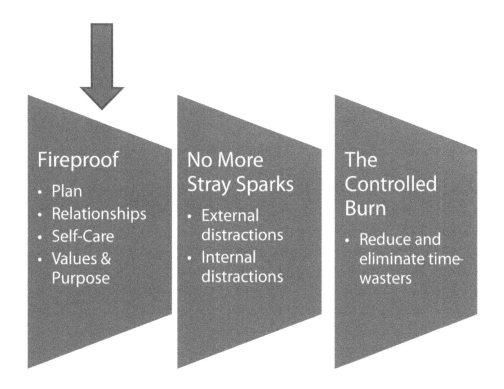

Now we know that constant emergency firefighting is exhausting and counterproductive, how do we prevent fires? By taking the time to clear away the underbrush, building firebreaks and keeping the grounds from drying out. You may see all the dried growth and say, "I'll take care of that later;" or "I don't have time right now." But this is how fires start and spread. In the new paradigm, we look to the future to improve our present: we consciously prepare and plan so as to eliminate those emergencies, or greatly reduce their occurrence. When you spend time fireproofing and planning to reduce and eliminate future fires, you work from a mindset of responding rather than reacting. You increase the space between the stimulus (outside event) and response (your choice of action based on the event).

This is a primary goal of time management—seeing what is before you and considering what response is best in the circumstance, rather than merely reacting. In order to shift to a mindset of **responding** rather than reacting, we must slow down enough to see the situation (stimulus) and give ourselves time to formulate our next move (response). A reaction is unconscious. A response requires that we stop, consider, and consciously choose our next move. All of the tools listed in this section will assist with this endeavor. They are:

(a) Fireproofing Tool #1—Planning and preparation
(b) Fireproofing Tool #2—Taking care of relationships
(c) Fireproofing Tool #3—Taking care of yourself
(d) Fireproofing Tool #4—Clarifying your values and your purpose

The new paradigm is based on shifting your choices of where to spend time so you spend less time on **emergencies** and more time on those things that are **meaningful** in your practice and your life. Those things that are **meaningful** will make the greatest difference to you and serve to improve your overall time management and quality of life.

The new paradigm requires conscious choice. In the above example, Jake's choices are from the old paradigm and are, therefore, largely unconscious. He says "yes" to all of the tasks given him out of unconscious motivation to please or to ensure his job security. He sometimes even finds himself unmotivated to work after a deadline has passed because of an unconscious feeling that he cannot name. These are habitual reactions to the situation. They are choices he makes that are unconscious to him; i.e., "reactions." He chooses largely from an **emergency** mindset rather than asking what is the most **meaningful** task to complete at this moment.

The new paradigm allows Jake to consciously implement new practices that enable him to do things differently. In the new paradigm, Jake plans his time by focusing not on **emergencies**, but on what is most **meaningful** or important. He begins to shift from emergency activities to meaningful and important activities.

Four Fireproofing Tools

a. Fireproofing Tool #1—Planning and Preparation

The most effective way to focus on what is meaningful and to purposefully manage your time is to plan and prepare. **Looking ahead will keep you from getting behind.** In this chapter, we will offer various tools to help you plan ahead and avoid emergencies. Choose what works for you. You may even come up with your own ideas that fit with your personality and your practice.

The failure to plan and prepare over the long term results in many attorneys "organizing" their time as follows: (1) They put items on their "to-do" list without consciously stopping to ask what they can manage and complete in a timely fashion. (2) They choose what to work on based on what is due the soonest. (3) They calendar due dates but do not actively use a calendar to manage their time in the process. (4) They do not maintain a consciousness of all of their other work while they tackle an emergency.

One of the most useful ways of planning and preparing is to actively **calendar your work** and to **overestimate your time**.

For example, if you have a project that is due in three weeks, ask yourself how long it will take to complete it. If your answer is twenty hours, add 50 percent to that and allocate thirty hours to the project. Next, take out your calendar and mark out blocks of time over the next three weeks that add up to thirty hours.

After you have overestimated your time for a while, you will start to learn if you need to add 50 percent, 20 percent or 100 percent to your initial time estimate. You may even learn how to accurately estimate your time, though many do not. The goal is not necessarily to learn how to accurately estimate your time. The goal is to learn how much time you need to *add* to your estimate to be most accurate and give yourself enough time to complete a project.

Many attorneys are resistant to blocking out time on their calendar to complete a project. Often they are afraid they will learn they do not actually have enough time to complete the project. But denial will not assist you; it is this mentality that causes you to accept projects when you cannot complete them on time. It is how fires are created in the first place. Part of being conscious is learning what you can and cannot do. You must discover the truth about this for yourself. It is far more effective to know you do not have the time in your schedule to finish a certain project than it is to say "yes" to it and not complete it on time.

In terms of planning and preparation, we find the best tools for most attorneys are the calendar and a running "to-do" list. This follows the big rock/small rock concept articulated by Stephen Covey.[1] It also tracks with a concept called "what gets scheduled gets done." And the corollary—"what doesn't get scheduled, doesn't get done."

Here is how it works:

1. First, look out into the future. If you are starting today, look one month out and see what deadlines are on the horizon. Then look out three weeks, two weeks, and one week. Get a feel for what is due and when.

---

1.   If you go on line, you can see Mr. Covey give the big rocks/small rocks demonstration, which he attributes to another time management/ leadership presenter. In the demonstration, Covey shows how a certain amount of large and small rocks can fit into a jar, depending solely on the order in which one puts the rocks into the jar. When we start by pouring the small rocks into the jar, there is not enough space for all of the large rocks. However, by simply putting all the large rocks in first, we leave plenty of room for the small rocks to be poured in. From a time management perspective, this means that if we schedule the most meaningful tasks first (the large rocks), we will find time to complete the smaller tasks as well. But if we spend our time on small tasks, we will never find the time to do the more meaningful projects.

2. Plan your upcoming week on the calendar. Do this at a time when you will not be interrupted. Some people like to do it during the weekend; some on Friday afternoon so they can leave work with a clear understanding of what they have planned for the week ahead; some on Monday morning when they first arrive at work. Experiment with what works best for you.

3. Then schedule in your calendar all the meaningful and important tasks you need to accomplish in order to meet the upcoming deadlines. These will be things like preparing the brief and the opinion letter, research and writing, meetings with clients, etc.

For a more in-depth discussion of how to use the calendar and running to-do list to effectively prepare and plan your time, see, *Pt. III—How to Implement the New Paradigm*, 188.

b. Fireproofing Tool #2—Taking Care of Relationships

One of the main factors affecting our time is our relationships with others. Consider the effect on your time of unhappy clients versus happy clients; an opposing counsel who employs a "scorched earth" approach to litigation and one who is cooperative; an employee or partner who is unclear and one who takes the time to explain what he or she wants; a child who is going through the volatile teen years versus the ten-year-old who is oddly compliant. All day every day we interact with others. And this is one of the greatest, if not the greatest, factor affecting our ability to be effective with our time. That is because most of our day is communicating or interacting with others and dealing with the results of poor communication and interaction.

Building and Maintaining Relationships

An important aspect of fireproofing is purposefully building and maintaining strong working and personal relationships. Often you spend time with a client fixing a problem that arose because you did not originally spend enough time explaining what he could expect in the case. Or you "save time" by not returning phone calls and ultimately spend more time repairing relationships with those callers who now believe they are unimportant to you. Or you don't take the time to make sure your secretary understands what you want— or to let her know how much you appreciate her—because you are "busy." It takes a lot more time to clear up misunderstandings than it does to be clear in the first place. The same is true with your home life, which will interfere with your work life if you do not take care of those relationships. Investing time to create, develop and maintain strong relationships will ultimately save you time.

Imagine the difference between settling a case for a client with whom you have forged a strong relationship and one with whom you have not. The latter client may not trust you enough because you avoid him, don't call him back, or have not fully explained the intricacies of the case to him. As such, it will take far more time to get him to agree to settle the case (if you ever do).

In summary, the most important strategies in taking care of relationships are:

1. **Schedule and spend time with people who make the biggest different to you.** Time invested with clients, family members and office mates is an investment in the relationship that will pay off later. Strong relationships help you avoid those emergencies that are generated by the other person feeling out of touch with you.

2. **Learn the art of deep listening and effective communication (see chapter 8, Communication Skills for Lawyers).** The better you listen, the more others trust you. The better you understand what others want, the fewer mistakes you will make and the less time you will spend asking unnecessary or repetitive questions. The clearer you are, the more likely it is that others will understand what you want and give it to you.

3. **Learn to build trust with others (see chapter 11, Trust in our Profession).** The more people trust you, the less time they will spend questioning your advice or your decisions and the more they will let you do what you need to do. The more that you trust others, the less time you spend micro-managing them and the more you can let them do what you have asked.

4. **Give and ask for feedback.** By giving and receiving regular feedback, you create an environment in which everyone knows where they stand. This results in fewer time-consuming misunderstandings.

5. **Create clear agreements with a time element.** One of the major ways in which attorneys waste time is that they tell their staff what to do, but are either unclear about the specifics ("this needs to be served on all parties"), or do not include a time element ("do this by Friday"), or both. The attorney then spends unnecessary time following up and "micromanaging." If you give an employee a time deadline and you keep track of it, you do not need to check in unless and until the deadline is missed. Of course, be sure to give your employees deadlines that are early enough that it can be missed without dire consequences so you do not add stress and emergency to your day if the deadline passes without the work being done.

It may seem like these relationship techniques will actually consume, rather than save time, but these are all highly important time management skills that will ultimately pay off. Many of these techniques involve an investment now to save time going forward on a consistent basis.

Consciously Choosing Client Relationships

When we consider the causes of lost time, we must also consider time spent on difficult clients and cases that do not advance your practice. We have said proactivity will save you time in the long run. How can you be proactive in choosing your clients? One way is to take your purpose and vision statement (ch. 9, Purpose and Vision) and consider what kinds of cases you want to take and what kinds of clients you want to work with. Consider what you are looking for in a client and be selective in the clients and cases you take.

Before taking on a new case or client, you should determine if it will be worth your time and energy. Ask yourself whether this client will advance your purpose and your practice or whether he or she will be a time-consuming distraction from your other cases. Learn about the new client. Is he or she likely to pay your bills on time, or at all? Also, how did the client find you? Was it from a reliable referral? Good clients tend to refer other good clients. The friend of that troublesome client who didn't pay his bills and refused to listen to you may not be worth your time. Other important questions include these: What does this client expect of you as their attorney? Is this the type of case that you understand and/or enjoy? Will this client listen to you and follow your advice? These are inquiries that, left unconsidered, could lead to huge time losses in the future.

Also determine if you will be the first attorney on a new case or merely the latest in a series of attorneys the client has hired. If you are not the first attorney, find out why your client left her former attorney. This can be the sign of a litigious client or of one who may later sue you if she doesn't get a favorable result. Other red flags are if the client is in a big hurry or if the case is an "emergency." Often these clients will not care that you have other work to do and will continue to deem everything an "emergency" throughout your relationship. Also determine if the client is overly angry or motivated by revenge. These clients tend to bring a lot of emotion to the case, requiring you to spend an inordinate amount of time dealing with their feelings. Or they may want you to take actions that are not productive to the case merely to "rattle" the other side.

Also determine whether the client is accountable at all (i.e., taking any responsibility for the result she has) or blames everyone else, including the system and the other side/attorneys. Clients who blame everyone and everything will also blame you eventually. And note whether the client was on time and prepared for your meeting. A client who is not prepared for the initial meeting is unlikely to be timely with discovery responses.

Your goal should be to have the majority of your clients be cooperative people who listen to you, are not overly demanding of your time or energy, and pay their bills on time. You should strive to have the majority of your cases be those in the area in which you prefer to practice and which tend to generate a high level of income. Consciously choosing these cases and clients will heighten your productivity and increase your enjoyment in practicing law.

c. Fireproofing Tool #3—Taking Care of Yourself
This is so important we have devoted an entire chapter to it. But this is also a

time-management principle. If you do not take care of yourself, you will be fatigued, burned out, and low on energy, both physically and mentally. This makes you slower and less motivated. When you are less motivated, you are less productive. Time management, as we have stated, is energy management. The higher your energy, the more efficient and productive you are. We suggest you refer to the self-maintenance chapter for tips and tools on how to get the most out of the supremely important machine that is your body and your mind.

d. Fireproofing Tool #4—Clarify your Values and your Purpose

In chapter 5, we taught you how to determine your values. In chapter 9, we will help you craft your purpose. These exercises also have practical effect on time management. When you live by your values and your purpose, using them to guide your decisions, you will consciously limit what you choose to take on. When you make choices from your values and your purpose, you consciously decide the direction in which to go, rather than have a direction choose you. You may determine there are certain types of cases, and certain types of clients, you do not want to bring into your practice. And you will clarify the clients and cases you *do* want.

Why is this a time management technique? There are two reasons. First, a lot of time is wasted when we do not have a clear direction. For example, if I have not clarified my values and my purpose, I might take a new client whose case is contrary to my values, and then spend additional time and energy either trying to extricate myself from the case or handling a case I don't like, thus taking time away from my productive cases. Second, when we do not have a clear vision for our practice and our future, our tendency is to take whatever comes. This creates a likelihood that we will not be doing what we are passionate about. When we do work we do not love, often our energy wanes. When our energy wanes, we do not work productively. Even if you know you will make good money, we tend to avoid that which we do not enjoy.

Purpose is useful motivation. Purpose helps us see the bigger picture. Imagine you are talking to the designated representative for a corporate client, who you do not enjoy working with. If your main focus is your dislike for this person, talking to him will feel like drudgery. In that case, you are likely to avoid the conversation, distract yourself, and waste time both before and during the meeting. But when you look at the larger purpose, you see that talking to this representative improves your relationship with the corporate client. You value being able to represent this client, which ultimately supports your larger purpose of, say, advancing ecology concerns on the planet. When you connect with your greater purpose like this, you are less likely to avoid or waste time on a task.

It is also useful to have a purpose statement for both your business and your life overall. These purpose statements will help you to put your time expenditures in perspective and will help you make choices that support your overall life vision and purpose. For more on drafting a purpose statement, see chapter 9.

After you have put together a purpose statement and identified your values, you will undoubtedly notice that certain of your clients and cases are not in keeping with those values. And you may notice that those clients and cases tend to be time-wasters. What can you do about that? First, stop taking these types of clients and cases! Second, extricate yourself from those time-wasters. For those clients who have stopped paying you, give them an ultimatum and then act on it. For others, you may need to allow the case to run its course, hastening it as you go. Those time-wasters are likely cases and clients you have been avoiding, so there may be an advantage in either working the case toward its finality or suggesting the client find another attorney who is not so "busy." One caveat: be very careful when extricating yourself from clients and cases. Make sure that you are doing so in a way that is in keeping with the ethical rules of your jurisdiction and with your fee agreement. A malpractice action or state bar complaint can be the biggest time-waster of all.

3. Eradicating Stray Sparks—Reducing and Eliminating Distractions and Interruptions

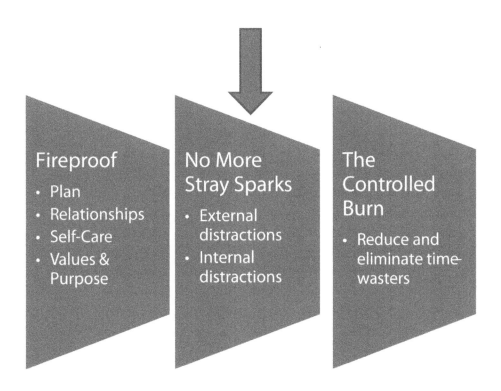

We have recommended you spend your time on meaningful/important tasks (fireproofing) and that you make a clear distinction between meaningful tasks and emergencies (firefighting). When you spend the majority of your time fireproofing, you avoid the need for firefighting. This strategy can be challenging to implement at first, because you likely have several fires before you and may wonder where you will find the time to start preparing, planning and improving relationships.

One answer is to eliminate distractions: the stray sparks that lead to additional fires. In this section we recommend that you track your time and see where you spend it. You may be surprised to learn how often you are distracted and derailed by things that do not need your immediate attention. We call these distractions and interruptions "stray sparks." There are two main ways that fires get started. The first is a lack of fireproofing. Failing to prepare and plan is akin to allowing the dried brush to lay over the land—fires will start. The second cause is stray sparks: those distractions generated by others that seek your time and attention.

Often you will be faced with seeming "emergencies", but when you look more closely at them, you realize they do not need your immediate attention. Generally speaking, we call these "other people's urgencies." Imagine that you are working diligently on a brief that is due in two weeks—planning ahead to avoid a later emergency. You look up to see an associate standing in your doorway. He says "I have a question for you" and walks in. Most attorneys react to this kind of situation as if it is urgent. When someone asks to speak with us, most of us say, "yes." If you say, "yes," to a request for your time right now that came out of the blue and which you did not plan for, you are treating that request as an emergency: dropping everything to attend to it. This throws you off track and causes you to lose focus on the current task, so that when you come back to your brief, you need time to remember where you were. This is like allowing a passing motorist to throw a lit cigarette on the dry grass next to the road. Next thing you know, you are battling another fire.

Consider this alternative to eliminate the stray spark: say to him, "You know, John, I would like to help you. But I am right in the middle of something and I know I will not be able to give you my full attention right now. How about later today?" Then the two of you can agree on a time. Once you estimate how long your meeting with him will take, you can plan this chunk of your day and continue to focus on what you were doing.

Sometimes other people's urgencies will be important to you at that moment and you will consciously decide to attend to the interruption. It is important for you to become *conscious* so you can decide if this urgency is truly important enough to handle *right now* or if you might schedule it for another time, or even delegate it. When your mindset is one of handling urgencies *whenever they arise* and you don't stop to ask if that is the best use of your time, then you will immediately handle anything that appears urgent to you without thinking (i.e., unconsciously).

For example, there are certain clients who are more demanding than others. Often we take care of the demanding client's needs first in order to get them to stop bugging us. Meanwhile, there are other clients and tasks quietly waiting, which we often do not serve in as timely a manner simply because they are not making trouble for us at that moment. When something seems urgent, it usually causes a visceral reaction in us; it is like hearing someone cry "Help!" We are immediately propelled into action. In order to truly manage your time, you must learn to interrupt that tendency. When something seems like an "emergency," ask yourself "is this really the best place for me to spend my time right now?" This is how you interrupt the tendency to act on whatever interruption arises. If the answer is "yes; this is important to me right now," then work on it. But you must first ask the question in order to consciously choose where to spend your time.

If you are very emergency-oriented, you might not see the difference between the following:

- A brief that is due tomorrow
- Preparing for a meeting that starts in an hour
- A client who wants to talk to you about her case right now
- An ex parte motion
- An associate who is standing in your doorway with an urgent question
- A ringing phone
- An email that just came in dinging on your computer

When you consciously assess these "urgencies," though, you will probably notice that certain of them do not actually *require* your attention at that moment. These may include the following:

- The client who wants to talk to you right now
- The associate standing in your doorway
- The ringing phone
- The email dinging on your computer

Learning the difference between true emergencies and items that you can schedule for later requires practice. Start asking yourself if those things that just "came up" really require your immediate action.

Three Steps to Eliminating Stray Sparks (Finding and Eliminating Distractions)
   1. **Self-Observation**
   2. **Managing External Interruptions**
   3. **Managing Internal Interruptions**

Step One—Self-Observation
Before you can eliminate distractions, you will need to see where they are arising. A good way to do this is to keep track of your time for a week. You must know where you are before you can figure out where you want to go. Use the Activity Log (found on our website, www.mclarencoaching.com/bookdownloads/) to track your time and see where you are actually spending it. The log is designed to see how much of your time is planned versus responding to emergencies or interruptions. Once you know this, you will see where to make changes.

Activity Log			
Date	Activity Description	Duration (Hours)	Planned? Emergency? Interruption? Distraction?

After you track your time for a week or two, you will see how often you are distracted or interrupted. Column four is an important piece of information. The next step then is to develop a plan for each of these interruptions and distractions.

Step Two—Managing External Interruptions
Let's say you have a bell on your computer that alerts you every time an email comes in, and you discover from tracking your time that you are distracted ninety-five times in a day by incoming emails. Chances are good that you have trained yourself to react to the bell by checking your email. That sound creates in you a Pavlovian sense of urgency, regardless of whether an actual urgency exists. You immediately look at the email to see if it needs your attention. And once you look at it, you are likely to read and even respond to it, regardless of whether it is urgent or not. And there goes another ten minutes of your day. This does not even include the further likelihood that once you read and respond to the incoming email, your attention will then be pulled to other emails in your inbox and you may decide (unconsciously) to then spend the next hour on email, before you realize that you have stopped doing the work you had planned to do.

The goal of time management is to:

1. Eliminate emergencies, to the extent possible
2. Make conscious choices as to where you spend your time
3. Plan ahead
4. Manage your energy
5. Feel in control, less stressed, and produce better work, and participate in new activities if you so choose

Imagine that you do look at every email as it comes in. The first thing to do is look at how you are creating the emergency mindset—in this case regarding email. If you did not have the sound on your computer and did not know that emails were coming in, they would not disturb you and you could spend two hours writing that brief. By setting up your computer to alert you to every incoming email, you have transformed non-urgent matters into "emergencies."

As we noted above, many of Cami's clients have started a practice of checking their email only two to three times per day or once every two to three hours. They block half an hour or so to read and respond to emails, which (1) is more efficient and less time-consuming than reading and answering them as they come in; (2) allows the attorney to handle other tasks quickly and efficiently because they are not shifting their focus back and forth between email and other work; and (3) eliminates one area where the attorney is reacting to self-created "emergencies."

At first response to this suggestion, most attorneys will say, "But I need to know what is coming in at all times because *it could be an emergency*." And yet email is simply a mode of communication. If the people sending you emails think you will respond within a few minutes, you have taught them to believe that. If people are sending you "emergencies" via email, it is because you have shown them you will react quickly to email. Now is the time to teach them something new. This is where you make a conscious choice about what would work better. Use this as an example of how to deal with an interruption that you are creating or allowing others to create for you in which you react rather than respond. Use this example for other areas in which you allow others to dictate when and where you spend your time, such as the following.

Typical interruptions:

- Family phone calls
- Office mates who want to chat
- Associates who have a question
- Clients who want to talk right now
- Incoming phone calls

Don't get us wrong. We are not saying you should ignore all human contact and eliminate all outside influence so you can work. Indeed, if you look above, under the Fireproofing suggestions, we recommend that you manage and maintain your relationships—with family, office staff, and clients—in a proactive and intentional way. As with the example regarding your emails, you will not ignore your relationships in favor of your work; you simply approach them in a proactive manner so that others get what they need from you at a time that is appropriate for *both of you*.

Thus, when a member of your family calls, you can train your staff to tell them when you will call back, unless it is truly an "emergency." In that case, you may say, "I have about five minutes right now." If an associate comes to you with a question, tell him or her that you want to devote your full attention to the issue, but your attention is on something else, and have them come back at a certain time.

Socializing is important, as are office relationships. Lunch is a great time to take a break from work and engage in some "face time" with your colleagues. It is also a great time to address those "urgent" issues they may have. Questions from associates and staff are important. Formal staff meetings can be useful. You might train your staff to write down and keep questions until the meeting, or email you more "urgent" questions—and you can respond during a designated time. Experiment to find whatever is appropriate for your office.

Other ideas on handling distraction: one attorney puts a sign on the outside of his door when he does not want anyone to interrupt him. During this time all calls go to voicemail. He returns calls when his "blocked work time" is over. You can set an alarm to go off five or ten minutes before you need to leave for a meeting or a court appearance, so you are not constantly checking your watch. Have someone else open your mail. Have a set time to return phone calls. Work on short-term projects like drafting letters or discovery motions until they are done, and then move on to the next task so they are not hanging over your head. As we have noted, shifting from one thing to another wastes time—and is distracting.

Bottom line: do not react to what is around you. Be in control of what you do and when you do it, to the extent possible.

Step Three—Managing Internal Interruptions

The techniques listed thus far are designed to help you to make conscious choices about where to spend your time, to not be distracted by others' supposed urgencies, and to reduce the number of emergencies you have, with the goal that you can comfortably sit down and work on one thing at a time.

But many attorneys put these practices in place only to discover, as they close their door for a two-hour block of time, that they are uncomfortable and actively seeking distraction. These are often the same attorneys who work furiously on an impending deadline and then, when the deadline passes, sit at their desks unmotivated to work on other projects.

While this is not true for all attorneys, it is very common. We believe this is largely a self-trained addiction to urgency. Having spent so much of your practice working under the gun, you may have lost the ability to work slowly and purposefully. Do not worry. The addiction to urgency is a habit. And like any habit, you can develop a new habit to replace it.

Cami has clients who want to lose weight, but they hate to exercise and lead very sedentary lives. They have an addiction to inactivity. It is often challenging for them to begin exercising because it is not what they are accustomed to doing. They have literally trained themselves not to. However, for most of them, once they begin to exercise, there is a neurological change that takes place and they have a new experience that is usually rewarding. Many of them continue to dislike exercise, but they feel better when they are done. After a few weeks, they have developed a new habit and they continue to exercise on a regular basis even though it is not their favorite thing to do.

It is the same with changing your addiction to urgency. Old habits fall away as you develop new ones. New neural pathways develop in your brain and new chemical systems are set up that reward you for the new activity. Every choice you make—whether to close your door or leave it open; turn off your email bell or leave it on; take the call or let it go to voice mail; sit at your computer to work for a thirty minute block of time or get up and walk around every five minutes—is either part of the old habit or part of a new habit. This is actually true throughout your life: everything you do is part of an old habit or a new habit. You get to decide.

Here are techniques to develop the new habit of managing internal distractions:

A. **Keep a notepad nearby.** As you work on a project, you will be distracted by your own mind, which will remember many other things you need to do. Simply write them down. Our brains do a great job of retaining information but it often comes out at inopportune times. Our brain reminds us of unfinished projects to make sure we finish them. This simple solution is very effective: every time you think of something you need to do, write it down. Your brain will stop bringing it up, and you can stop being distracted by it, because now your brain is confident you will do it later.

B. **Take conscious breaks and increase your ability to focus.** If you are following the guidelines in this chapter, you are now working on projects that have not yet become emergencies; you are being proactive and planning your time. If you find yourself seeking distraction, discipline yourself and build up your stamina. This is a bit like exercise to a person who is out of shape. The first week, you may wish to work in twenty minute increments. Set up your two hour time block. Set a timer for twenty minutes. Then take a one–three minute break. It is most effective to stay in your office: stretch, check Facebook or email, whatever feels best to you. If you venture outside your office for a cup of coffee or to take a quick walk around, be vigilant about returning within the time you have set for your break. Then work for another twenty minutes. **Be sure to time it.** Then take a break. Make your next block of time twenty-five minutes. You can increase your stamina here as on the treadmill.

C. **Set up accountability systems.** For many people, it is the external pressure that causes them to work hard and furiously on a project that is due soon. It is the fear of being late and having to answer to someone else that drives them to work hard and complete something on time. You can use this to your advantage when you start being proactive and working before deadlines. Set up your own deadline and tell someone. Let others know that you will finish the project by a certain time. The consequence of telling other people you are going to meet a particular deadline will often produce enough motivation for you to continue working. What other accountability systems could you set up?

D. **Learn when you work at your best.** Some attorneys work best at 6 a.m. when it is quiet and they are fresh and having their first cup of coffee. Some like to take a late lunch and work through the lunch hour. Some find themselves energized after a client meeting or a staff meeting. Still others are "night owls" who do their best work after most people have left for the day. Recognize the most productive time of day for you. Also notice when you are most distractible (i.e., resistant to sitting down to work). Learn to go with what works. Do your most challenging work when you are at your best.

4. The Controlled Burn—Reducing and Eliminating Time-Wasters

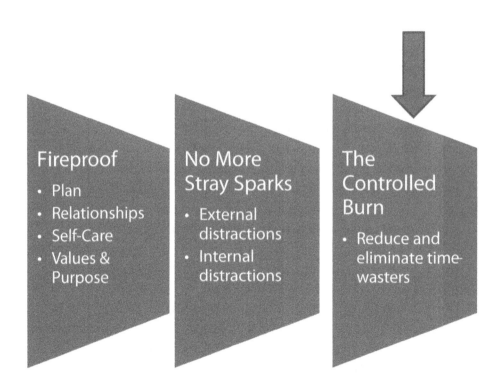

What is ironic about time management is that we race around putting out fires and then "find ourselves" on Facebook or cruising the internet or watching television for hours at a time. Some attorneys "find themselves" chatting with others in the office or wading through meaningless emails and then chastising themselves for wasting so much time.

Why would we do this? If you are operating from a paradigm that says work as fast and as hard as you can, then why would you waste your time on non-meaningful activities? Think about it: the paradigm we operate under says work as fast and as hard as you can to get caught up. But for most of us that paradigm also includes the knowledge that we can *never* be caught up. There is never any breathing room. And so the paradigm is a set up for "crashing." Often "crashing" translates into wasted time on meaningless activities.

If you go as fast as you can for as long as you can, you will ultimately run out of energy. This is when you "find yourself" doing something that is purely a waste of time: neither an emergency nor a meaningful activity.

This type of "crash" is an indication that you are working more than can be sustained. It is a cry for help, so to speak. It is a sign from your body and your mind that a break is needed. As we say in the self-maintenance chapter, if you do not take breaks, they will take you. The forest with too much undergrowth and dead wood will eventually be cleared by an uncontrolled fire, if controlled burns are not employed regularly.

As such, we recommend that when you find yourself wasting time, you ask yourself what you need in this moment, honoring the fact that your "time wasting" indicates you need some sort of break. We call this the "controlled burn" because it recognizes that fire has its place: when controlled, it clears the underbrush and old dead trees to make room for new growth, as well as protecting against larger, more disastrous fires. In the same way, allowing yourself to "waste" time can be very nourishing for your psyche if done in a conscious manner and within certain limits.

The "Controlled Burn" Means:
(1) **Take care of yourself**—rigorously and religiously. Time management *is* energy management. You must manage your energy.
(2) **When you find yourself wasting time, heed this call** and ask what you need, then make a conscious decision to answer the message you are receiving. This not only honors what is really true for you, but it gives you more control over what is happening. For example, when you find yourself on Facebook, you might ask yourself, "what do I need right now?" (Rather than telling yourself to get back to work and calling yourself a slacker.) You might need to take a break. Then you can say to yourself, "Ok; what kind of a break would be best right now?" And you may find that you need to get some fresh air or take a walk; you may realize you are hungry or thirsty; you may need to stretch or move or lay down and close your eyes; you may need to talk to someone who is neither lawyer nor client; or you may find that you really just want to be on Facebook.

This allows you to figure out what you need and go get it. It also (1) sends a message to yourself that you are listening, paying attention, and fulfilling requests for what is needed; (2) rejuvenates your energy so you can come back to work fresh; and (3) allows you to set a time limit and make conscious choice about taking breaks.

Part III—How to implement the New Paradigm

Up to this point in this chapter, we have offered you a new paradigm—a new way to approach your time and tasks. Rather than offering specific ways of doing things, we have outlined a framework that will assist you in making choices and experimenting with what works best *for you*. This framework is illustrated by the firefighting chart set forth above. Now we will specify tools and techniques you may use to implement this new paradigm, reiterating that you should experiment with these tools and techniques, but ultimately find what works best for you.

1. Use A Calendar

The first tool we suggest you use is a calendar. You may use an electronic or paper calendar—whatever works best for you. Many attorneys use their calendars only to schedule depositions and court appearances, client appointments, and due dates. We recommend going farther than this. We also recommend you take full ownership for your calendar. This means you (not just your secretary) look at it every day, and look out into the future as well. Why use a calendar? When we do not schedule our time, we do things in a fairly haphazard way. If you have only a vague sense of what needs to get done, you are most likely to work on whatever is right in front of you. When you do this, you do not necessarily choose the most important tasks; you choose the most urgent. Not scheduling your time feeds the emergency mindset.

It is important to have a calendar with due dates on it. Most attorneys keep this type of calendar—with drop-dead dates. The problem is that when a due date is a week or two away, the project often doesn't qualify as an "emergency" and we don't work on it. Better than just *having* a calendar with due dates is to look at the calendar regularly. Even better is having a calendar with due dates that you look at regularly *and* a to-do list that includes everything you have to get done that isn't on the calendar.

This is still not the *best* system. A better system is to use your to-do list and your calendar in conjunction with one another. Here is one way to do this (remember our suggestion, though, that you experiment and find the way that works best for *you*.)

Steph: In addition to having a bound booklet-type calendar in which I put my due dates, meetings, court appearances and the like, I also print up each of the next several months on a separate sheet of paper. For instance, in September, I will have three sheets of paper: one for September, another for October, and one for November. On this calendar I insert due dates for different projects, and for each day, blocks of time on which I am working on those projects. For instance, if an opposition to a motion for summary judgment is due on the third Friday of October, I will have blocks of time in early October in which I am working on it (i.e., Monday from 1:30 to 3:30; Tuesday from 9:00 to noon, and so on). This calendar only blocks off about half of my available working time to work on upcoming projects, which gives me the flexibility to respond to those stray sparks, as well as engage in other fireproofing tasks. Because the calendar for any given month is only on one sheet of paper, I can always print another one if circumstances change (i.e., the hearing on the MSJ is continued or the case settles).

2. Prepare at the Beginning of Your Week

Most overworked and stressed-out attorneys say they don't have a spare hour to plan their week or ten minutes to plan their day. However, in our experience, one hour invested at the beginning of the week to create a plan saves countless hours later in the week, just as ten minutes spent planning your day will save you at least an hour spent non-productively thereafter. As with much of what we suggest, you must try it out and see how it works, and then tailor it to your specific circumstances. You will likely not be convinced just by reading this book. You will need to experiment. But beware: if you are afraid it won't work, that is just a voice in your head that is worried, overburdened and sometimes panicked. **You must try it out to see.**

Pick a time—Sunday night, Friday afternoon, Monday morning, or whatever works: Sit down with your calendar and see what is coming over the next month or two. As you are getting started, look at each week over the next three months. Looking a week or two out will provide context to your days. Often when we are working on a specific project we lose sight of the greater benefit this will create. When you plan your day in the context of your week and beyond, you keep the bigger picture in mind and add meaning to your choices for today.

Before you schedule new tasks in your calendar make sure the appointments are already there—court dates, client meetings, etc. Then schedule the most important and meaningful things for you to do. This includes planning ahead, self-care, maintaining relationships, marketing, staff meetings; things of this nature. Ask yourself, "what will make the biggest difference this week? in two weeks? 3three weeks? in my life?" Those are the most meaningful tasks for this week. Remember: not all emergencies are the most meaningful thing to spend your time on right now.

Why schedule the most meaningful tasks ahead of time? By and large, unless they become emergencies, those meaningful tasks that are not scheduled **will not get done.** We suggest a system where you:

1. Identify the most meaningful tasks for your week.

2. Calendar those tasks.

3. Stick to your calendar.

4. Keep a TO DO list of less important tasks that you want to get done, but you do not schedule.

It is interesting to note how most people achieve their tasks in the absence of a system. When we do not have a system, such as a calendar, a list, or some other way of capturing and scheduling tasks ahead of time, we work on emergencies first. We also do smaller and less meaningful things first. If you have the choice between starting a brief that you believe will take up to twenty hours to complete and is due in two weeks, and making a phone call where you do not even think the person will answer, you will likely choose the latter. If, however, you schedule a one to two hour block of time to *begin* work on your brief and it is in your calendar, you are far more likely to do it.

This is similar to the system referred to above and attributed to Stephen Covey called scheduling the "big rocks" first. The idea is when you schedule your more important tasks into your calendar, your smaller tasks can be done in the gaps. But if you do not schedule your important tasks, you tend to work on the smaller items, which then fill up your day, and the important tasks simply do not get done. This is what keeps us reactive and under the gun.

When we say schedule the most meaningful tasks which tasks do we mean? In part, we are talking about scheduling fireproofing activities. In part, though, the question as to what is "meaningful," is personal and one that you will have to answer for yourself in your own practice. Here are some inquiries that may help.

1. What will make the biggest difference **in my practice** if I get it done this week?[2]

2. What will make the biggest difference **in my life** if I get it done this week?

3. What will make the biggest difference **in my family** if I get it done this week?

4. What will make the biggest difference **in my health** if I get it done this week?

5. What are the **fireproofing** activities I want to complete this week (hint: it's a good idea to schedule all of them, as listed above)?

---

2.   In thinking about what will make the biggest difference, you may want to consider the Pareto principal which says that 80% of our results typically come from 20% of our efforts. If this is true, then carefully choosing those 20% of actions can greatly leverage your time. Find a way to put more focus on the 20% of meaningful activities rather than the 80% of less meaningful activities. For example, planning your day will save time otherwise spent wondering what to do next. When you plan your day, you will not spend so much time on less important tasks simply because they are in front of you and you have not specifically decided to do something else. If you have something important to do and you plan it at the beginning of the day, it is far more likely to get done. Planning your day is one of those 20% of activities that produces 80% of results.

What to Include in your Calendar

These are suggestions. After answering the questions above, and coming up with your most meaningful tasks for the week, consider the following as big rocks to include in your calendar.

(i.) Fireproofing

Be sure to schedule time for self-maintenance (this in particular tends not get done if it is not scheduled); relationship-tending (e.g., time to contact clients, sit down with your associate to go over cases, take your secretary to lunch, etc.); future projects planning (see the "Chunk it Down" insert for how to do this most effectively).

(ii.) True Emergencies

As you start this new system, you may see things that have "snuck up on you"—things that you need to complete this week. Go ahead and schedule them. Scheduling "emergencies" can give you a greater sense of control.

(iii.) Marketing

Most attorneys have "business development" and "bringing in new clients" as a part of their long-term plan. Most attorneys appreciate this is necessary to sustain their business. And yet most attorneys do not feel they have the time to market. But marketing is a proactive step that keeps your business healthy and sends the message to **you** (and your colleagues) that you can and will care for your business. It is also a great way to see the big picture and not focus solely on what is just in front of you. If your business is full and has been for some time and you do not need to market, you may disregard this suggestion. But before you do, ask yourself if your business is in line with your purpose and vision. Do you have the kinds of clients and cases you really want?

This is also a place where you might delegate, training your assistant or another person in your office to make appointments for you at lunchtime from a list of contacts you have procured.

(iv.) Staff and/or File Review Meetings

Another great time-management activity that may seem like it "takes too long" under the old paradigm is conducting regular staff meetings. But the better your communication with your staff, the more efficiently they will operate; the more aware you will be of how they are operating; the more you will be able to see problems before they arise; and the clearer will be the expectations of all employees.

You might also use case-review meetings to make sure everyone involved stays up to speed on each file. This is also a great time to delegate and to track your delegation, saving a lot of time in the long run.

Planning for Projects Technique—"Chunk it Down"

For each project (trial, brief, deposition, etc.), determine when it is due, estimate how long it will take (remembering to add a percentage to your initial estimate so you are sure to give yourself enough time), break it down into component parts (research, review of file, writing, etc.), and schedule these parts in your calendar.

This is called "chunking down" in NLP (neuro-linguistic programming) terms. We each have a "chunk" size that works best for us. The best size for you will be a personal matter. You can tell your chunk size is too large is if you feel overwhelmed when you think about doing the work. This feeling of overwhelm is a sign that (1) the chunk size of the project you are considering doing is too large; or (2) you have too many "open loops"—unfinished projects. (Regarding open loops, see below under "completion.") If you feel overwhelmed by the size of a project, chunking down will help you feel better. If you feel better about the project, you are more likely to do it.

Calendar your Chunks

Once you have chunked your projects down, place the component chunks in your calendar. A few tips on this:

1. When you schedule a block of time to work, put in a few minutes (five or ten) before and after the block in order to give time to transition to what is next. This is useful between all activities scheduled in your calendar. Don't back things up against each other. Planning to go directly from one project to another creates stress. Transitions take time and unforeseen circumstances will arise. You want some flexibility in your schedule.

2. Schedule your work time strategically. If you know you are a good morning worker, schedule your work time early. If you prefer to start your morning by checking your email, getting coffee, and following up on calls, schedule your blocks of work time after that. If it is quiet in your office around 4 p.m., and you enjoy working at that time, schedule it then.

3. Close your door! This is a tip Cami's clients taught her. The vast majority of Cami's clients find that simply closing their office door while working on projects makes them more productive. There can be resistance to this idea, from the attorney and often the staff. But you can work it out by communicating with your staff and letting them know what you are doing and why you are doing it. Enroll them in your plan by asking them when they think is the best time to do it; and asking them what they need to work efficiently while you do so. Also, be clear what constitutes an emergency and justifies your being interrupted when your door is closed. You may even decide how long to work on a project with your door closed based in part on how long you and your staff believe you can be out of communication. Let your secretary know when you will return phone calls so she can communicate that to callers. (Be sure to return calls when you say you will!) Be sure to turn off your landline, cell phone, and email. There should be no interruptions during your project production time, except for strategic breaks. See chapter 6 on strategic breaks.

Now that you have created your calendar for the week, **stick to it.** Barring true emergencies—an ex parte or a child's broken leg—you *must* stick to your schedule. Due to the specific attorney "drift" (see chapter 1), many attorneys have trained themselves to be motivated by the press of external deadlines. To manage your time well, you will need to motivate yourself in a different way. For this system to work, you cannot look at your calendar, see that from 2 to 4 p.m., you have scheduled "Brief-Drafting" and say "I'll do that tomorrow." You must respect everything you place in your calendar as if it were a court hearing or a deposition. It may be challenging at first, but you can train yourself to do this.

Putting it into practice

Calendar Chunks

Your MSJ is due on October 31 and today is October 1. You estimate it will take you **20 hours** to complete. You adjust your time estimate by adding 50% so that you now estimate **30 hours** to complete the project. You have about **4 weeks** to complete it. You divide the amount of time by 4 and determine you need to spend about **7 hours a week** on this project. Then you can choose how long you want to work at one sitting. Do you work best for one hour? Two? Is it good for you to lock yourself away for seven hours?

Then on your calendar write "Smith MSJ" in appropriate blocks of time on as many days as you need between now and October 31. Then, most importantly, you must stick to it.

---

3. Prepare at the Beginning of Your Day

Now that you have planned your week, you are set up to be productive. Next you will want to have a daily system in place. We recommend that you spend 5 to 10 minutes in the morning reviewing your calendar to see what you have scheduled. Some prefer to do this the day before. Then look at your TO DO list for the day. Ideally the TO DO list contains items that are not urgent and are small enough to fit somewhere in your day. Be sure to keep your TO DO list accessible at all times so you don't forget about it.

Use a TO DO List

What is the value of this list? It helps you be present from moment to moment. Remember earlier in this chapter we suggested that you not multi-task, but that you be present with what you are doing? There are two facets to being present. One is to do only one thing at a time. Another is to only think about what you are doing. Both are important. It is difficult to be fully present when we have something on our minds or are trying to remember something. Our brains usually remember what we want them to, but not always at the right time. This means that often, when you are working on that brief, you suddenly think, "Oh! I need to call that client back!" and you stop working on the brief in order to call the client. And while you are looking for the client's number, you remember some research you wanted to assign to your law clerk. You can try to remember to do these things later, or you can write "Call Smith" and "assign Jones research" on your TO DO list, then forget about them and fully focus on your brief. Write down everything that crosses your mind that you need to do, because anything you try to hold onto in your head will get in the way of your concentration.

There are many ways to approach a TO DO list. Steph chooses three or four things she intends to accomplish that day from her TO DO list and circles them. Then she crosses them off as she completes them. Crossing items off your list has significant psychological value. (See "Completion" below.) The sense of "completion" that comes from crossing items off your list gives you more energy to move forward with other tasks. This is why it is also valuable to cross out items in your calendar when they are complete. The value in choosing only three or four things from your list to do in one day is the sense of satisfaction that comes at the end of the day when you have completed all you set out to do. You will feel more energetic if you meet the goals that you set for the day. It is not psychologically satisfying to have a list of twenty things that continue from day to day and only cross off a few. When you don't feel you are getting ahead, you lose energy to continue forward with enthusiasm.

Another useful tool we call "do the worst first." Choose that task that you've been avoiding, that is the most unpleasant-seeming to you, and do it first thing in your day. This gives you energy for the rest of the day. When you avoid things because they make you nervous or you don't like them, you send yourself the message that you can't do it. Psychologically, this will drag you down. From a time management perspective, it's best to feel like you can accomplish anything. When you accomplish something daunting or scary first thing in your day, you will feel very confident after that. This psychological mindset is empowering and will have you move more purposefully and efficiently and get more done!

Finally, Cami's clients' advice is to deal with your list in the way that works best for you. One of Cami's clients had her list on the computer with small colorful icons by each task and would delete them at the end of each day. Another client had an 8½ x 11 piece of paper and he scribbled his "to do" items all over it and folded it up into a very small square and carried it in his breast pocket. If the judge asked him to do something, he would literally take the piece of paper out of his pocket and write it down. Whenever the paper got too tattered, he replaced it with a new one. This practice made a big difference for this busy trial attorney; he went from allowing things to "slip through the cracks" to getting done everything he agreed to do.

4. Close Down Your Day Effectively

Many attorneys do not realize that how they end their work day has a significant effect on their energy level. If you are like many attorneys, you typically leave at a certain time each day, say 6:30 p.m., so you can get home for dinner. Like most, you probably work until the very last second, leaving everything mid-work as you rush out the door. When you return in the morning, your computer is still on and your desk is covered with files and paper. This has a negative effect on your energy for several reasons. First, you are going home in a mindset of non-completion. When you leave in the middle of something (or multiple things), you tend to mentally take work home with you. This is particularly true if the case is challenging or worrisome to you, or if you are not sure when you will get back to it. Second, it is mentally discouraging to walk into your office and see your desk in a mess. You have to sort through what you were working on in order to get yourself up to speed. If you are like most attorneys, your desk contains more than one unfinished project.

At a fundamental level, seeing a messy desk does not make you want to go in and start working. Psychologically, the best thing you can see when you enter your office is a clean desk. It just feels better. And this cannot be overemphasized: the feeling you have when you walk in the door has a large effect on your ability to start being productive. Your state of mind will reflect the state of your desk and office. If your desk and office are cluttered, your mind will likewise feel cluttered. If you see a clean neat desk and floor, your mind will similarly be clearer. No kidding: **Try it!**

We recommend you consciously close down at the end of each day. Your goal at the end of the work day is to leave your office such that (1) you feel good; (2) you leave work at your office so you can be fully present for your evening activities; and (3) you have maximum energy for the next day. We will outline the process below. The steps are as follows:

(a) Go through the completion assessment.
(b) Acknowledge yourself.
(c) Celebrate your accomplishments.

a. The Completion Assessment

When we use the word "completion," it is in a somewhat different context than you have typically heard the word used in the past. It is different from being "done" with a project. Completion is a way to close some of the open loops from the day. "Open loops" are not only tasks, projects, and activities that are unfinished. When something is an "open loop" you do not have a clear plan for how or when it will be finished. Having too many ongoing projects will ultimately drain your energy. They are like open windows on your computer. Too many open loops or windows slows everything down. Every time you close a loop, you release energy and will feel more ready to take on the next task.

Completion is a state of *being*. You know you are complete by how you feel. Of course, *finishing* something will make you feel complete. But that is not always possible at the end of the day, especially when you are proactively working on projects that are not due right away. **The idea is for you to feel *complete* when you are *not necessarily done*.** The feeling of completion is like a sigh; a release; a letting go. We know we are complete when we feel we can move onto the next thing. You will likely feel you are complete at the end of the day when you think, "Ok; now I can go home." If you pay attention, you might notice that leaving in the middle of a task makes you feel incomplete, nervous, and perhaps a bit anxious about going home.

As you can see, poor time management is not solely the result of having too many things to do; it is about having too many open loops. The more things you complete, the better you feel, the more energy you have, the more productive you are. While there is a small number of incompletions we can comfortably and effectively manage, there comes a point when it is just too much. How will you know? The main sign is a lack of energy, enthusiasm, and motivation.

This is why we recommend at the end of each day you get yourself "complete" on the projects you have pending. Here's how. (See our website for the form, www.mclarencoaching .com/bookdownloads/.)

Completion Assessment:
1. **Write down what you worked on today,** whether or not it was on your calendar or TO DO list for the day.
2. **Go through your TO DO list and cross off all items that are entirely done.**
3. **Schedule the incompletes.** Go through your list of remaining (incomplete) items and write down what action(s) you will need to take in order to finish each one. If it is something small and easy, you may go ahead and do it and claim that energy! For larger items, anything you can't finish now, state the actions still needed and—this is important—put them on your calendar, on your TO DO list, or in a reliable place so you know *when*, and you trust that you *will* take the action to finish the project. Once you have calendared these next actions, you will feel better; you will feel complete. This will enable you to go home and leave work at work.

b. Acknowledge Yourself

Look at all you have completed today and acknowledge yourself. Do not skimp on this step. Completion releases energy. Acknowledgement creates the excitement and motivation to complete something else. As you cross items off your list, consciously congratulate yourself, even if it is a small task. Say, "I am glad I got that done." If it was challenging or you didn't think you could do it, acknowledge that you did it. Acknowledging yourself is very important. If you don't do it, you will feel unappreciated and your energy will start to dwindle. (See the Self-Maintenance chapter for more on the concepts of acknowledgement and celebration.)

c. Celebrate Your Accomplishments

Now that you have (1) crossed off what you completed for the day; (2) acknowledged yourself for the completions and anything else you worked on; and (3) scheduled those things that are undone, it is time to celebrate. This is slightly different than acknowledgement. Celebration requires a physical act. See the self-maintenance chapter for ideas.

At Thesaurus.com, we found the following synonyms for "celebrate":

- beat the drum
- bless
- blow off steam
- carouse
- ceremonialize
- commend
- consecrate
- dedicate
- drink to
- eulogize
- exalt
- extol
- feast
- glorify
- hallow
- have a ball
- honor
- jubilate
- kick up one's heels
- laud
- let loose
- lionize
- live it up
- make merry
- memorialize
- observe
- paint the town red
- party

- praise
- proclaim
- publicize
- rejoice
- revel
- revere
- ritualize
- solemnize

In the self-maintenance chapter, we recommend celebrating large and small accomplishments. Here, as a mode of completion, we recommend you simply celebrate your day: that you got up, you went to work, you did the best you could, you came home. For many of Cami's clients, after doing this for a while they learn that this is the celebration of a day of living and working. It becomes a celebration of life and gratitude for what we have. This is a *great* way to end your workday and prepare energetically for the next day.

Putting it into practice:

Completion Assessment:
1. Today I worked on the Smith MSJ; met with my secretary for a case review of 10 open files; and wrote a letter to Jones. [Cross off what is complete.]
2. The MSJ is Incomplete. The case review is Incomplete. The letter has been mailed and is complete so I cross it off my list. [Note what is incomplete.]
3. I think the MSJ has about 20 hours left on it, and I have already scheduled the time in my calendar so I am complete on this for now. As for the case reviews, I think we have about one more hour on this, so I will insert it in my calendar for Monday at 10 am and send my secretary an email right now letting her know that. [Schedule what is incomplete.]

Acknowledgement: I acknowledge that I finished the Jones letter and that is off my plate. I also acknowledge I did a lot of work on the MSJ, which I am proud of because I implemented the closed door policy and it worked well. I got all the research done today and that is more than I thought I could finish.

Celebration: I am going to go home and have a glass of wine and spend half an hour reading my favorite book!

5. Learn to Delegate

"The best executive is the one who has sense enough to pick good men to do what he wants done, and self-restraint enough to keep from meddling with them while they do it."

Theodore Roosevelt

What is the value of delegation? When you can reliably have some of your work done by another competent professional, you are leveraging your time. Truly successful and wealthy people know the art of leveraging. This is because the amount of work you can do yourself is limited. You may be able to get a lot of work done, but it is still a finite amount. On the other hand, you can get a lot more accomplished if you have others doing work so you don't have to.

This begs the next question: why so many attorneys are poor delegators. Most attorneys are afraid that if they do have someone else do work for them:

- It will be done wrong
- It will be late
- They will have to do it over again
- It will not be the quality of work they require
- It will take longer to explain it than to do it
- They delegated once and it was a mess!

While these may be real risks, you can never leverage your time until you are willing to take the leap and begin delegating. When you start delegating, try this effective process:

a. Evaluate if You *Really* are the One For the Job.

Obviously there are certain jobs only you can do. But what are they? Are you being over-expansive when you name the jobs only you can do? Take some time right now and create a list of everything you believe *only you* can do. Then have someone else check it for you. This is a reality check as to those things that only you can do.

b. Decide What and How Much to Delegate

You do not need to delegate entire projects. You might delegate portions of projects. Also, you will not delegate work to each person to the same degree. People will need to earn your trust and the degree to which you trust them will determine the degree to which you delegate to them.

There are different levels of delegation. There may be employees who you do not trust to make a substantive decision, but you can ask them to bring you the facts so you can make the decision. (These are probably employees operating to some degree outside their expertise; or could be employees who are very new and you want to learn what their decision-making ability truly is.)

There will be employees who have great ideas and initiative, but who you still would like to double check. You may have them conduct analysis and give you input, but you ask them to come to you before making the final decision so that you can be sure you align with their plan of action. (These are largely employees in training to move to a higher level of autonomy.)

The next level are those employees who make decisions, but report them to you so you can track and even jump in if necessary. (These will be employees who are close to autonomy.)

You may even have employees who have been with you long enough and have the experience to actually make important decisions and operate with a high level of autonomy.

You will need to assess which tasks to give which employees.

c. Determine the Frequency of the Task

If a task is common and recurrent, you will save yourself a lot of time in the long run by delegating it to someone even though you may spend some initial time in training. Under the new paradigm of time management, this is time invested in the short term to earn long-term time savings. If your project is a one-time occurrence, it may be quicker for you to do it yourself.

d. Be Clear!

Imagine you are feeling overworked and harried. So you tell your associate, "Do this project for me." And then you leave. That is not going to ensure that she understands what you want. One of the main problems attorneys have with delegation is they feel it takes too much time. That is why delegation is a part of the new paradigm. In the old paradigm, we are running and doing as much as we can as fast as we can. We don't have time to give instruction to anyone. In the new paradigm, we understand that time invested now to give clear instruction is time saved in the long run.

Ideas:

1. Set a meeting where you and your employee are present and not distracted.
2. Give the assignment as clearly as possible.
3. Ask if she has questions. If so, answer them.
4. Once she says that she understands, have her repeat the assignment back to you. Be sure it is completely accurate.
5. Ask her to return to her office and type up the assignment as she sees it and email it to you within the next two hours. Be sure you have included specific time lines for each part of the assignment.

6. Set yourself a reminder to check at the end of the day and make sure she has emailed you. If she has not, ask why not. Do not prompt her to do it or scold her for not doing it. Ask *her* to figure out why she did not follow through, and ask *her* put a process in place so she will follow through on agreements to communicate with you in the future.
7. When you receive the email, review it closely to make sure it is accurate.
8. Track the follow-up times. (See next section.)
9. If it is recurrent and similar to projects that are common in your office, create a system and written instructions.

e. Trust Allah, but Tie Your Camel

It is challenging for some attorneys to let go of work. But to effectively delegate, you must be willing to assign the task, then watch what happens so you can see the gaps in the employee's performance. You will need to trust sometimes where you are in doubt and then watch closely. This is distinct from micro-managing. There is a spectrum of ways to delegate. Neither end is the most effective.

Micro-managing	*Complete Abdication*

On the micro-managing end, you watch, worry, and "nag." "Are you done? Do you have any questions? Did you do this? Did you do that?" On the abdication end, you delegate and you never check back and you don't find out there is a problem, if at all, until it is too late.

When you are empowering your employees, they are more likely to do a great job for you. When you are micro-managing, they will not feel empowered and will not make decisions on their own, will be doubtful, and will rely heavily on you. So the first thing you need to do as a delegator is to let go.

Next, observe and track their progress so you can see where the gaps are in their performance. One of the biggest problems delegators run into is that they let go completely and do not discover problems in a timely fashion. Create a tracking system for everything you delegate. It could be a sheet of paper that states the project, the task, the date delegated, the date due, and how the delegatee will report. Make the employee responsible for the reporting so that you are not micro-managing. But have a tickle system (perhaps a notification on your Outlook or in your calendar) that tells you when the project is due so you can see whether it has been completed. If, the day after the project is due, there has been no communication by the employee, find out what happened and ask him how he could be more reliable in the future. Again, make the employee responsible for figuring out how to change. The more you tell others how and when to do things, the less likely the change will stick and the more likely you will spend your time nagging and following up.

The goal is to produce motivated employees who are empowered, feel ownership for their projects, and are in regular communication with you about the status of those projects.

f. Use Your Staff Meetings

Your case review meetings are also a great time to delegate and to track your delegations. This will also enable those in your firm to see what others are doing.

6. Create Systems

How much of what you do is repetitive? The way you open a new case or file? The information you need from clients? How you conduct a deposition? How the phones are answered in your office?

You will save time in the long run, be more proactive, and create consistency when you have systems, such as a checklist for file setup or review. This way, rather than training each new staff member over and over or relying on the staff with the most longevity or the best memory to know how you like things done, you achieve consistency; you save the time of having to repeatedly explain how you do things; and you save the time of having to rescue things that fall through the cracks.

Look at where you spend your time. For *everything* you do, ask, "could I create a system for this?" Have your staff ask the same thing. Then devote a certain amount of time each week to creating those systems. Involve staff in the creation. Their ideas are usually very much in line with what goes on in the office, and they are often the ones who will need to carry it out. Again, of course, this is time spent now for huge savings in the future.

A good system will inform each person who looks at the file or project what needs to be done and what has been done. The checklist should include what must be done and by when, a designation for who will do each task, and a line to initial when done. In this way, the checklist prompts those whose duty it is to do certain tasks, and it communicates to anyone who looks at it what has been done. This provides greater communication, fewer mistakes and greater consistency—all time-saving devices.

Homework

1. Keep a log of your activities for at least one (preferably more) week. (Activity Log is found on our website, www.mclarencoaching.com/bookdownloads/.) Once you get the information, experiment with changes to be more effective.
2. Employ a completion process at the end of each day.
3. Find one thing this week that you and/or your staff do repeatedly and begin the process of systematizing that task.

4. After keeping a log of your activities for a week or two, experiment with planning your week as set out above.
5. Make a list of your big rocks and schedule them every week.
6. Teach these time management concepts to the people in your office. Not only will all of you be on the same page, but you yourself will learn them more thoroughly by teaching the ideas to others.

Time Management Tips

A note about the tips: These tips were compiled from Cami's associates, clients and a multitude of websites and books. What is important in managing time is that you experiment until you find what works for you. What works for someone else may not work with your personality or have a positive effect on your day or your project load. The purpose of this list is to give you numerous time-management tips so you can experiment and see what works for you. Try different ones for a week or a month and see which work for you. Ideally you will come up with some of your own.

1. **In order to figure out how much time to leave for (or to start a project), count back** from the time you need to be there (or to finish the project). This will give you your start time. Remember tip #2!
2. **Add 10 percent to time estimates** as a cushion for activities you already know how to do or have experience with, and 30 to 50 percent to time estimates for activities with which you are unfamiliar. Block the full time in your calendar and stick to it.
3. **List everything you need to get done.** Pick three or four tasks to complete in a day so you feel you have accomplished something at the end of the day. Take inventory in the evenings and acknowledge yourself for your accomplishments and plan when to complete what you have not finished.
4. **As Stephen Covey says, sharpen the saw.** You will be much more effective and efficient if you get enough rest, eat properly, and take time to yourself. It may seem counterintuitive when you feel under the gun, but it works.
5. **Try meditating.** You will feel more rested and improve your ability to focus, which will also save you time in completing projects.
6. **Don't read every email the minute it comes in.** It takes more time to follow them as they arrive because you keep interrupting your train of thought as you shift gears. Instead, try this: set aside a specific period of time to go through and respond to emails—an hour in the morning and an hour at night, for example. Surprisingly, you will spend less time on emails than by checking them as they come in. And *turn*

off the auditory indicator that alerts you when emails come in! It's an interruption and a distraction.

7. **Keep your work area organized.** When you have completed something, put it away. Disorganization and clutter interferes with your ability to stay focused and complete tasks quickly and efficiently. Mentally, clutter can make a task seem larger than it actually is.

8. **Plan each day.** Planning your day can help you accomplish more and feel more in control of your life. Don't plan every minute, but do set your intention for what you will accomplish. In the evening, compare your outcomes with your morning intention.

9. **Do one thing at a time.** Multi-tasking is a fiction. You cannot do more than one thing at a time. You can only go from one thing to another quickly. This splits your energy and concentration and makes you less effective and less efficient at each task.

10. **Use the 80–20 Rule,** originally articulated by Italian economist Vilfredo Pareto, who noted that 80 percent of the reward comes from 20 percent of the effort. The trick to prioritizing is to isolate and identify that valuable 20 percent. Then, prioritize time to focus your work on those items with the greatest reward.

11. **Say "No" to nonessential tasks.** Consider your goals and schedule before agreeing to take on additional work. Remember your short and long-term priorities.

12. **Delegate.** Look at your to-do list and consider what you can pass on to someone else. No matter how small your business is, there's no need for you to be a one-person show. For effective time management, you need to let other people carry some of the load. This includes chores you do at home. What can your children do? Can your spouse do certain tasks more easily than you? Don't be stopped by the initial thought that you can do it faster or better than someone else. Time invested now teaching someone else is a huge savings of time in the long run.

13. **Break large, time-consuming tasks into smaller ones.** Work on them a few minutes at a time until you get them all done. This is a neuro-linguistic programming technique known as "chunking down." Mentally, we will avoid things if they seem too big. If we break them into more manageable pieces, we are more likely to do them.

14. **Practice the ten-minute rule.** Work on a dreaded task for ten minutes each day. Once you get started, you may find you can finish it.

15. **Do the worst first.** Do the most dreaded task of the day *first* and as early as possible.

16. **Evaluate how you're spending your time.** Keep track of everything you do for one to two weeks in order to determine how you're spending your time. Look for time-wasters that steal time you could be using much more productively. What are your time-bandits? What patterns do you see? Where can you make change?

17. **Limit distractions.** Block out time on your calendar for big projects. During that time, close your door and turn off your phone and e-mail.

18. **Take a break when needed.** Too much stress can derail your attempts at getting

organized. When you need a break, take one. Take a walk. Do some quick stretches at your workstation. Take a day of vacation to rest and re-energize. The key is to do this consciously rather than becoming so stressed that you unconsciously engage in time-wasting activities just to get a break. If you choose consciously, you can also limit the length of the break.

19. **Use time management tools.** Whether it's a Day-Timer or a software program, the first step to physically managing your time is to know where your time is going and to plan how you're going to spend it in the future. A software program such as Outlook, for instance, lets you schedule events easily and can be set to remind you of events in advance, making your time management easier.

20. **Set time limits for tasks,** especially those that could consume your whole day if you let them. Instead, set a limit and stick to it.

21. **Be sure your systems are organized.** Are you wasting a lot of time looking for files on your computer? Take the time to organize a file-management system. Is your filing system slowing you down? Reorganize it so you can quickly access what you need.

22. **Don't waste time waiting.** From client meetings to dentist appointments, it's impossible to avoid waiting for someone or something. But don't just sit there and twiddle your thumbs. Always take something with you, such as a report you need to read, a checkbook that needs balancing, or a pad of paper on which to plan your next marketing campaign. Technology makes it easy to work wherever you are; your smart phone and/or ipad will help you stay connected.

23. **Spend fifteen minutes every night before going to bed making a list of things you need to do the next day.** Prioritize the tasks, and mentally figure out what you need to finish them. The next day, you will know what to do first and what you need to finish your job.

24. **Have a list of your to-do items in your wallet all the time.**

25. **Close open loops.** Complete as many projects as you can. Having an incomplete project will sap your energy. The more open loops you have, the more your energy is drained. Finish everything you can—even the small jobs.

26. **Reward yourself for your accomplishments.** Even for small successes, celebrate your achievements. Promise yourself a reward for completing each task and for reaching each goal. Then keep your promise and enjoy your reward.

27. **Find the "right time."** You'll work more efficiently if you figure out when you do your best work and do most important tasks then. Are you a "morning person," a "night owl," or a late afternoon "whiz?" Knowing your best time and planning to use that time of day for your priorities (if possible) is effective time management.

28. **Communicate your schedule to others.** If phone calls or text messages are proving to be a distraction, tell your friends that you are only available at certain times of day and not to expect a response at other times. Set and maintain these boundaries.

29. **Set goals.** Goals give your life, and the way you spend your time, direction. When asked the secret to amassing his fortune, one of the Hunt brothers from Texas replied: "First you've got to decide what you want." Set goals that are specific, measurable, realistic, and achievable. Optimum goals are those that cause you to "stretch" but not "break" as you strive for achievement. Keep your goals in front of you at all times.

30. **Be flexible.** Allow time for interruptions and distractions. Time-management experts often suggest planning for just 50 percent or less of one's time. With only 50 percent of your time planned, you will have the flexibility to handle interruptions and the unplanned "emergency." Schedule routine tasks for times you are more likely to be interrupted. Schedule priorities for those times you are least likely to be interrupted.

31. **Eliminate the urgent.** Urgent tasks have short-term consequences while important tasks are those with long-term, goal-related implications. If you reduce the number of urgent things you must do, you'll have more time for important priorities. Flagging or highlighting items on your to-do list or attaching a deadline to each item may help keep important items from becoming urgencies. (See Stephen Covey's *First Things First* for more on urgency vs. importance.)

32. **Practice the art of intelligent neglect.** Eliminate from your life trivial tasks or those that do not have long-term consequences for you. Can you delegate or eliminate any items on your to-do list? Work on those tasks that you alone can do.

33. **Avoid being a perfectionist.** In the Malaysian culture, only the gods are considered capable of producing anything perfect. Whenever something is made, a flaw is left on purpose so the gods will not be offended. Yes, some things need to be closer to perfect than others, but paying unnecessary attention to detail can be a form of procrastination.

34. **Take a time management course.** If your employer offers continuing education, take one on time management. If your workplace doesn't have one, find one in a local community college, university, or community education program.

35. **Read *First Things First*, by Stephen Covey,** to shift your paradigm regarding time and where you spend it. Covey spends less time on specific "how to" items and more on changing your perception in order to discover your own answers.

36. **Read *Getting Things Done*, by David Allen,** for ideas on how to do things in a way that produces the greatest results. Unlike Covey, this book contains many practical ideas on "how to" manage time.

37. **Hire a coach.** She will assist you in finding the best way to work *your* schedule and *your* life so that you are efficient and balanced.

Chapter 8

Communication Skills for Lawyers

Why Read this Chapter?

1. People on your staff are often confused by what you ask of them.
2. Your employees often do not produce the results you believe you have asked for.
3. You get feedback at work and at home that you do not listen well.
4. You want to improve teamwork and productivity among your team.
5. You don't know exactly how to be with clients when they are upset.
6. You are having a conflict with someone and want to learn how to resolve it.

David

David is often frustrated by judges who just don't seem to "get" his arguments. He just lost a motion in which the judge explained that David had not properly addressed an issue that the judge had earlier stated was important. David thinks that issue is irrelevant and does not remember the judge even talking about it.

Sue

Sue's family seems upset lately about how much she is working. She believes she has been up front with them about the amount of time she needs to be at work and her frequent need to work at home on the weekends. But her husband and children are often surprised and disappointed when they plan a weekend or evening event and she is unable to attend. It has caused strained relationships at home, which is starting to affect her work.

Introduction

Communication has two basic parts to it: listening (receiving a message from another) and transmitting (conveying a message to another via speech or in other ways). We divide communication into these two "basic" parts for ease of instruction. However, these two parts are intertwined and each affects the other to a great degree.

Why do lawyers want to learn about communication? All aspects of your life are affected by your ability to communicate. Attorneys rely a great deal on their ability to communicate well. Whether you win or lose depends in large part on your ability to get your point across and to have your arguments heard and understood. Whether you bring in new clients is largely a communication issue: how you convey the value of your services. Whether your staff works well together, is productive, and stays in your employ is mainly the result of your ability to convey appreciation, motivation, and specifics about the job.

In short, all of your practice is affected by your ability to communicate. But we are not trained to communicate well. Not by our parents; not in elementary school, high school or college; and certainly not in law school. We learn by imitation. We model others who have an influence on us. As such, we pick up habits of communication from them. And unfortunately, there are very few people who communicate well.

This chapter will give you techniques for better communication. But here, perhaps more than anywhere else in this book, you must *practice* what you learn. Communication is one tool that is almost impossible to learn just by reading about it or hearing about it. You must do it. Find a partner and have someone else read this chapter and practice with you. Do the homework. Commit to improving in this area. If you do, you will stand out.

The Art of Listening

To improve communication, first and foremost, we must learn to listen well. For many attorneys, this will be disappointing news and hard to believe; isn't communication about being understood? However, once you practice, you will find that listening well actually increases the effectiveness of what you have to say. If you listen closely to a prospective client, you will find it easier to say the things that will have him hire you. If you listen closely to opposing counsel and her arguments, you are far more likely to be able to craft a persuasive counter-argument and prevail. If you are curious and open to what the judge is telling you, you will increase your ability to speak in a way that persuades him.

Why is listening so important?

- People will not listen to you until they feel heard. As such, speaking is a waste of time until you have listened.

- You will learn things you would not otherwise. You will get the information you need. We often feel we are hearing people without really listening. We are not.
- When people feel you are listening to them, it builds their trust in you.
- When people are angry or upset, their emotion will subside more quickly if you really listen to them.

Listening is the first skill to learn in good communication. This does not mean that what you say and how you say it is not important. It means that the *foundational* skill in good communication is listening. You will get a chance to talk; don't worry. But listen first!

Listening, in Three Stages

1. **Fully focus on the person speaking:**
   - Listen—and only listen—when someone is talking.
   - Give up **the focus** being about **you.**
   - Forget about **your agenda** for a moment.
   - Give up your attachments and your **judgments.**
   - Don't assess the speaker's **values, beliefs,** and **agenda,** which may be very different from yours.
   - Know what distracts you and **limit distractions.**
   - Don't offer advice.
2. **Be curious what they are saying:**
   - **Don't assume** you understand.
   - Have a **curious** mindset.
   - Ask curious **questions.**
3. **Listen reflectively**
   - Listen to the **words** and the **feeling.**
   - **Reflect** back the words and the feeling.
   - Make sure you are correct.

Before we begin to lay out the steps and tips on listening, let us acknowledge that this is a lot of information to process. Cami has had clients say, "How can I listen when I am *thinking* so much about *how* to listen?" We recommend you read through this material entirely and then go back and take one piece at a time. Any of these tips will improve your ability to listen. So, simply begin with one. And next week try another one. Notice which make the biggest impact on your ability to listen fully. This is a process. It took a long time to learn the habits you have. It will probably take some time to learn new habits.

1. Stage One: Fully Focus on the Person Speaking

The first step in listening we call tuning in. The idea, shocking as it may seem, is to listen to people when they talk, to offer them your full attention, to do only one thing when you are listening, and that is to *listen*.

Here is the challenge: according to most authorities, human beings can listen at a rate of approximately 500 words a minute. However, most people speak only about 150 words per minute. As such, our minds move so quickly that they are able to "sort of" listen and still do something else. So there is a great temptation to think we can listen while doing other things. But we cannot do this well. If you are doing something else, no matter how mundane, you may be aware that someone is talking, but you are not getting the full import of what they are saying. If you train yourself to fully listen, your conversations will be quicker and more to the point. You will understand more fully and spend less time clearing up communication breakdowns.

a. Practice #1—Listen, and only listen, when someone is talking

Attorneys are typically multi-taskers who believe it is quicker to do more than one thing at a time. If you read our time-management chapter, you will learn that this is not efficient because our brains are not designed to focus on more than one thing at a time—at least not well. When another person is speaking, many of us think this is a prime opportunity to do something else. If we are on the phone, we may check e-mail or read over a brief. But when we do this, we really are not listening fully.

Therefore, the first practice is to actually listen—and only listen—when someone else is talking. This will take patience and practice. But it is well worth it.

b. Practice #2—Give up the focus being about you

Most people are self-referencing. This means that when we hear or see something, we internally ask ourselves, "How does this affect me?" Or "How am I involved?" Or, "How does this relate to me and my life?" We spend much of our time during conversations thinking about ourselves. For example, you have a colleague who is telling you about the grueling trial he just completed and how unhappy his wife and kids were that he was home late every night. Your response? "When I go to trial I always stay in a hotel so my family can think of me as out of town for the week." Or, "Really? That's nothing. I had a two-week arbitration and we stayed late every evening. It was snowing and every night my car was buried and I never arrived home before 2 am."

Practice #2 requires you to focus only on the other person and what he is telling you, without relating it to your own life. In the example above, even if in your mind you start to think about your own trial experience, set that aside and focus instead on what the other person is telling you; be curious about *his* experience. You might ask him how he handled his family's frustration or what he found to be the worst part about the experience.

Asking these curious questions will help you let go of thinking about yourself and increase your ability to truly listen.

c. Practice #3—Yours is not the only agenda

In our conversations and communications, we usually have an agenda. Even if it is only to get the conversation over with, we usually have something we *want*. Therefore, we often listen not to learn and understand, but to move toward our outcome. If you are in a rush and give your secretary an assignment and she begins to ask questions, you may get nervous, thinking "I don't have time for this; I just want her to do one thing; I made it clear enough; I need to get back to work." And so you do not listen. Your agenda is to quickly give her an assignment and get to your next appointment. You are not listening for the content of what she is saying. You are listening for a way to extricate yourself from the conversation. You are focused on your agenda.

Practice #3 requires you to recognize that communication is a two-way street, and that your agenda is not the only one, and that the conversation may take a different turn depending on the other person and his or her agenda.

d. Practice #4—Give up your attachments and your judgments

We assess. It's what we do as people. We evaluate what we see and hear in terms of right/ wrong; good/bad; a winning argument/a losing argument. And this is another way in which we fail to listen when others are speaking: we are often so focused on our assessments of what they are saying that we do not truly hear them. Imagine you have formulated an argument in a case and your associate proposes a different argument. From the moment he begins, you decide it is a losing argument. From then on, you are not listening in order to hear what he has to say. You are listening in order to discredit the argument and show him that he is wrong. Once you decide his argument is wrong, you stop listening.

Practice #4 requires you to be aware of your judgments and to notice when you stop listening and start arguing internally. Often you will realize this when you notice you are formulating a response and you can't wait to say it. Once you have this awareness, you have the opportunity to notice, to stop assessing and instead become more curious about the other person's position and understand it fully.

e. Practice #5—Don't assess the other person's values, beliefs, and agenda, which may be very different from your own

This is why many people have a rule—never talk about religion or politics. We have such a hard time just listening to something when it conflicts with our own values and beliefs that often we cannot even talk about it. If someone is telling you their opinion on the environment and you realize it is vastly different from your own, you will almost certainly not listen curiously; instead, you will be thinking about how wrong, stupid, or misinformed the other person is.

Practice #5 involves recognizing that the speaker is a different person from you and is entitled to his own beliefs. For attorneys—who are constantly assessing arguments, points, and facts—this can be the hardest practice of all. And yet mastering it can often be the most valuable.

f. Practice #6—Know what distracts you and limit distractions

The first five listening practices have to do with internal thought patterns. Practice #6 has to do more with your environment. If you are in your office and an associate comes in to talk to you, you may be distracted by your computer if the screen is still on. Or you may see a squirrel outside your window that distracts you. These are visual distractions. You may be distracted by voices in the hallway or your telephone ringing. These are auditory distractions. You may be distracted because it is too cold in your office or you just got some disappointing news. These are called "kinesthetic" distractions because they have to do with your feeling state.

The key to Practice #6 is to notice what typically distracts you and to limit the input of these environmental factors. If you know you are distracted visually, shut off your computer screen and turn yourself to face the person in your doorway. If you are often distracted auditorily, ask him to close the door and put your phone on do not disturb. If you are distracted kinesthetically, you might put on a sweater if you are cold or tell the associate now is not a good time to talk and ask that he come back at a later specified time, so that you can be emotionally present when you listen to him.

What is important is you notice and limit distractions when others are speaking.

g. Practice #7—Don't offer advice

So many of us, especially attorneys, listen with a focus on "fixing" whatever is being discussed. While you may feel it is your job in a particular relationship to solve the problem, you will do a much better job of it if you truly listen first. Also, people often do not feel heard when you offer them advice. And if you really feel you must give your opinion, it is best to ask if the speaker would like to hear your advice before offering it. You may be surprised how often others really don't want advice; they just want you to hear them.

2. Stage Two: Be Curious About What the Other Person Is Saying

What does this mean? It means being in a mindset of "Tell me more." It is this "curious" mindset that will enable you to bridge the gap between the 150 words per minute that people speak and the 500 words per minute that is your listening capacity. You can use that 350 word per minute differential to listen from a very curious place. As you are listening, have an internal mindset of investigation and learning. Ask yourself, "What is she really trying to tell me?" "What is most important to him right now?" "What can I learn from this?" "What am I not understanding?"

Part of being curious is not assuming we understand what the speaker is telling us. You would be surprised how often we think we know what someone else is saying, or where they are "going" with the conversation, only to find out we were wrong. Being curious and not assuming we understand allows us to be open to what the speaker is actually seeking to convey to us, rather than what we think he or she is saying.

You can train yourself to be very curious. Like any of these skills, it just takes practice. You can achieve the curious *mindset* by asking "curious questions" such as, "What makes you say that?" "Why is that true?" "What else do you know about that?" In this way, you not only demonstrate to the speaker that you are interested, but you send the message to your own mind as well. The more you ask questions and listen to the answers, the more you train your mind to focus on *listening*. Like anything else it is a habit.

3. Stage Three: Listen Reflectively

Reflective listening employs the practices we have discussed above—it involves tuning in, listening without distractions, letting go of your own beliefs and agenda, and being curious—as well as an extra step: that of reflecting back to the speaker what you believe he or she is seeking to convey to you.

Reflective Listening in a Nutshell

Reflective listening, as described below, is not necessarily a linear process. You will listen, reflect, check in, and begin again until you are sure you have heard your speaker.

1. **Listen without judgment or reaction in a curious fashion.** See stages one and two above where you focused on your listener and being curious. Now you will use these skills as the first step in the reflective listening process. Do not come from judgment or assessment or disagreeing or agreeing with the speaker. Come from a place of pure intention to understand and connect with your speaker.

2. **Listen to the words only.** Separate the words and the emotions. Listen to the language. Make sure you have really heard the words.

3. **Listen to the feeling.** What is the speaker's feeling being conveyed underneath the words? Look for emotions, tone, and concepts.

4. **Reflect the words, but also paraphrase and check for accuracy.** Check in with the speaker to determine if you have heard correctly. Make sure you are not simply parroting the words but are paraphrasing in your own words.

5. **Reflect underlying feelings.** This will likely not be something they have specifically said. It will require listening on a deeper level. You may ask, "It seems like you feel _____. Is this true?" Again, check for accuracy.

6. **Begin the process again.** Tune in and listen deeply as they state the parts they feel you are not clear about and then reflect that back and ask if you have understood fully.

1. Fully focus on your speaker. Listen without judgment or reaction.

We have described this step in detail above. Essentially, focusing means "minding your mind"—being aware of yourself and what distracts you, letting go of your own agenda, and truly listening for what the speaker is saying. As we state above, do not assess, judge, agree, or disagree with the speaker; come from a place of curiosity, a place of pure intention to understand and connect with your speaker. As we stated above, it is helpful to *be* truly curious about the other person and what they want you to know (as opposed to *acting as if* you are curious). If you focus on *being* curious, you are less likely to focus on your own judgments and agenda.

2. Listen to the words only.

At this point, you want to hone in on precisely what is *being said*, as opposed to your interpretation of what is being said. For this step, listen to the words and note if there are any words that you do not understand. Note if there are words that the speaker seems to be giving a particular meaning to. You will want to come back to this later and *ask for clarification.* Guessing or assuming we know what our speaker means by particular words or phrases generates confusion.

Also, separate the words and the emotions. In this step, listen only to the language. Then after you have learned to hear the words, listen to the feeling underneath.

3. Listen to the feeling.

Now listen to what is underneath the words: the emotions, tone, and concepts. Regardless of what kind of conversation you are having, there will always be some emotion underlying the words. Obviously, it's easy to hear rage and grief, but in all conversations (business and personal) there is some underlying emotion. This could be excitement, interest, anxiety, or even boredom. Listen for it.

4. Reflect the words, but also paraphrase and check for accuracy.

Once you believe you have heard the words and the emotion, check in with the speaker to determine if you are correct. Make sure you are not simply parroting the words but are paraphrasing in your own words. Repeat back what you believe the speaker has said, checking in to see if you are right:

- "What I think you are saying is _____"
- "Is this correct?"
- "Did I hear you say _____?"
- "Is this what you meant by _____?"

The repeating back is not mimicry. You will paraphrase such that you are stating their concept in your own words. This way your speaker can tell you whether you have understood him or her.

Two important points:

a. When you reflect back, do not tell the speaker what they are saying; tell them what you have heard. **Do not** say, "You want to settle the case only if we can get $100,000," as if you are the authority on their message. **Ask,** "Are you telling me that you want to settle, but only if we can get $100,000?" You want the speaker to know you are listening. If you get the message right, they *will* know you are listening. If you get the message wrong, but do not inquire as to what they truly meant, they will know you are not really listening, and instead are putting your own interpretation on their communication. If you reflect back what you think they are saying in a manner that indicates you want to know if you don't quite have it right, they will know that you are truly interested in hearing them.

Your tone of voice can influence if they believe you are really listening; be sure not to sound sarcastic or critical. And having a more questioning tone and a less declarative one will be more conducive to your speaker believing that you are open to him saying you have not accurately heard what he sought to convey.

b. Be very careful about your own interpretation. After you tune in and you let go of your own agenda and judgments, you still will want to *interpret* their statement—you will see it through your own filter. You must look at where your filter comes into play and set it aside so you can hear what the other person is really trying to convey. (See Filter, below.)

5. Reflect underlying feelings.

This is likely not going to be something your speaker has actually said. You will need to listen for the underlying feelings beneath the words. Then reflect them, saying, for instance, "It seems like you feel anxious about going to trial. Is this true?" This requires you to listen to more than just the words the speaker is using, but also to her tone, inflection, facial expressions, and body language. As such, this tool is sometimes called "deep listening." It is important to listen for and reflect back feelings because most people will not necessarily tell you their feelings (i.e., "I am frustrated at how this case is going"). But when you hear and reflect a person's feelings accurately, the speaker feels heard.

6. Begin the process again.

After you ask the speaker, "Is this what you are saying?" he or she may say, "No; it is more like this." At this point, you want to again tune in and listen deeply as they further explain the parts they feel you have not clearly heard. Be curious, listen to words and emotion, and then reflect back what you heard the second time. Finally, ask if you have understood fully. Be committed to asking and listening until you are sure you got the message.

Example

One of your colleagues is telling you that his brand-new car was just sideswiped in the parking lot.

1. **Fully focus on the speaker. Listen without judgment or reaction.** A likely reaction in this scenario might be for you to make this about you. For example, "My car got hit out there too" or "I remember when my car got sideswiped." The antidote for this is for you to be very curious. In your mind you can turn off your self-referencing by saying to yourself (and perhaps to him as well), "I wonder where he was parked? I wonder how old the car is? I wonder how he feels?"

2. **Listen to the words only.** Here you are listening for the facts of what happened and may ask some questions to make sure you understand. Ask in a natural way, not mechanically. Ask more with the flow of the conversation like, "Wow! So what happened?"

3. **Listen to the feeling.** Is he angry? Sad? Frustrated? Or does he find it funny? This requires you to tune into his body language. Is he laughing, crying, gritting his teeth? Speaking quickly, slowly?

4. **Reflect back the actual words and also paraphrase.** "So this was the blue Mercedes you just got a week ago? And it was hit here in this parking lot yesterday?"

5. **Reflect underlying feelings.** "You sound really unhappy about your car." Then you allow your colleague to correct you if you are wrong: "Not so much unhappy as really pissed off". And you reflect again with this new knowledge: "Gosh, your brand-new car is all dented now. Wow, I can see where you would be really angry".

Feedback is very important in this process. Most people assume they are good listeners; they are typically wrong. Enlist friends and family to give you feedback as you go through these processes. After a conversation, ask them how well they thought you were listening. Ask them what worked and what did not work in whether you seemed to be hearing them or not. What specifically made them think you were listening or not listening?

Interpretation is the Enemy of Listening

Now that you have learned how to listen and reflect back, you are ready to go practice. But first let us alert you to a problem that arises in listening and will probably come up when you begin practicing reflective listening. The problem is this: We do not see or hear what is actually before us; instead we see and hear our own *interpretations*. Very little gets through our interpretation. As is stated in the Talmud, "We don't see the world as it is; we see the world as we are." When another person speaks, you hear your interpretation of what they are saying, as opposed to what they are actually saying or intending to convey. Learning to recognize your own interpretations and filters is a great way to start paying more attention to what is really being said, and less to what you think is being said.

The Feedback Loop

The feedback loop is an NLP (neuro-linguistics programming) concept that addresses this issue of interpretation in communication:

Ms. Jones and Bob Smith

Ms. Jones is telling her associate, Bob Smith, about something that happened in one of his cases. Following is the type of feedback loop that occurs in most conversations when the parties are not tuned in and practicing effective listening:

Ms. Jones: Bob, the way this case was handled did not work out well for the client or for the firm. [Bob Smith hears]: You are about to get fired. You really screwed up. [As a result of his interpretation, he says]: Well, you know it was really Sally who did the majority of work on the case. [Ms. Jones hears]: This was not my fault and I am not going to take responsibility for it. [So she says]: Okay, I'll go talk to Sally [thinking, "Bob is not reliable and willing to take ownership for what happens in his cases. That could be a problem."]

How would this conversation be different if Ms. Jones and Bob Smith had training in how to listen?

Ms. Jones: Bob, the way this case was handled did not work out well for the client or for the firm.

Bob Smith: I am wondering, when you say it "did not work out well," what do you mean?

Ms. Jones: You know, it just didn't bring in the kind of money we were expecting and the client is disappointed about this as well.

Bob Smith: It sounds like both the firm and the client expected a higher award and the client is upset.

Ms. Jones: That is true.

Bob Smith: I am curious what you think our next steps should be?

Notice in the second example, although Bob Smith might still have had some initial fear that he had made a mistake and that the firm and the client were mad at him, he set that aside and appeared to Ms. Jones as curious and collaborative. And the result was different than he expected. Also, there is a saying: "What we fear we create." This is based on the principle that we interpret situations in such a way that we often see what we expect to see. In the first iteration of this conversation, Bob's fear was that he had made a grave mistake. Because that fear was so strong, he interacted with Ms. Jones in a way that *caused her* to see him as irresponsible and not accountable for his results. His fear of getting fired actually led her in that direction. Had he been more curious, as in the second example, he might have found out that things were different than he feared.

Interrupting the Feedback Loop

As demonstrated above, being curious and employing the tool of reflective listening help break the cycle of [mis]interpretation and filtering. Another related way of doing this is to become familiar with your own personal filter. Then when you notice that you are filtering a speaker's words through it, set it aside so you can listen more fully.

Your Personal Filter

Everyone has a unique way of viewing the world. This creates the *filter* through which we hear, see, and otherwise experience people. No two people have the same filter. And yet it is human nature to assume others see the world the way we do—that our filters are the same. Exploring another's point of view will help you communicate much more effectively. As we see where others are coming from, we begin to understand their behavior and the positive intention behind their behavior. We do not misunderstand so often *and* we learn to speak in a way that others can hear.

There is an NLP presupposition that says, **"The map is not the territory."** Our "map" is our interpretation. The "territory" is reality. Envision the GPS in your car. It is a representation of the road you are travelling, but it is not the actual road. It does not show hills, traffic signs, or structures. The GPS filters a lot of information because it gives you only a certain category of information—what it believes you need to get from point A to point B. It does not tell you if there is a traffic accident on your street, or what the weather is like. It is a representation, not reality. And if your disc is old, it may not even be an accurate representation. Like the GPS, our minds delete certain information so that we don't have too much to think about. We do not see all of reality; we see what we look for and expect to see. Our minds bring *our* definitions to certain words and bring *our* history to events, so that we are not seeing what is really happening, but our beliefs about what is happening.

The Development of Your Filter

Why is it important to learn about your own filter and those of other people? Because we cannot fully listen to people through our filter. We must educate ourselves about our filter so we can recognize it and learn to set it aside so we can hear people.

A filter is developed from the moment you are born. It is developed from the circumstances and events you experience and your internal reactions to them. The positive aspect of having a filter is it makes things easier for you. If you don't have to interpret a circumstance or event for the very first time every time it arises, then you are freed up to focus on other things. Of course, as we have said, the downside of your filter is that you assume you know what people mean without asking.

There are six predominant factors and influences that create the filters through which we see, hear and experience the world. They are: **current situation, history,** goals, **long-term vision, values and beliefs,** and **attitude.** Knowing these elements will give you some questions to consider in becoming curious about personal filters—yours and others'. When considering these questions in order to determine another person's filter, you may not know all the answers. The greater value really is in exploring and being curious about the answers so you remember *other people are not you.* They do not have your history, your present, your concerns, your beliefs or your way of seeing the world. Other people (even those in your family, your firm and your church) do **not** interpret circumstances, language and communication the way you do. This is one of the *major* problems in communication: the assumption that other people see the world the same way that you do. They do not. Recognizing this is the first powerful step in really hearing others when they speak to you!

Fill in the blanks below to start learning about your own or another person's filter. (The questions are framed to have you look at your own circumstances, etc., but you can use this for anyone.)

1. Current Situation
What is happening in your life right now? What issues are foremost in your mind? What demands are being placed on you at present?

_____

_____

_____

Example: If you are in rush mode on a brief that is due on Friday and an associate comes in to ask you for time off, you might think, "Time off!? I am working 15 hours a day on this brief! How can he ask for time off?" This is a filter based on your immediate situation. It may be that if he approaches you when your load is not so heavy, you will understand why he wants time off and happily consider it.

2. History

How have you been impacted by your personal experiences and/or your cultural or social influences?

_____

_____

_____

Example: Many attorneys have a filter based on a social influence of practicing law that tells us we must work long hours. So when your spouse asks you to go to Hawaii for two weeks, you see that as an impossibility. Rather than curiously asking her how that could work, you immediately say NO, because you don't see an option based on your filter.

Or perhaps you grew up with several siblings and not much money. Even though you are financially secure as an attorney, you are still extremely frugal. This not only affects how much money you and your family spend, but it affects your willingness to spend money on your practice or on self-improvement, which might net you more income. In this way, your filter limits the choices you make and even the choices you see.

3. Short-Term Goals

What are your short-term goals (i.e., those in the next few weeks or months)?

_____

_____

_____

Example: Your short-term goal might be to prepare for the big trial you have starting at the end of the month. Your long-term goal might be to improve staff relations in your office. By focusing on one to the exclusion of the other, you might have trouble reaching both. Both of these goals affect how you see your life. If you feel you need to spend a lot of time and energy preparing for that trial, you will filter your ability to listen to certain people. For example, if your secretary tells you she needs to take time off to care for a sick parent, you may see that as unreasonable through the filter of your short-term goal.

4. Long-Term Vision

What is your vision for your future?

_____

_____

_____

Example: If you see yourself as the managing partner of a large firm making lots of money, there are certain things that you will not see. You may filter out most pro-bono cases. You may decline taking those cases that could be interesting to you, but will not yield a high return. There is nothing wrong with this, but it does affect your ability to see what is before you.

5. Values and Beliefs

What are your values? What are your prevailing beliefs?

_____

_____

_____

Example: If one of your overriding values is having financial security and one of your strong beliefs is that hard workers make a lot of money, you might scoff at your friend who is planning to leave his high-paying job to work for a non-profit organization. You also might put in a lot of hours and be unable to see other ways to make money.

6. Attitude

What is your general attitude, mood or frame of mind? Do you tend to be positive, rushed, worried, peaceful? What do you *believe* is *possible*? What *choices* do you believe you have? Are you more glass half-empty or half-full as an approach to life?

_____

_____

_____

Example: If your general frame of mind is one of worry, you may see circumstances as more dire than do others who do not have this attitude. So when your client tells you he would like to consult with another attorney on a matter you are handling, you immediately become concerned that the client will fire you, and balk at his suggestion to consult another attorney, ultimately causing him to lose trust in you.

The Speaking Part of Communication

We told you communication has two parts: transmitting and receiving. We have spent a lot of time discussing the receiving (listening) portion, as that is often overlooked and underdeveloped. Now, at last, we focus on most people's favorite part of communication: the transmission (speaking). In this section we offer some ideas on clear speech. We will focus on speaking in a way that gets you what you want. Remember: although we have separated out listening from speech, they do go together. The foundational step is always to listen first.

The Non-Verbal Portion of "Speaking"

In considering the part of communication called "speaking," note that "speech" is simply a way of conveying thoughts, ideas, beliefs or positions to another person. As such, the "speech" part of communication is not all verbal. In fact, according to some authorities, our outgoing communication is about 55 percent body language; 38 percent tone, speed, and volume of voice; and only 7 percent the actual words we say.

As such, you must pay close attention to the 93 percent nonverbal portion of your "speech" when you have a conversation. If you are not aware of your non-verbal communication, you may not realize when it does not match up with your verbal communication. Imagine you are angry that your secretary is late and you approach her to discuss it. Though you might say, "I am not mad; I just want to talk to you about how you might be on time in the future," your anger will be communicated non-verbally. Therefore, the communication will not be what you wanted it to be, which is a neutral exploration of why she is late. Because non-verbal behavior constitutes such a large percentage of communication, your anger will come across more strongly than your words—"I am not mad."

Note: You may not even be angry *at* the person with whom you are speaking. It doesn't matter; your anger will come across. Imagine the same scenario, but you have just had a fight with your spouse on the phone when your secretary walks in an hour late. If you go and talk to her about it, while still angry with your spouse, your anger will come across and she will *interpret* your communication as angry. While you are talking to her about her tardiness, she is likely to interpret your non-verbal behavior as anger at her for being late.

A Model of Effective Communication

We believe the first step in effectively communicating with another person is to think about what you want to convey *before* starting the conversation. This will allow you to not only plan what to say in order to get your point across clearly, but also to determine if you are in the proper frame of mind to deliver the communication. This is important because we can only control our non-verbal communication to a certain degree. If you are upset, it will come out no matter how hard you try to smile and modulate your voice. As such, you should be checking for what, in NLP terms, is called "congruence" between what you are saying and what you are feeling. In checking for congruence, ask, "Is my internal state in line with what I want to convey?" If it is not, then perhaps the conversation should wait.

Before you have a conversation with someone, consider the following:

1. **What is my desired *outcome*?** What do I want to achieve as a result of this conversation? This is your destination—where you want to end up—so it is important to be very clear. Imagine yourself at the end of the conversation that went exactly as you wanted. What is your result? In other words, what are you walking away with (information, feeling, etc.)? What is the other person walking away with?

Following are examples of the same scenario, but different desired outcomes.

Example #1: As an outcome, I want my secretary to think about what is making her late and to choose a different process for getting to work in the morning so that she will solve this problem herself and start to be on time. As a further outcome, I want her to know it is unacceptable to be late because it lowers staff morale, puts us behind schedule for our day, and is in contradiction to the agreements we have made.

Example #2: As an outcome, I want her to start being on time immediately and to know she will be fired if she does it again.

2. **What is my *intention*?** Consider why you are having this conversation. What is your purpose or your reason?

Example #1: My purpose is to have everyone on the same page about being to work on time, working as a team and raising office morale. I want my secretary to look at the problem and be empowered to solve it. I also want to have this conversation to show that we will not ignore these kinds of things.

Example #2: My purpose is to demonstrate a zero tolerance attitude for tardiness, so she will change her behavior or be made an example so others do not believe they can come in late or break other rules.

3. **Am I in the right *frame of mind/emotional state*?** It is important to do these steps in order. Now that you know your intention and desired outcome, notice how you are feeling about the situation and see if you are in a state of mind that will facilitate the outcome you are after.

Example #1: If I am feeling angry, I do not believe it will help me get the result I am after. So I will wait until I have cooled off.

Example #2: If I really am mad at my secretary for being late, I may believe that letting her see this anger will be helpful in getting the result that I want. As such, I may consciously choose to talk to her when I am angry.

This model allows you to observe your internal state and make a conscious choice about whether to talk to another person in this state or not.

Specific Speech Tools

Although the most important part of communication is listening, we certainly will need to speak at some point. And when we do, it behooves us to be clear. Since we know that only 7 percent of our outgoing communication is the language we use, this is all the more reason to be *clear*.

How to Make an Effective Request

It is very valuable to be able to ask for, and get, what you want. That seems fairly obvious. All day long we make requests—in our firms, to the court, to the client, to our secretary, to our spouse, to our children, to the barista at Starbucks. It is a fundamental element of communication. It is how we move things forward and achieve what we are after. And yet, strangely, most people are not adept at the skill of clearly asking for what they want. Indeed, we are often very imprecise with our language, particularly when making requests.

Do we have your attention? This is important. Most people make requests poorly, if at all. Making effective requests is one tool that Cami has seen *transform* law offices. She has seen law firms use this tool such that:

- everyone understands what is expected of them;
- staff candidly tell their superiors whether they can realistically complete a project by a particular deadline; and
- people know and understand what agreements have been made and trust that others will honor them.

This skill has two elements to it. The first, which we will not discuss here in much detail, is the willingness to ask for what you want. Many people are reticent to ask for help, support, or whatever will give them the ability to do what they want easily and efficiently. It is immensely valuable to realize that people are some of the best resources we have.

The second element of getting what you want and need is a step-by-step process for making an effective request. This will lend clarity to your conversations and to your agreements. Imagine the effect on your practice when you learn to make requests that are fully understood by your partners, associates and staff. Imagine the effect on your personal life when you are able to make requests that are fully understood by your friends and family members.

How to Make an Effective Request

You will need:
1. A present and focused speaker.
2. A present and focused listener.
3. Terms of fulfillment, including a time element.
4. A specific answer to your request.

1. A present and focused speaker.

This is you. You must be fully present with your listener, without distractions. This means do not make a request while working on the computer. Do not shout it into your associate's office as you walk down the hall. Do not make a request of your spouse or child while you are in another room in the house.

This also means know what you want and think about it ahead of time. Before you make your request, be prepared and know exactly you are asking for.

2. A present and focused listener.

Make sure that your listener is tuned in to you and not watching TV, on the phone, or leaving the room.

What if you are making a request via email? You do not actually know if you have a present or focused listener. You therefore will need to think of ways to determine if that person is "present." Many of Cami's clients tackle this challenge by asking the email recipient for a response to the email by a certain time. For example, "Please let me know by 5:00 p.m. today if you accept my request." The value of doing so is that (1) people often respond to emails asking for an answer by a certain time; (2) by 5:00 p.m., you know if you do or do not have a present and focused listener and if you do not, now you can simply call the person.

What if you are in a meeting and you say, "I would like someone to take care of this project." If you do not get a response, you have no way of knowing if your listeners are present and focused. In that case you must either wait for someone to answer, ask for someone to answer, or ask a specific person to answer.

3. Terms of fulfillment, including a time element.

This should be familiar to you as an attorney, as it is very similar to contract creation. Clearly express what you want from your listener—all terms specifically. One way to do this is to think about how you will know when the request has been fulfilled. For example, my request will be fulfilled when a hard copy of the completed brief is on my desk and an electronic copy on which I can make changes is in my computer twenty-four hours before I need to file it. Therefore, I ask for the brief to be **on my desk and in my email inbox by Monday at 5 p.m.**, in a format that will allow me to make changes. Note this includes a time element.

Be clear when you want the request fulfilled. All too often, we hear attorneys ask for something without any kind of timeline: "Will you prepare this brief? Will you make this call? Will you fix my computer? Will you schedule a depo?" You have not made an Effective Request if you have not specified the time expectations. As such, when the other person says "yes," you do not have a clear agreement. When this happens, you are envisioning a certain time frame and the other person is envisioning a certain time frame, and they are likely not the same.

4. A response.

Possible responses from your listener are "yes," "no," or a renegotiation. If the response is "yes," you have an agreement. If it is "no," you do not have an agreement. The third possibility is your listener says "I cannot get that to you by Friday, but I could get it to you by next Tuesday. Is that okay?" If you say "yes," now you have an agreement. Or you might continue negotiating.

Note: if your listener does not respond when you make a request, **you do not have an agreement.** Another breakdown in communication occurs when the speaker says "Will you...?" and then leaves the room without getting an answer.

This happens often in a group setting where the leader says, "I would like someone to ___" and does not wait for a response. There is no agreement, and thus a high likelihood that no one is going to fulfill the request. As a leader in your firm, this is a good thing to know.

How to Make an Effective Promise

Our promises are the basis of trust and integrity. If you do not keep your promises on a consistent basis, people will not know what to expect from you. This will diminish their ability to trust you and will likely affect the relationship and whether they want to do business with you. Often the problem is that we do not make clear promises. It seems simple, but can be challenging.

How to Make an Effective Promise

You will need:
1. A present and focused speaker.
2. A present and focused listener.
3. Terms of fulfillment with a time agreement: "by when."

---

1. A present and focused speaker.

As above, if you are going to make a promise, you need to be present, without distractions, and clear on what you want to communicate. If you are making a promise, know that you are making a promise. This element is important. If you review the trust chapter, you will see that often we lose trust with people because we are not careful and conscious of when we are making promises.

2. A present and focused listener.

Make sure your listener is tuned in to you and not watching TV, on the phone, or leaving the room. Wait until you have their full attention. This is important because if your listener is not fully present when you are making a promise, there is a good chance that they will not understand what you are promising, which can lead to problems when you do not fulfill your promise in the way they expected.

3. Terms of fulfillment, including a clear time element

Clearly express what you will deliver. Be very clear about the terms. "I will get you the brief by Friday, June 17, at 5 p.m. I will email it to you at ____ email address." Or "I will bring it to your office." Or, "I will put it in the U.S. mail postmarked on that day."

Think about where misunderstandings could occur in your language. For example, if you say "I will try" to do that for you, some people will hear that as a promise. When you make a promise, be clear and use language such as "I will do that" or "I promise." By the same token if someone makes a request and you are not sure if you will be able to fulfill it say, "I am not promising" or "I am not sure if I can do that, so do not count on me." Many associates, wanting to please their partners (and attorneys wanting to please their clients) say "I will try to do that" or "I hope I can get it to you on time." And they get in trouble when the other person hears this as "I will." Be clear if you are saying "No." Be clear if you are saying "I will try." That is not a Yes. You are not making a promise. So be clear about it. You are responsible for how your communication comes across.

Think about where misunderstandings could occur in your promised behavior. For example, lack of clarity such as "I'll get the brief to you" without defining what that means. The partner may be very disappointed to find a hard copy of the brief on his desk at 5:00, when he was expecting a soft copy on his computer. Clear up any potential misunderstandings at the time you make the promise.

Dealing with Communication Failure

What is a communication failure?

When we talk about communication failure, we are referring to a problem in a relationship that involves communication between the parties. Most conflicts and relationship challenges are the result of a communication failure. How do you know you are in the midst of a communication failure? You might have a negative feeling towards another person. You might not want to talk to him anymore. You might avoid him. You might stew over a conversation you had with someone and feel bad about it. You might think about a situation with another person and be unsure of what to do.

On the other hand, you might notice that another person is avoiding you, or that they have a "tone" when they talk to you, or that something has changed, or they stop doing business with you or calling you.

Even in the best of all possible worlds, there will be communication disruptions and failures. This stems mostly from a failure in understanding and appreciating other people's filters (as explained above). There is an NLP (neuro-linguistics programming) presupposition that says, "Every behavior has a positive intention." This means that people rarely set out to hurt or upset you. They typically have a good reason—a positive intention—for behaving as they do. However, our filters are so vastly different that we often do not see the other person's positive intention and assume a bad motive.

Conflict Arises from Mis-Interpretation and Mis-Communication

Ms. Chang and Mr. Butler

Ms. Chang is a partner in the firm; Mr. Butler is an associate. Mr. Butler is late on a "soft" deadline (he did not get her the brief for review two days before it needed to be filed, like she had asked). Ms. Chang calls him into her office and speaks to him in a direct and firm manner, raising her voice and letting him know the problems this causes for her and that this is unacceptable behavior that will not be tolerated. Ms. Chang does this not out of anger, but because she believes the way to train an associate is to clearly state the rule and that it was broken and articulate the problems it caused. This is based on her filter. In her first law firm a particular partner was hard on her. Ms. Chang remembers the partner with fondness and believes he taught her valuable lessons that have made her a good attorney. Moreover, because of Ms. Chang's personality, directness and a firm tone do not bother her at all.

Mr. Butler has a different personality and a different filter. He experiences Ms. Chang's directness as disrespectful and harsh. This interpretation of her behavior is based on his own filter. He grew up with people who rarely raised their voices or spoke in a harsh manner. In his home, his private Christian school and even his first job, he was taught to believe that harshness and direct criticism were disrespectful. Additionally, Mr. Butler's personality tends to be non-confrontational. He begins to complain about Ms. Chang to other associates because it makes him feel better to talk about it and he doesn't have to approach her directly. The gossip begins to circulate, and makes its way back to Ms. Chang. Because of her filter, she believes that if Mr. Butler is upset with her, he should talk to her directly and that it is childish and insubordinate for him to talk about this behind her back. She becomes upset and now there is genuine conflict between Chang and Butler, which you can see is based on behavior that arose from how each of them has interpreted the situation.

Why It Is Important to Resolve Communication Failures

What happens when we allow communication problems to continue unresolved? Think back to a time when you were upset with someone and you did not clear it up. How did you feel around that person? How was it working with him or her trying to get something done? Unresolved communication issues tend to fester; when we are upset with someone, we tend to look for more reasons to get upset with them, creating a "bonfire" effect—our upset causes us to look for more wood to throw on the fire, thus proving we are right to be upset.

Prices we pay for unresolved conflict:

- **Weaker Relationships.** You may lose the relationship; or at the very least, communication will be poor which causes problems if you have to work together.

- **Lower Morale.** Others can see conflict and will be affected by it; also, those who are experiencing unresolved conflict tend to talk about it, and this undermines morale in the workplace.
- **Less Cooperation.** If you are avoiding someone with whom you work or spend a lot of time, you cannot collaborate with them; if you need to work with them directly, this will be very challenging.
- **Less Productivity.** If you are in conflict with a co-worker or superior, your productivity—and often theirs—plummets.
- **The Toll on Your own Health.** It does not feel good to be in conflict with another person; it can generate loss of sleep, changed eating habits and other physical stress symptoms.

Benefits of clearing up communication disruptions:

- **Learn something new.** When you take the time and effort to resolve a communication issue, you will definitely learn something—about that person, about the situation, or about how you see the world, giving you clarity and the ability to move forward productively.
- **Higher self-esteem and self-confidence.** The message you send to yourself, and often to others, when you do not clear up communication problems is that you cannot handle it. Psychologically, this will take its toll on you. On the other hand, you will gain a feeling of power when you respectfully and calmly work to solve the problem, especially if this is challenging or frightening for you.
- **Strengthened relationships.** When you work with another person to solve a problem, you gain trust with that person through collaboration. You may even gain trust with others who see how you have handled the situation. Often through this type of experience, the relationship gets even better than it was before the communication problem began.
- **A feeling of relief.** It's hard to hold onto anger and upset, especially if it is with someone you see on a regular basis. You will feel relief if you move through it.

How to Address Communication Failures/Conflict
"The best way out is always through."

Robert Frost

Summary of the process:

1. **Manage your emotions.**
2. **Consciously respond to conflict.**

3. **Problem solve.**

Step One: Manage Your Emotions

Self-awareness is critical in preventing and, when necessary, addressing conflict situations. The better you know yourself, the more you will avoid non-productive conflict. We all have certain "triggers" or hot buttons: things that cause us to get upset in any given situation. For example, you might be bothered by a certain tone of voice that signals disrespect to you. You might find lateness to a meeting offensive. You might hate when people interrupt you while you are talking or are engrossed in something else. You might have issues with the disorganization of the common areas of your office or home.

Think back to the last three times you were upset with someone else. What are the **main sources** of conflict ("triggers") for you?

_____

_____

_____

Awareness—**How did you know that there was a problem?** (Internally, how did you feel? Externally, how did you act? What are *your* signs that you are upset? For example, your heart beats faster, or you tend to avoid the person.)

_____

_____

_____

When you think back to your last three examples of conflict, you should be able to realize that you can identify conflict because of how you *feel*. Our emotions tell us when something is wrong. Many people are somewhat disconnected from how they feel; we often deny or disregard our emotions in favor of rational thought. Emotions reside in your body; you can get insight into them by noticing how you physically feel. For example, nervousness and excitement can manifest as butterflies in the stomach. Some people experience anxiety as a tightening in the chest. A gritting of teeth can often signify anger. It is very useful for you to notice and observe how you physically feel when you begin to get angry, frustrated, or upset. The sooner you realize this, the more able you are to manage your emotions consciously and address conflict early.

Professionals often wonder why we need to talk about our feelings in a business context. But consider your work environment. Consider the conflict that has arisen in your work environment. All conflict implicates how you feel. If you were neutral (without positive or negative emotion) about everything, you would not experience conflict. Emotions are a part of every area of life, especially at work, where we spend a lot of time solving difficult problems and being with the same people for long periods of time. If ignored, emotions will cause problems in the business environment. The emotion most often involved in conflict is anger. Frustration, irritation, and annoyance are all related to anger.

In case you have not noticed, anger runs a particular course. As we start becoming angry, we often have very little awareness that we are even upset. As we build momentum, we become more and more angry and will ultimately reach a peak of all-out rage if we do not interrupt the process. After that peak, the anger begins to subside.

There are several things to note about this process. First, if you can detect the onset of anger early enough, you can interrupt it, or at the very least avoid interactions with others. (One example of this tactic is from a show many of us watched as a child, called "The Incredible Hulk." It was about a mild-mannered doctor who, when he became angry, turned into a huge green monster with no control over his behavior. His strategy was to get away from people when he knew this was about to happen. He became adept at seeing it coming.) Second, it is good to know that the process will run a predictable course: you will build up steam and eventually your anger will die away. This is not true, however, if you stay in the situation and engage with the person you feel is making you angry. In that case, the anger will not subside, but often will become far worse. Two other matters of note: First, you *cannot* think rationally or communicate intelligently when you are in the throes of anger. Don't try it. It always turns out badly, often with you saying things you later regret. Second, at the end of this process, most people feel bad about what they have said and done; so again, it is good not to talk to anyone when you are feeling angry.[1]

As you learn more about your feelings and gain more awareness, you will hone your ability to know when to talk to others and when not to. (Note this is useful in using the above Model for Effective Communication, page 197, as that model suggests you determine how you are feeling before you begin communicating with another person.)

How are you feeling right now? Take a moment to answer this question. Remember: emotions are revealed in the body. First check all parts of your body and answer this question literally (Example: My arms feel heavy, my chest is tight, my leg itches). Then see if you can identify any emotions—well-being, peace, concern, stress—and tie them into how your body is feeling. (Example: my chest is tight and I know this is a sign of stress because the motion is due in twenty-four hours and I still have a lot of work to do on it.)

_____

_____

_____

If you cannot tell how you feel at this moment, take this on as homework. We are always experiencing something. As lawyers, in a very intellectual profession, we are often disconnected from how we feel. It is very valuable to learn to recognize how you feel. As

---

1. *Cami:* I first learned this concept in a book called THE JOY OF CONFLICT RESOLUTION, by Gary Harper, which I can highly recommend. It is entertaining, very easy to read, and highly useful for solving conflict in business. Harper calls this concept "anger mountain."

an exercise, every day at a particular time of day (or two or three times a day), stop and ask yourself how you are feeling. If you do not know, scan your body and look for physical feelings and emotional feelings.

Why is it important to know how we feel in dealing with conflict? First, if you are angry or upset about something, you are more likely to *cause* conflict with others. If you recognize these feelings, you will know to stay away from people. Second, when you are in conflict with another person, unmanaged emotion will block communication and prevent resolution. Because conflict often *causes* anger, if you feel it arise, you can take a break from the situation and resume when you feel you can be calmer.

Step Two: Consciously Respond to Conflict

There are many ways to respond to conflict. These behaviors exist on a spectrum and are based mainly on our personalities, and to some degree on our histories. Knowing where you fall on the spectrum will enable you to work with your natural and learned tendencies to find a more conscious and useful way of dealing with conflict. The spectrum of conflict behavior is this:

Avoidance	*Aggression*

The Spectrum of Typical Conflict Responses

Start where you are. When you go to the mall and you look at the map that tells you where all the stores are located, there is always a dot that says "You are here." Without knowing *where you are*, it is virtually useless to know where you want to go. Knowing your particular conflict style is like stating, "I am here." Once you do that, then you can decide if you want to go somewhere else; that is, develop a way of dealing with conflict that works better for you.

The following are typical responses to communication failures or conflict. Note that you may have different responses in different environments or to different people.

1. Avoidance/Withdrawal

This style typically responds to conflict by leaving it. This can mean actually leaving the scene or refusing to engage in discussion, often with the implication that the other person "wins." Sometimes, this style may leave everything to chance, hoping the conflict will just "go away." The last thing the avoider wants is to face the problem head-on.

The problems with this method of dealing with conflict are: (1) the conflict can (and usually does) recur because nothing has been resolved; (2) the person walking away feels he or she has "lost" and usually retains some anger; and (3) there is often little resolution for the other person even if he or she feels they have "won."

Personalities most likely to use avoiding: those who are by nature reserved, often intelligent and in-their-head types; these are typically not litigators.

Example of Avoiding: Angela

Angela is very studious and detail-oriented; she is quiet by nature and is fearful of conflict. She is having a dispute with her client's insurance carrier, who is refusing to pay a claim that Angela believes should be covered. The insurance representative has accused Angela's client (and Angela) of lying about the claim. During a telephone conversation, the representative has gotten rather heated. Angela is uncomfortable arguing with him and makes an excuse to get off the telephone. The result of her avoiding the conversation is that the carrier now believes Angela has agreed that the client's claim is not covered, and he has no intention of paying on the claim.

2. Smoothing/Acquiescing

This style is defined by acting as if everything is okay even in the face of real and serious conflict. When all parties to conflict openly participate in smoothing, it is often called "agreeing to disagree." The smoother, like the avoider, would like the conflict to go away, but instead of leaving, the smoother works to "make it all better."

Smoothing does not work as a long-term strategy, as the problems and conflicts do not really "go away" because they are not really being addressed. Often, the conflict reappears later even more forcefully. But there are occasions when smoothing or agreeing to disagree can be a useful, *temporary* strategy: for instance if emotions are running high or if there is simply no time to problem solve.

Personalities most likely to use smoothing: those whose main motivation is to get along with others; those who are primarily relationship-oriented (i.e., people for whom relationships are the guiding force, as opposed to those who are more task-oriented). These people like to make sure everyone is happy.

Example of Smoothing: Dave

Dave is a real "people person." Given the same dispute with the insurance carrier above, Dave is more likely to tell the insurance representative that he will talk to the client and get more information and get back to him, but then not do so. The result of this strategy is likely that the claim is not paid, but the issue continues to linger in the background of the client's case. At some point, the client will question what is happening with the claim, may become "rather heated" with Dave, and then Dave will try to smooth things over with the client possibly making vague promises as he did with the insurance rep.

3. Forcing/Pushing

If smoothing is the most passive strategy for dealing with conflict, forcing is the most aggressive approach. "Forcing" means engaging in full-fledged battle that is expected to result in a winner and a loser, and the forcer intends to be the winner. This style is characterized by simplistic, black or white stereotyping of others as "enemies" with little or no concern for those "others."

Forcing is rarely a productive strategy for an organization, and this is especially true if "winners" must work with "losers" in the future. It is also a poor strategy because the forcers, when dealing with avoiders, will always seem to have "won," and nothing will ever really be resolved.

Personalities most likely to use forcing: Those who tend to rush and push through tasks and meetings. Those who do not spend a lot of time considering *how* to say things and who don't worry how they come across to others. They are often litigators, as they do not mind conflict.

Example of Forcing: Parker

Parker is considered a bit of a "bulldog" by other attorneys. Given the same dispute with the insurance carrier, Parker is likely to become confrontational, threatening to sue the insurance company for bad faith. The result depends on the personality of the representative. He may become defensive and set in his opinion and the possibility of resolving the claim short of litigation becomes almost zero. Or he may become fearful and acquiesce verbally but not take the promised action. In any event, the representative will become reactive and the chances of solving the problem are slim.

4. Arguing/Fighting

Some people, faced with conflict allow their emotions to take over and try to win at all costs. Different from "forcing," this behavior tends to be emotion-based and is not about getting one's way but about winning. Often the arguer will bring up other matters, or even make personal attacks on the other person in order to "win."

This strategy, like forcing, does not work because it often produces a winner and a loser, and thus no real resolution. Additionally, the arguer will almost certainly have to deal with hurt feelings from the other person, who often feels personally attacked.

Personalities most likely to use arguing: Those with "big" personalities, often strong-willed, but also emotionally volatile. These are people who are often easily offended and unafraid to show their emotions. They are, by the same token, very expressive with positive emotions like affection and enthusiasm as well.

Example of Arguing: Ed

Ed can be a lot of fun when he is in a good mood, but a bear when he is in conflict. Given the same dispute with the insurance carrier, Ed might first try to garner the representative's sympathy for the client, noting that the client has been paying premiums for years. When that does not work, he might bring up other cases in which other carriers have paid similar claims and may even implicate the representative's ethics and intelligence.

5. Compromising

Typically this style involves negotiation aimed at reaching some sort of a solution in which both parties give something up. While each party "loses" something, each also makes certain gains. Often a third party may be involved as a mediator or arbitrator. The third party sometimes has the responsibility of proposing a specific compromise and in some cases may have authority to enforce his or her decision (e.g., binding arbitration).

Compromising is typically seen as a mature way of dealing with conflict, since ideally all parties feel they have gained more than they lost. However, true conflict resolution does not mean everyone has to give up something.

Personalities most likely to use compromising: all may do this, but it is more likely with those who are less volatile.

Example of Compromising: Jane

Jane is considered a good negotiator because she can usually get people to compromise. In the above example, Jane may ask if the insurance company would be willing to pay certain portions of the claim. The result may be that she negotiates away portions of her client's case unnecessarily.

6. Problem-Solving

Problem-solving is ideal. Although it is more difficult than any of the other strategies—and requires more skill, more time and more commitment—problem solving is the *only* approach to conflict that research has shown to have consistent, positive benefits. Stephen Covey labeled this a "win-win" or looking for the "third alternative." According to Covey, the best method of resolution does not involve winning, losing or giving anything up (compromise). It involves acknowledging the alternatives desired by each party and then finding a *new alternative* created collaboratively by both parties together.

Step Three: Problem Solving

1. Prepare Yourself.

Before you set a meeting to problem-solve, prepare yourself mentally. Ask the following questions. Really spend time reflecting on each one. It would be useful to journal your answers as well. It is important to have a full understanding of yourself and the other person before having the conversation.

- Why do I want to meet with the other person?
- What's in it for the other person in approaching this collaboratively?
- When and where is the best time and place to meet?
- What can I say or do to set a positive tone?
- What do I want to talk about?
- What is the source of the conflict for me?
- What interests and needs do I have in resolving the conflict?
- What might be the source of the conflict for the other person?
- What do I believe are the interests and needs of the other person in resolving the conflict?
- What interests and needs do we have in common?
- What is the other person's positive intention (the positive reason he is doing what he is doing)?

2. Establish Rapport and Positivity

Once you have prepared yourself and the other person has agreed to meet, the first thing to do is make sure that the other person is comfortable and knows that your intentions are positive. If you do not start out on the right foot, a person who is already in conflict with you will feel distrustful right away.

Let the other person know why you are raising this issue; for example, to clear the air, improve the working relationship, or build understanding. Maintain a kind and inviting tone and body posture. Meet in a neutral environment, perhaps a coffee shop, or take a walk. Direct eye contact tends to increase the tension. Remember your rapport-building skills from the enrollment chapter.

The problem-solving process is not linear and you must always make sure the other person understands and feels your positive intention. If you start to feel you are losing rapport during the conversation, take time to regain it.

3. Listen to Their Story

Part of problem-solving is getting it all out on the table. The best (possibly the only) way to do that is to listen first. Listen in a curious fashion, with an open mind and the intention of learning where the other person is coming from. Ask curious questions and reflect back. (See Reflective Listening on page 213 of this chapter.) Listen for the other person's positive intention. This means focus on hearing where he is coming from, why he feels and acts how he does. Once you know this, you will feel better about the situation *and* you will have an easier time knowing what it takes to resolve it.

This cannot be overstated. When emotions are high and there is misunderstanding, reflective listening is invaluable. Reflective listening will help the other person feel comfortable and heard. It will also help you to understand the source of the conflict for that person.

4. Share Your Story

After the other person has shared all they wish to share, it is your turn. Tell the person how you see the situation, in a neutral fashion. Begin with "From my point of view..." or "How I see it..." or "How I interpreted that...." Your intention here is to share your *point of view* not your *position*. This is not an argument. It is important to remember that at the end of the meeting, you want a resolution. The intent in problem-solving is not to win.

5. Collaboratively Decide What Needs to be Resolved

Once both stories are on the table, decide together what issues to discuss. There may be issues that are important to one person, but not the other. Make sure each of you agrees as to the issues you are seeking to resolve.

6. Create a Plan

Work on a plan through mutual brainstorming. Look for a scenario in which you both feel you have "won." Come up with agreements and a plan. Each person should restate their understanding of the plan. Reduce the plan to writing. Be sure the plan involves both of you taking action and follow-up. Agree to and set the next meeting.

Example of Problem Solving

Lucy and Pete

Lucy and Pete, two young attorneys, have been assigned a case. Lucy believes she has done more of the work, and that Pete is taking more of the credit. On one hand she does not want to "make waves;" on the other hand, this is an important case and Lucy wants to show her boss what she can do. And she does not want Pete to get in the habit of taking credit for her work. Rather than ignore the problem or get in a fight with Pete, she employs the problem-solving technique.

First, she prepares herself. She wants to be in a neutral frame of mind and not angry, but ready to stand up for herself. She spends time journaling on the preparation questions above. Her own needs include looking good to the managing partner and doing a good job on the case. She believes these are Pete's needs as well. Both of them will look bad if they cannot work collaboratively. She tells Pete she wants to talk to him, and arranges to meet in the conference room at 6:00, after most of the support staff has gone home. (She chooses the conference room because it is neutral territory. She asks Pete if this is a good location for him as well.)

Second, when she meets with Pete, in order to create rapport, she sits next to him, rather than across from him. She asks how his day has been and about a different case he is also working on. She tells him that she really respects him as an attorney and thinks he has a lot going for him, and explains that she wants to be able to work with him toward having a great outcome in their case and is hoping they can talk about their work together on the case.

Third, in order to hear his story, she asks him how he likes working on their shared case, and how it has been for him working with her. She is very curious and asks a lot of open-ended questions. She lets him know he can open up to her, explaining that she knows sometimes she can come across as a bit bossy. She asks him what kinds of things might not be working for him in their work relationship. She listens and reflects back what she hears.

Fourth, after she has listened to Pete, and he seems to have shared everything he would like to share with her, Lucy tells her story. She explains that it is important to her that both of them do a good job on the case, and that they are able to share credit where credit is due. Then she explains that sometimes it seems like Pete is not doing all he could be, and has taken credit for certain work she has done. She provides specific examples of these situations, and does so in a neutral, non-judging way. As she speaks, she watches Pete's reaction. She explains that the reason she is telling him this is because she wants to be able to work with him not only on this case, but in the future.

Example of Problem Solving (cont.)

Fifth, she asks Pete if there are other issues he thinks they should discuss besides those she has put on the table.

Sixth, she asks Pete for his thoughts on what the two of them (not just Pete, but both of them) can do to meet their shared goal of doing a good job and impressing the managing partner. It turns out that Pete has a new baby at home and feels pulled two different directions: he needs to be attentive to his wife, but he also needs to do a good job at work. After discussing the matter, the two of them agree that in furtherance of their shared goal, they divvy up the tasks in a way that seems fair to each of them, and agree to keep open the lines of communication. They agree that Lucy will tell Pete if ever she has concerns about the amount of work he is doing, and that Pete can tell Lucy if he is having a problem with one of his tasks. In that event, Lucy agrees to help him if she can—which Pete will acknowledge not only to Lucy, but to the boss. Lucy agrees that she will support Pete and will tell the boss that Pete worked hard on the case and did a good job. Each states the agreement and plan as they believe it to be. They agree to meet again in one month to review their progress on the plan.

Conflict arises and relationships are often strained anywhere people work together. But it can be more pronounced in law firms, where there are time pressures and the nature of the business is already conflict-ridden. Most conflict in any setting is largely due to miscommunication or a lack of communication. It takes a degree of courage to leave your normal conflict-dealing behavior and turn to problem-solving. It is much more rewarding, though, in the long run. The people at your firm are people you need to work with every day. It can be exhausting to have ongoing conflict, and it is a waste of time and money.

Example of Problem Solving

Ms. Chang and Mr. Butler

Using the example above of Ms. Chang and Mr. Butler, Ms. Chang may approach her problem-solving conversation with Mr. Butler as follows:

First, she prepares herself. She wants to be in a neutral frame of mind and not frustrated with Mr. Butler. She knows that because he is an associate and she is a partner, he likely has different concerns than she does, and yet they both want to be able to work together at the firm. She tells Mr. Butler she would like to take him out for lunch. This allows them to be in a more neutral setting, rather than at the office, where she is the "boss."

Second, Ms. Chang selects a restaurant two blocks from the office, and they walk together, side by side, thus establishing physical rapport. As they walk, Ms. Chang discusses the weather and how nice it is to be outside. When they sit at the table, they are across from one another, but Ms. Chang continues to make "small talk" as they look at the menu. After they have ordered, she explains that she and the other partners like his work and asks him what some of his favorite cases have been so far.

Third, she asks him how he likes working at the firm and particularly with her. She asks how it compares to some of the other jobs he has had and other people he has worked for. She is very curious and asks open-ended questions. She explains that she really wants to know where he is coming from and that she wants Mr. Butler to be able to tell her, and/or the other partners, what may not be working for him. Ms. Chang recognizes (although she does not verbalize) that due to the partner-associate relationship Mr. Butler simply may not feel comfortable completely opening up to her, but she makes him as comfortable as possible.

Fourth, after she has listened to Mr. Butler, Ms. Chang tells her story. She tells Mr. Butler about her first job as a young attorney and how hard her first boss was on her, and that she feels that has made her the successful attorney she is today. She explains that she knows she can sometimes come across as a bit "harsh," but that she does not believe in "sugar-coating." She tells him that one of the differences between a good attorney and a great attorney is that the great attorney never stops improving. She tells Mr. Butler that he has the capacity to be a great attorney and she would be doing him a disservice by not addressing his tardiness on delivering the brief. As she speaks, she watches Mr. Butler's reaction to determine if he is receptive to what she is saying.

Example of Problem Solving (cont.)

Fifth, she asks Mr. Butler if he has concerns that he would like to share with her. She says she would like to discuss the best way for them to work together, including how he can get his work in on time; how she can best support him if he doesn't; and how to avoid office gossip.

Sixth, she asks Mr. Butler for his thoughts on what the two of them can do to make their working relationship better, and specifically what they can do to avoid gossip in the future. Mr. Butler acknowledges that he took her chastising about the brief as criticism and he did find it to be harsh. He explains that he is doing the best he can and feels pulled in many different directions at the firm. He tells her this conversation has been very helpful because now he will view Ms. Chang's directness as helpful, rather than criticism. Ms. Chang explains that she will be more sensitive to Mr. Butler—and the other associates at the firm—and recognize that her directness can be misinterpreted. Mr. Butler agrees to tell Ms. Chang well ahead of time if he thinks he'll be late on a deadline. She is clear with him that deadlines must be met and he must tell her if he cannot meet a deadline. Each states the agreement and plan as they believe it to be. They agree to meet again in one month to review their progress on the plan. They leave the restaurant with a newfound respect and understanding for one another.

Note: We realize this is not a typical partner-associate approach. The drift in law firms is for partners to dictate to associates rather than talk to them; to ask for more work than an associate can do without staying late into the night; and to cause associates to believe their jobs are on the line if they don't come through on time. Associates tend to believe there is no room for discussion about whether the associate already has too much on his plate when another assignment is put on his desk. But imagine the type of environment in the firm if these kinds of discussions did occur between partners and associates. If you are a partner, consider what would happen if there was collaboration in your firm.

Homework

1. Practice reflective listening every day.
2. Practice making promises and making requests daily.
3. Regarding Homework 1 and 2, meet with members of your firm and teach them these tools, and make an agreement that you will all begin to use them. Communication in your firm will improve dramatically when you are all using the same tools.
4. As lawyers, in a very intellectual profession, we are often disconnected from how we feel. And yet it is invaluable to be able to recognize how you feel. In order to learn to do so, begin this practice: Every day at a particular time per day (or two or three

times per day), stop and ask yourself how you are feeling. If you do not know, scan through your body and look for physical feelings and emotional feelings.

5. Examine your firm and elsewhere in your life to see where you can resolve a communication problem. Use the six-step problem-solving model and solve it. Start with the easy or minor challenges to get comfortable resolving problems.

Chapter 9

Purpose and Vision

"Nothing contributes so much to tranquilize the mind as a steady purpose—a point on which the soul may fix its intellectual eye."

Mary Shelley

Why Read this Chapter?

1. You are not sure if what you are doing professionally is your highest calling.
2. You want to be sure that your career path is aligned with who you are.
3. You do not always feel satisfied and fulfilled in the practice of law.
4. You would like a guiding principle to assist you with your daily, weekly and long-term decisions.

Jonathon

Jonathon is feeling burned out. He has practiced employment litigation for 10 years, but feels something is not right. The constant antagonism is starting to wear on him. He is finding himself angry a lot of the time, even at home and when he is by himself. He is not sure if he should stay in this line of work or change practice areas.

Raymond

Raymond is fresh from law school and just passed the Bar. Now he is in the process of deciding what to do with his degree. He is not sure how to approach this decision.

Introduction

In this chapter, we will discuss the value of knowing your purpose—in your life, in your work, and in any given task. We will teach you how to determine your purpose and how to use it to keep you on track.

Purpose is a guiding principle that will help you understand what is most important in your life and help you make choices in keeping with that importance. Knowing your purpose will enable you to live all areas of your life with greater meaning, which in turn makes decision-making easier, and results in greater fulfillment overall. Knowing and living your purpose will assist you in "taking a stand" against other people's (and your own) drifts. (See chapter 1.) Having a purpose will also help you cope in a profession in which you are always either winning or losing and where people are not always civil. Your purpose provides you with a central guidance system, which makes you less likely to be swayed by other people's agendas or to get off track.

We also address purpose in the time management chapter (chapter 7) because when we know our purpose and are consciously purpose*ful*, we make much better choices about what to do with our time. Often the sense of feeling overwhelmed and not having enough time to do everything arises from doing whatever seems most urgent, rather than purposefully deciding what will make the biggest difference in your life and in your practice.

What Is Purpose?

Purpose answers the question WHY? On a task-specific basis, we ask, "Why am I doing this?" For example, "Why do I want to take this new case?" "Why do I want to grow my practice?" "Why am I going to this particular networking event?"

On a broader basis, we might ask "Why am I here?" (i.e., in this law firm, in this relationship, on this planet) or "What am I supposed to do?" "What is most important to me?" For example, in the practice of law, we may ask, "Who am I really meant to serve?" In life, we may ponder, "What is most fulfilling to me?" "What offers me the most satisfaction?" "What do I feel I am meant to do?"

Purpose can have a deep meaning or a surface meaning. It can range from, "Why do I want to practice law?" to "Why do I want to work in this part of town?" to "Why am I having chicken for dinner?"

Knowing your purpose allows you to be ***purposeful***. Purposefulness is intentionality and conscious choice. It gives us focus and direction and usually makes us far more effective. When we are purposeful, we make conscious choices as to what to do and what direction to take rather than just waiting to see what shows up.

It is also useful to know your purpose because purpose is what motivates us. If you have a strong sense of purpose behind what you are doing, you are more likely to bring your energy and dedication to completing it efficiently and well. Think of something in your life to which you are fully committed, something you never waiver on, something that you always complete. Then ask yourself, "Why do I do this?" For example, you might be very committed to spending time with your children or your spouse each day. Why? What value do you get from doing so? You may say it is because you love them, you enjoy their company, and you want them to know you care about them. If so, then this is your ***purpose*** for spending time with them: to connect with and enjoy them so they know you love them. Because it is so important to you to feel that connection, and that your family knows you appreciate them, you are committed to spending time with them and it is easy to stay committed.

Cami: I am committed to the viability of my coaching business. Why? When I started, I spent a lot of time asking this question. I wanted to be sure I would have a high level of commitment and build my business based on something important to me so I wouldn't tire of it or give up when it became challenging. I am committed to my business because it feels good to serve and empower others and I receive great satisfaction when my clients get what they want from working with me, particularly in building their own businesses. I believe this is because I also am a small business owner and have passion in this area. I get satisfaction from coaching attorneys and seeing their lives get easier and more fulfilling. I think this is because I know what it is like to be an overworked, stressed-out attorney. I also get satisfaction from the creative process, such as writing, on topics I am excited about and that I know help people make important changes in their lives. I love creating and teaching classes. So, my WHY is: I get satisfaction from knowing I make a difference; from being creative; and from challenging myself.

My purpose is "To **serve** others, while **challenging** myself, **creating wealth and abundance, inspiring** myself and others, using my innate **creativity** and **standing** always for **unlimited possibilities**." It is on the wall in my office. I look at it frequently to ground myself and to make sure I am moving in the right direction.

What does it mean for me to know and live this purpose? I know that I get great satisfaction being in **service**. Not only does this drive me in my coaching practice, but it motivates me to volunteer in other areas, and is a driving force for me as a parent. The best times in my life have been when I was **challenging** myself. I believe in **abundance** and am inspired to help others also experience abundance. I feel deeply fulfilled when I am **inspiring** others to make change and get what they want. I feel most alive when accessing my own **creativity.** And some of the most exciting times in my life and my career have been, and continue to be, when others begin to see all the **possibilities** available to them. These are all elements of who I am and what brings me joy in my life. When I am working, marketing, networking, with my family, alone, anywhere, I can ask myself if this purpose is being satisfied. When I feel dissatisfied or tired or annoyed, chances are I am not honoring my purpose. When I feel happy and peaceful and energized, it is always when I am acting and behaving in a way that is consistent with my purpose.

Now let's move toward creating *your* purpose statement. This will be an overall purpose statement. It will be a statement that informs your decision to practice law, as well as what type of law to practice, *and* it will inform much of what you choose to do in your life. When you have a purpose statement and you honor it, practicing law (or any other profession) will become more fulfilling and easier.

Creating a Purpose Statement

There is no real formula to creating your purpose statement; there are many ways to do it. There are coaches and other people who have devoted their professional lives to assisting others with this undertaking. We will defer to them if you wish to do in-depth work in this area. See our bibliography for some great books on the topic, including *The Purpose-Driven Life*, Rick Warren; *The Passion Test*, Atwood and Atwood; and *Finding Your Own North Star*, Martha Beck.

We have provided three different exercises in order to help you determine your purpose. Alone or together, they will assist in discovering your purpose. For the most clarity, do all three. In order to really delve into this work, we recommend you block out time where you will not be disturbed.

Part A: Timeline of Your Life
We are driven to live from purpose. It feels good to live a purpose-driven life. And yet, we often get off track. Looking back over your life, you can find clues about when you were on purpose and when you were off purpose. This will help you begin to understand what your purpose is.

Get a large piece of paper and draw a horizontal line across the middle of it. Mark the left end as the year of your birth and the right end with your current age. This is the timeline of your life. Go back to your youngest memory and begin to write down the significant events in your life. It is helpful to divide the timeline into five-year increments.

Think about the significant events in each increment. If an event was positive, fulfilling or energizing for you, write it above the line. If it was negative, draining, or dissatisfying to you, write it below the line.

Steph: For instance, I wrote "running Boston Marathon" above the line. Below the line, I wrote "middle school."

We recommend that you start the exercise by writing down those things that pop into your head first; then walk away from it. Over the next one to two week period, spend some time with it each day, and allow this project to remain in the back of your mind. If you remember an important life event at an odd time, go ahead and jot it down. This will help you remember a lot more of the events of your life.

When you are done with your timeline, look back over the entire thing and search for patterns. Those events that are above the line typically indicate a time when you were honoring your purpose. So for each event, ask yourself WHY this event was fulfilling. Look for the deeper meaning in the event. Your purpose will **not** be about the actual activities that brought you satisfaction in these areas, but about your internal experience of the event and what it meant to you on a deeper level.

Steph: I realized that running the Boston Marathon was a fulfilling event in my life because one of my purposes is to constantly challenge myself. My purpose statement does not include "to run marathons." It does include "to challenge myself."

Draw the distinction between the activity on your timeline and the internal experience or internal motivation behind it. In the end, your purpose statement will identify concepts such as "fulfillment," "collaboration" and "creativity."

Cami: For example, I wrote above the line my time in college and law school. While I found the specific experience satisfying, when I looked at it from a purpose-driven perspective, I asked, "What was the internal experience that was satisfying to me? Was it challenging myself? Love of learning? Contributing to other people? Excelling? Intellectual pursuits?" In my purpose statement, this translated to challenging myself.

Note that both of us discovered a purpose to challenge ourselves, but see how different the experiences were that led each of us to this purpose. And indeed, what we each mean by "challenge myself" may be very different as well.

Next, look at the events below the line. Search for patterns. These are times you were not honoring your purpose. For example, if your time in a particular relationship is below the line, ask why. What did you not like about the relationship? Maybe you felt taken advantage of. From this you might discern a purpose that involves "honoring the intrinsic worth of human beings," including yourself. Or maybe that person did not like the outdoors and you really missed giving that up. So you might note that your purpose involves being outdoors, communing with nature or the like.

Steph: It was not necessarily the act of going to school in sixth through eighth grade that was intrinsically unsatisfying. It was that I was not intellectually challenged and had very few friends. I realized that not only is one of my purposes to challenge myself, but to have connection with others and challenge them as well. I learned this by having the experience of NOT being challenged and NOT experiencing connection.

Jonathon

Jonathon creates a timeline, noticing that his significant events above the line include organizing the recycling program as a fundraiser for his twentieth college reunion, participating in a 100-mile relay run in the mountain trails with seven other people, and helping his friend from law school try a pro bono environmental case. Those events below the line include being stranded alone in an airport for several days during a bad snowstorm, watching his father slowly die of cancer, and his brief stint at an oil refinery when he was seventeen years old. The pattern he sees is that he really enjoys nature and is at his best when he is working with other people to achieve a joint goal; and that he cannot stand pollution and is at his worst when he feels alone and ineffectual. This leads him to conclude that his purpose involves being a part of nature and working with others. He realizes that part of his frustration with his work is that he is a sole practitioner whose human interactions are often limited to conflict with opposing counsel and his often-challenging clients, and that he is not communing with nature.

Part B: 14 Reflective Questions

Answer each of the following questions in detail, listening for WHY you do what you do, WHY you want what you want. It is important that, as you go through these questions, you continue to ask yourself "Why is this true for me?" "What does this say about me and what is important to me?" Some of the questions will seem redundant, but are asked in slightly different ways to trigger different thoughts and reflections. If a question seems duplicative of another question, do not give the same answer. Find another way to interpret the question.

Note that many of these questions refer to your business. If you are retired, or not working, answer by looking at your life in general.

1. **What makes you happiest in your business/line of work? What do you do that you are passionate about?** [*Why this is important*: your passion derives from your purpose.]

_____

_____

_____

_____

2. **Why does this make you happy?** Look for deeper qualities in yourself that are being satisfied. (For example, "I like drafting briefs because there is an analytic part of me that loves logic and a creative part of me that enjoys crafting a superior piece of writing. Part

of what drives me, then, is the desire for logic and to be creative.") [*Why this is important:* Here you are translating what you do into a deeper motivation.]

_____

_____

_____

_____

3. What activities make you lose track of time? [*Why this is important:* When you lose track of time, you are thoroughly engaged and likely acting from passion and purpose.]

_____

_____

_____

_____

4. What kinds of people do you love (or hate) to be around? (List three people who you really enjoy being with and another three whose company you do not enjoy. What are the specific qualities or personality traits of each that you enjoy or dislike? For example, greedy, loud, kind, thoughtful.) [*Why this is important:* People you enjoy usually have qualities that resonate with your purpose. People who you do not enjoy typically exhibit qualities that are contrary to your purpose.]

_____

_____

_____

_____

5. What makes you feel great about yourself? [*Why this is important:* When you feel good about what you are doing, you are typically living your purpose.]

_____

_____

_____

_____

6. Who inspires you most? (Anyone you know, or know of, living or dead. This might be family, friends, authors, artists, leaders, etc.) What qualities of this person inspire you? [*Why this is important:* You will be inspired by qualities that resonate with your purpose.] (For example: Martin Luther King, Jr.—you might say, courageous, a leader, inspired change; Mother Teresa—you might say kind, selfless, in service; Uncle Joe—you might say entrepreneur, takes chances, philanthropic.)

_____

_____

_____

_____

7. What are you naturally good at? (Skills, abilities, gifts etc.) Think about areas in which you excel and on which you have been complimented. What particular talents make you unique? [*Why this is important:* Your talents and skills often indicate your purpose, especially if they are talents you seem to have had all your life.]

---

8. Why are you in your particular line of work? When did you decide, and what made you decide, to take this professional path? [*Why this is important:* It is important to know whether you are in this line of work because you thought you "should" be; or because it resonated with a deeper purpose; or because it was something you "fell into."]

---

9. What are the best times you have ever had in this business? [Why this is important: Thinking about specific aspects of your business that are most fulfilling may point you toward elements of your purpose.]

---

10. What are the aspects of your work you do not like and/or wish you didn't have to do? [*Why this is important:* Often when we "push through" things we don't like, it is because they are not part of our purpose. Of course, sometimes there are things we need to do in order to fulfill our purpose that we do not particularly enjoy. But more often than not, most aspects of our purpose bring us joy.]

---

11. Looking at your answers to the previous questions, why do you want to continue in this career/business/line of work? [*Why this is important:* When you can state clearly why you want to be in a certain line of work and it comes from an inner joy or conviction, you will be closer to stating a business purpose.] **If you do not want to continue in this business, state why. If you are not currently employed and have been answering these questions about other aspects of your life, state why you want to continue doing these things.**

---

12. **What do you expect to achieve by continuing in this line of work? And when you achieve it, what will it give you? And when you achieve THAT, what will it give you?** (For example, if I continue in this line of work, I expect to make millions of dollars. That will give me financial security. Financial security will give me freedom. Freedom will allow me to travel and do other things in my life. Therefore, part of my purpose may be to attain security and freedom.) [*Why this is important:* When you "dig down" and ask these questions, if you keep going to the next level and then the next, you will arrive ultimately at a specific purpose-type word, such as freedom, security, service and the like.]

13. **Imagine your 90th birthday party—what do you want people to say about you?** [*Why this is important:* The most fulfilling way to live is from purpose. Therefore, what you want others to say about you will reflect your purpose.]

14. **What did you love to do as a child? Who did you pretend to be?** For example, Cami loved pretending to be a teacher. Looking back, this made sense to her, as her purpose is to serve and inspire others to make positive change and she loves to be in front of a room full of eager learners. [*Why this is important:* We are born with a sense of purpose. Children tend to act out their purpose from a young age.]

Part C: Values

Determine your values. In Chapter 5, we have given you various exercises to determine your values. Use this list of values to create your purpose statement. For example, if your values include honesty, creativity and service, your purpose will likely align in some way. Your purpose statement need not (though it might) use the same value words, but your purpose will be consistent with your values.

What is Your Purpose Statement?

Now take the information you learned from the prior three exercises and distill it down into a statement that reflects your deeper WHY—why you do those things you do when you are living in a way that fulfills you.

Some tips about formulating your statement: Finding your purpose is important, but don't make it *hard*. It does not need to sound or look a certain way. It does not need to be perfect. It may also change and morph over time. Make this easy and even fun. Go with your gut.

Consider your answers to the foregoing questions, your discoveries from the timeline exercise (i.e., looking at the times that you felt most alive, the people you enjoy being with the most), and the values that you hold most dear. If you coalesced that information into a single statement, what would it be? What were you experiencing in those fulfilling moments and who were you "being"? How would you describe those experiences in general terms rather than specific terms? (For example, achieving self-mastery vs. learning karate.)

Many people believe purpose to be primarily about what you DO. We disagree. We believe purpose is more about who and how you want to BE in the world, in your work, and in your life. Purpose is a context for our lives that describes the type of person we want to BE. There are many different paths of "doing" that will allow you to live in accordance with your purpose. It is best to frame your purpose in terms of *who you want to BE*, and then find things to do that allow you to be that person.

Words that appear in a purpose statement are typically what we call "being" words, rather than "doing" words. Some people have a hard time with this concept, being far more familiar and comfortable with concepts of *doing*. To understand this, you might think about a state of being as a foundation for your doing. At any moment, stop and look at what you are doing and ask (in a grammatically awkward fashion) "Who am I being right now?" There will always be an answer. If you are writing a brief, maybe you are **being productive**. Taking a break? Perhaps you are **being balanced**. Planning ahead? **Being proactive**. Having dinner with family? **Being connected, healthy,** or **present**. There is always a state of being underneath our doing. When you learn your purpose, then you can consciously and proactively DO from the most fulfilling state of BEING. It will change everything.

Being words include:	
Purposeful	Loving
Healthy	Confident
Caring	Abundant
Kind	Teachable
Accountable	Resourceful
Giving	Creative

Being words include:	
Responsible	Charming
Respectful	Excited
Motivated	Connected
Committed	Cooperative
Interested	Collaborative
Curious	Productive
Inquisitive	Professional
Imaginative	Happy
Thoughtful	Peaceful
Communicative	Fulfilled
Trusting	Successful
Satisfied	Connected
Creative	In Service
Inspiring	Manifesting
Challenging	Secure

Some examples are the purposes listed below from Cami, Steph and Matthew. Note the being words in bold.

Cami: To **serve** others [BE in service], while **challenging** myself [BE challenging], **creating** [BE creative] wealth and abundance, **inspiring** myself and others, using my innate **creativity** [BE creative] and standing always for unlimited possibilities.

Steph: My purpose is to constantly **challenge** myself and to **assist others** in achieving their goals.

Matthew: The purpose of my legal, mediation, and collaborative practice is to be a **peacemaker** and **teacher, helping** clients find harmony and agreement in their lives, and **teaching** them skills to maintain peaceful relationships into the future.

Yours: My purpose is to

_____

_____

_____

Test: How to Tell if Your Purpose is Right for You

Now take your purpose statement and go back over the timeline of your life. As you review the fulfilling, positive parts above the line, were you living out this purpose? When you look at the unfulfilling experiences below the line, can you see that you were not honoring this purpose at those times?

Another way to determine if your purpose statement is accurate is to ask others who know you, is this me? Seek the input of those who have known you for a long time.

As you review your timeline and get input from others, you may wish to adjust your purpose to add certain words and change others. Remember: it does not need to be perfect! It may (and likely will) evolve over time. The main thing is, do not be derailed by making it too perfect. After you have done the exercises and played around with the language, live with it for a while; then revise it if need be. One coach we talked to advised, simply ask yourself "What is my purpose?" and write down whatever comes to your mind, then see if it resonates. If not, ask the question again, "What is my purpose?" Continue writing down phrases until you find something that really resonates for you. When you find the right statement, you will *feel* it. This is not as intellectual as it may sound. In the end, it will be something that "feels right" to you.

How to Use Purpose to Stay on Track and Make Decisions

So you have your purpose statement, or at least the beginnings of one. Now what do you do with it? You use it to make choices and decisions.

There are two basic ways to approach your business decisions from a place of purpose.

1. Check in each time you decide to do something in your business and ask "WHY am I doing that?" Then determine if the reason is in alignment with your purpose.
2. Write down your purpose statement, have it framed, put it on your desk and regularly ask yourself, "What must I do in order to be in line with my purpose?" Or, "Am I living and working in accordance with my purpose right now?"

Once you develop your purpose statement, you can use it in either or both of the above ways to guide you in your business and your life. Let's take a simple example: Suppose you have decided to go out tonight for fish and chips. Perhaps your purpose includes **to live a life of health, energy, and vitality and inspire others to do the same.** Using the first method above, you will ask yourself, "does going out to this meal align with my purpose?" And you might realize you do not feel energized after eating deep-fried food and what you know about this type of food causes you to believe it will not accord with your purpose of living a healthy lifestyle.

In using the second method above, if you want to go out to eat, you might consult your purpose first and then ask where is the best place to go? What restaurant or type of food would be consistent with my purpose of health, energy, and vitality? You can consult purpose for everything.

Let's go back to our first examples.

Jonathon

Jonathon is feeling burned out. He has practiced employment litigation for 10 years, but feels something is not right. He is not sure if he should stay in this line of work or change practice areas.

After doing the above exercises, Jonathon creates as his purpose statement, **"My purpose is to challenge myself, work with and serve others and always strive for the highest good in global and environmental matters."** This statement is fairly specific as purpose statements go. But Jonathon looked back over his timeline and found his greatest fulfillment was in working on environmental issues and feeling he was making positive environmental impact. He also saw that some of the least fulfilling times in his life have been dedicating himself to work that did not promote the environment and did not allow him to collaborate with others. Now he looks at his purpose and asks if employment litigation—particularly as a sole practitioner—serves that purpose. He sees it does not. He already had an inkling that he was not in line with his purpose because of his dissatisfaction with his work. Part of his purpose is to challenge himself and serve others. He decides that practicing law does challenge him and provides a service, but he decides to look into practicing environmental law at a firm with other people. He feels excited about this new endeavor.

Raymond

Raymond is fresh from law school and just passed the Bar. Now he is in the process of deciding what to do with his degree. He is not sure how to approach this decision.

Raymond's purpose is to **"Discover and promote innovative solutions to complex problems."** This is a fairly broad purpose statement. But he knows that he is most satisfied when solving difficult problems in innovative ways. As such, he considers three potential areas of law: complex business litigation, collaborative family law, and mediation. He believes complex business law will allow him to use his problem-solving skills to help others; that collaborative family law is a good fit because it is a new and innovative way of practicing family law; and that mediation would be a way for him to help others create unique solutions for their problems. Knowing he will need to practice law for a while before becoming a mediator, he decides to focus on complex business litigation and collaborative family law and later determine what it will take to become a mediator and if he even wants to go that direction.

Once you have a purpose, now you can move on to developing your vision.

Create Your Vision

"If you don't design your life plan, chances are you'll fall into someone else's plan. And guess what they have planned for you? Not much."

Jim Rohn (1930–2009, Author and Speaker)

What Is Vision?

If purpose asks the question WHY, then vision asks the question WHAT? Once you have a purpose—a WHY—for your business, the next step is to ask WHAT do I want it to look like, to sound like, to feel like? If, as we have stated above, purpose is a "being" state, vision is about doing and having. Although who you want to BE will certainly be an element, vision will focus more on what you want to HAVE and DO.

"Vision" does not suggest what already exists; it is about *creating something new.* When you create from purpose, the sky is the limit. Be willing to explore what you really want. In NLP, we say "Memory and imagination run the same neural pathway." This means that imagination is very strong; it is potentially as strong as memory and has a powerful generative quality. In other words, what you can envision you can always create. As Napoleon Hill said in his book, *Think and Grow Rich*, "Whatever the mind of man can conceive and believe it can achieve."

If you do not take time to create your vision for your business, your life and your future, you are unlikely to achieve or obtain what you want. Goal-setting is imperative to creating those things you want in your business and other areas of your life. Studies show that making written goals increases the likelihood that you will get what you want by close to 90 percent. And when you do not set goals, you will get whatever comes. You may like it or you may not. (This is discussed further in the WFO chapter.) Written goals are imperative to success. And written goals are preceded by written vision. Once you discover your vision and commit it to paper, then you can set the specific goals that will help you to achieve your vision.

Create a vision that is in keeping with your purpose.

Instructions:

1. Set aside thirty to forty minutes when you will not be interrupted. Turn off the computer and your phone and close your door.
2. Get out your purpose and look at it. Read it over a few times.
3. Get out paper and pen. Do not use your computer at this point.
4. Close your eyes for a few moments, and think about your business and/or other aspects of your life as you want them to be, all in keeping with your purpose. Allow yourself to dream and imagine fully. Don't impose limits on yourself. Get a clear

picture of your business and the rest of your life as you want it to be. Ask yourself, "When I am fully living my purpose, what will my business be like? What will the rest of my life be like?" If there is something you want that you do not think is in keeping with your purpose, don't worry about it. This is a dreaming process. **Do not censor yourself in any way.** By the same token, if there is something you want that you think you cannot get, allow it to be part of your vision. Your mind may want to be logical. This is not the time for that. There is no timeline on this vision. It is not a question of where you will be in a year or five years; it is what you want in your wildest dreams. What is the perfect, most amazing vision you can conjure up?

5. When you have a clear picture, open your eyes and write your vision on the piece of paper. It is important to write it longhand and not to type. At this stage, it is simply stream of consciousness; don't even worry about grammar.

6. Write your vision in the present tense. For example: "My business is thriving and I am making $1,000,000 per year. New clients come to me effortlessly. I practice exclusively civil litigation and my clients are friendly and easy to deal with. I look forward to coming to work each day. My wife and kids are healthy and happy and I am able to spend time with them when I wish."

7. Phrase your vision in the positive. This will energize what you want and cut off the flow of energy to what you don't want. For example: "I feel peaceful and confident" as opposed to "I do not feel stress or anxiety."

8. State your vision in a way that you can clearly see it, hear it, and feel it. Include all of your senses to get a full and complete vision. Be sure to include the following: What do you have? What you are doing? Who is around you? How you do you feel? What do you see? What do you hear?

   For example: "My business is thriving and I am making $1,000,000 per year. The bulk of my money comes from representing Fortune 500 companies. This enables me to represent battered women on a pro bono basis. I wake up every day excited to go to work. I work with people I respect and whose company I enjoy, who are smart, who challenge me every day, and who hold the same values as I do. Our office is in the business district with a view of the river. I take a walk every day at lunch, rain or shine. I am well-respected in the legal community and have won awards for my community service. My children are happy and excelling in school. My spouse and I get along well and I come home every night for dinner.

Matthew

Matthew is a Santa Barbara family law attorney. When he went through this process of creating purpose and vision, he came up with the following **purpose statement**:

The purpose of my legal, mediation, and collaborative practice is to be a peacemaker and teacher, helping clients find harmony and agreement in their lives, and teaching them skills to maintain peaceful relationships into the future.

After creating his purpose statement, he crafted the following **vision**. Notice how he states his vision in visual, auditory and kinesthetic (feeling) terms. Brackets are ours:

In One Year:

- I will get up each morning looking forward to spending the day doing my life's work.
- I will be proud of my office [kinesthetic]:
  - I will see a conference room with quality furniture that is comfortable for training and negotiating and that has a flat screen display [visual];
  - I will hear compliments from clients on its beauty and professional appearance [auditory]; and
  - My peacemaking purpose will be communicated through my office infrastructure.
- I will spend my day largely in meetings with clients and colleagues:
  - Feeling compassion for their needs and interests;
  - Centered and confident in my listening abilities [kinesthetic];
  - Open to tough feedback without pain or fear;
  - Hearing relief in the voices of clients who have shifted from being in a stuck place to being in a peaceful, harmonious place [auditory]; and
  - Hearing interest in the voice of my colleagues as I share with them the peacemaking skills I am learning [auditory].
- I will end my work day with pleasure in a job well done [kinesthetic]:
  - Remembering the relief on the faces of clients who have learned something positive [visual];
  - Knowing I have provided a service far superior to litigation; and
  - Knowing I have modeled behavior that I am proud of.
- I will refer to others all clients who must utilize the court system:
  - Confident that I have communicated all peaceful options; and
  - Confident in the abundance that skill and good karma can provide [kinesthetic].
- I will play a number of roles:
  - At least 10% of my practice will be providing pre-marital advice and training;
  - At least 10% of my practice will be drafting QDROs; and
  - At least 10% of my practice will be providing advice and assistance to pro-per litigants.

Matthew (cont.)

- I will be proud of the support team that allows me to focus on what I do best:
  - I will feel confidence in my secretary and/or legal assistant's ability to draft needed documents with minimal review [kinesthetic];
  - I will see files that are organized and professional in appearance and usage [visual];
  - I will hear my secretary accurately describe my skills and services to prospective new clients [auditory];
  - I will see meetings with clients and colleagues on my weekly schedule, all arranged by my secretary with minimum conflict [visual].

In Five Years:

- I will have no interest in being a judicial officer because I will be confident that my peacemaking impact in private practice is far greater;
- I will hear clients asking about collaborative practice before I explain it to them, and they will tell me they've been referred to me as the "go to" collaborative attorney;
- I will feel confidence in myself as a "master mediator," helping people to peacefully resolve their conflicts in areas beyond family law;
- I will proudly earn significant income training others:
  - As peacemakers;
  - In preparation for marriage; and
  - In preparation for business partnerships.

In Ten Years:

- I will only do projects that are interesting to me, having already begun my "I'll never retire" retirement routine.
- The majority of my work will be training in one form or another;
  - I will present seminars to large groups of people who are contemplating marriage;
  - I will conduct mediation training twice per year;
  - I will present trainings to collaborative professionals outside of Santa Barbara.
- My family law mediation and collaborative practice will be performed by partners and employees.
- My non-training work will largely be working with venture capitalists in managing the expectations of exciting start-up companies.

Matthew (cont.)

Note that Matthew's vision includes time frames. We recommend that you first write your vision statement without considering how long it will take you to achieve. When you get to the next step—the HOW—you can set timeline goals.

The Purpose and Vision Model

Implementing Your Vision

So far, we have (1) Created a purpose; and (2) Created a vision from purpose. The obvious next step is to (3) Implement your vision. Purpose is the biggest and most important piece. Vision is completely subsumed within purpose (i.e., the most effective and satisfying vision will be 100 percent aligned with your purpose). The "how" (action and implementation) part of your plan is a subset of vision. It looks like this:

Now that you have your purpose statement and your vision, the next question is, "how do I achieve my vision?" For example, if part of your vision is to have a comfortable office that is welcoming and spacious with a full staff, you will next need to figure out how to get there: how much staff do you want? Can you hire one person now and one more each year? What is realistic for you? Does your current office need remodeling or will you need to move? What will it cost to remodel or move? What is the first step in that process? In the "how" part of the process, you take your vision and chunk it down into manageable pieces.

Making Decisions With the Model

What is so valuable about this Purpose and Vision Model is the ease with which you can make decisions when you know your purpose and your vision. Taking a simple metaphoric example, imagine you want to go to Texas. The first question that most people ask themselves is, "**How** will I get there?" That question can be overwhelming because there are so many options. You could go by bus, train, plane, or car. Depending on how close Texas is, you could even walk or ride your bike. What will narrow your choices of HOW to get there is to ask WHY—what is your purpose in going to Texas? If your purpose is to vacation and connect with your family and relax, you can then ask, "What is my vision? When I close my eyes and imagine the Texas trip, what do I see, hear, and feel? I see myself touring the countryside; I hear myself and my family in conversation and laughing; and I feel relaxed." Then, and only then, you ask how you want to achieve that vision. You may realize that driving in the car is not very relaxing for you or your family. And flying will not allow you to see the countryside. So you might opt to take a train. Note that once you consider **why** you are going and **what** you want the trip to be like, your options for **how** to get there are narrowed down to fewer choices.

On the other hand, let's say your grandmother is on her deathbed and your purpose for going to Texas is to see her, create closure, say good-bye, and let her know you love her. In your vision, you see her, hear her voice, and feel a sadness and yet a sense of completion. Then, and only then, you ask yourself how you want to achieve that vision. Since your grandmother is close to death, you need to get there quickly and are not interested in seeing the terrain. Thus, as above, your purpose and vision guide your choices significantly and inform your ideas of how to get to Texas.

Notice how small the "HOW" section is in the diagram. The vastly more important question is purpose and then vision. The "how" simply follows as a method of achieving the purpose and vision.

Suppose you want to grow your practice, bringing in more clients and more money. If the first question you ask is HOW to do this, many options will present themselves and it may be difficult to decide which action(s) to take. For example, you may decide as the "how" that you will join several local bar associations and attend their mixers and introduce yourself to as many people as possible. But maybe you feel you are not very good at small talk and you are afraid that evening meetings will take even more time away from your family.

If, instead, you first ask *why* you want to grow your practice and bring in more money, you may realize your overriding purpose in doing so is to have extra money and time to spend with your family. You then ask what will my practice look like when it has grown, based on my stated purpose? You may see more money is coming in, but you are doing less of the work and spending more time with your family. You may then decide on a more passive form of marketing that requires an initial outlay of money but less of your time. You may also decide to hire a contract attorney to do some of the additional work, giving you more flexibility and income. That "how" will only present itself once you have your purpose for growing your business (to spend more time with your family) and your vision (to have work done at a lower cost by others whom you supervise) in place.

Formula for Effective Plan of Action

The above formula can be applied to any goal you have. Any plan of action will be quicker, more satisfying, and run more smoothly when you approach it in the following fashion, and specifically in this order. Using the above example:

1. WHY do I want to bring in more clients and money?
2. WHAT is my vision of having more clients and money, i.e., what will I see, hear, and feel when I have achieved this purpose?
3. HOW will I achieve that vision in line with my purpose?

This will dictate my actions.

Homework

For much of the homework in this book, the order in which you do it is unimportant. But here the order is important. As you have learned from reading this chapter, we start with purpose, then move to vision, and then to implementation. Thus, you should do the first three exercises in the order stated below:

1. Do the purpose exercises and draft your purpose.
2. Draft a vision of your business—how your business will be (what you will see, hear and feel) when you are living in your stated purpose.
3. Chunk it down—what steps must be taken to achieve your vision? What is the timeline?
4. Frame your purpose and put it somewhere you will see it every day. When you look at your purpose, ask yourself: how am I living my purpose right now?
5. Read your vision and your purpose daily.
6. Use the Purpose and Vision model to decide how to proceed in at least one activity daily. For example, if your purpose and your vision involve having a nicer office space that is close to the courthouse, you may always be keeping an eye out for buildings near the courthouse that are for sale or lease; you may e-mail or call friends and let them know you are looking for such a space; or you may check in with a realtor regarding available spaces.

Chapter 10

The Art of Enrollment

"Leadership is the art of getting someone else to do something you want done because he wants to do it."

Dwight D. Eisenhower

Why Read This Chapter?

1. You want to bring in more business.
2. You want your clients to take ownership for their part in their cases, let you handle your part, and listen to your advice.
3. You feel like you are not "on the same page" with other attorneys in your office.
4. Your secretary and other support staff seem not to want to do your work.

Doug

Doug has a case that appears to be headed for trial, but he thinks the clients should settle. Whenever he starts telling the clients about the problems with their case, they always cut him off and refuse to listen, adamant that they will prevail because they are "right." Lately these conversations have left Doug feeling frustrated and he has found himself almost yelling at his clients. He is contemplating withdrawing from the case.

> ## Lois
>
> Lois is a fairly young attorney and is having a hard time with her secretary, Jane, who is much older. Lois does not feel respected by her secretary, who sometimes questions Lois's decisions. Jane has also made derogatory comments to the managing partner about Lois's competence. Jane has been with the firm for many years and Lois knows the partners will never fire her. Lois now cringes whenever she has to talk to her secretary and is afraid if she confronts Jane, that Lois may lose her job.

Enrollment: An Introduction

Enrollment is a very important tool for attorneys and other professionals. Enrollment can be utilized for many purposes: to bring in new clients, to have employees *want* to perform at work, and to ensure that your partners and associates are on the same page with you, to name just a few.

When we use the term "enrollment," we use it in a way you may not have heard before. We define enrollment as follows:

> To form a partnership with another person, in order to support that person in attaining a result they desire; and in taking committed action toward that result.

This definition is quite broad and can cover many situations. The simplest examples have more to do with conversations akin to selling. For example, a potential client comes into your office for a meeting, at the end of which she gives you a retainer and signs a fee agreement. You have *enrolled* her in the value of your services. Or you come home tired after work and say to your spouse, "Let's just go out to dinner tonight." Maybe at first your spouse does not want to go out, but after speaking with you, agrees that going out to dinner is a good idea. You have *enrolled* her in this plan. Or the outcome might be different and she might *enroll* you in staying home for dinner.

When you look at the definition above, you might think, "how can I enroll someone in what I want if the definition is to support the other person in getting what *he or she* wants?" This is precisely the distinction between most kinds of selling and enrollment. It is a different way of approaching the situation. You may want a particular outcome— a new client, or to go out to dinner—but your result will be best if you *approach the situation* by finding out what the other person wants first and directing your conversation toward that. In this way, if the other person agrees, we say they are "enrolled." This means she did not just say, "Yes," to get you to stop talking, but she truly believes your idea is a good one *for her*. Note the distinction, which we will expand on later, between a person being "enrolled" in the result versus being "sold to" or "convinced." The person who is "enrolled" will stick to the agreed-upon course of action because she is clear on its value—for her. The person who is merely "sold to" or "convinced" may not see the value for herself and may ultimately back out.

Examples of enrollment:

- I enroll my busy friend in going to a Chinese restaurant with me for dinner
- I enroll a client in allowing me to represent her
- I enroll my law partner in the value of bringing a yoga instructor into the firm
- I enroll my client in the value of settling his case rather than taking it to trial
- I enroll the judge in seeing that my argument is the right one

Indeed we believe that you are, at all times, either enrolling others or others are enrolling you, *in something*. For instance, while I am seeking to enroll my children in cleaning their rooms, they may be seeking to enroll me in letting them go to a friend's house first. The result will reveal who enrolled whom in what.

The Definition of Enrollment

Let's break this definition into three parts:

(1) To form a partnership with another person, (2) in order to support that person in attaining a result they desire; and (3) in their taking committed action toward that result.

First: "**To form a partnership with another person**, in order to support that person in attaining a result they desire; and in their taking committed action toward that result." This is a different model of attaining agreement, bringing in new clients or winning an argument. What is important about this model is that we are focused on attaining **partnership**, which is different from how we usually approach a situation in which we want someone to do something in particular. We usually strong-arm others, wear them down, talk at them, even plead with them. However, if I am looking to establish partnership with the other person, then my agenda is not the only agenda. My agenda is important, but not primary. When I support another as a committed partner, what becomes very important for me is that person's agenda. This is why in enrolling others, we ask *a lot* of questions. If we do not ask a lot of questions then we do not really know what is important to the other person. We demonstrate partnership by *asking* and *listening*.

Here is the distinction:

Not Enrollment—An attorney talking to a potential client tells her all about the potential client's exposure and what a great track record the attorney has. He tells the potential client that he, the attorney, will "do battle" with the other side to get her the best result. Here the attorney is demonstrating his agenda—that this client should hire him to represent her to actively litigate the case.

Enrollment—If the attorney was focused on creating a *partnership* with the potential client, his main concern would be that the client get what she wants. As such, the attorney would need to know precisely what the client wants. (Many attorneys assume what the client wants is obvious. Often it is not.) Therefore, the attorney will ask this potential client a lot of questions, such as what is the best outcome for her? What is she most afraid of? How involved does she want to be in the case? How quickly would she like to resolve it? What is most important to her in this matter? This demonstrates the attorney's desire to fully learn the potential client's agenda, from all angles. This is a very important piece; it is how the attorney works *with* the client toward her specific desired outcome.

In the first example at the beginning of this chapter, Doug might want to ask the clients why they feel so strongly about trying the case and why they are not concerned about what he has raised as problems. He might walk them through different scenarios, asking them how they might react if certain evidence is introduced, or if the jury does not believe them. He might ask why it is important for the clients to go to trial. And he will be genuinely interested in their responses, instead of just using them to argue his own position in favor of settling. Even though he has represented the clients for some time, he might be surprised what he hears now that he is seeking to be in partnership with them.

Second: "To form a partnership with another person, **in order to support that person in attaining a result they desire;** and in their taking committed action toward that result." This means we find out what is truly important to the other person: what is the "result they desire?" It means we are genuinely motivated by a desire to assist the other person in getting what he or she wants. In the instance of enrolling a potential client, the attorney communicates that his overriding motivation is a caring concern for what the potential client wants, rather than communicating (verbally or not) that his motivation is simply to secure another client. Clients can tell your motivation. Most people can tell, on some level, when you are merely pretending to support them in getting what they want in order to further your own goals. (See chapter 8, Communication Skills for Lawyers: non-verbal communication is 93 percent of the message you convey.) To enroll you must care about the other person getting what she wants.

In the second example at the beginning of this chapter, Lois might inquire as to Jane's motivation for staying with the firm as long as she has, and what she gets out of her work. Lois might realize that Jane wants to feel important and knowledgeable, and is afraid that Lois might see Jane as "just a secretary" and might not value Jane's expertise. Instead of resisting Jane's attitude, Lois might use it to her advantage, asking Jane how she thinks Lois should approach a situation or structure a letter, given the secretary's lengthy experience in dealing with attorneys and opposing counsel. She might do things to demonstrate that Jane's knowledge and experience are important to Lois, now that she sees the result Jane desires is to feel important and necessary. This will lead to a very different outcome than had Lois just decided that Jane was obstinate and hard to work with and made up her own reasons for believing Jane was acting this way.

Third: "To form a partnership with another person, in order to support that person in attaining a result they desire; **and in their taking committed action toward that result.**" This means showing the other person that your service or product can assist them in getting what they have told you they want, and then encouraging them to take action in getting what they want. In the case of enrolling a potential client, this "committed action" is in hiring you and paying a retainer.

Enrollment is much more *collaborative* than just getting someone to agree with you or to sign a contract and plop down a retainer. You are working with another person to create a future reality he or she wants. The other person experiences you as on their side, as part of their team, as an essential piece.

In the first example in the beginning of this chapter, Doug might explain to the clients that he wants them to attain their goals and may show them how those goals could be attained—or potentially not—by going to trial and explore how those goals could be attained through settlement. In this way, Doug demonstrates that he is on board with his clients' agenda and is looking out for what they truly want, and is committed to helping them attain it.

In the second example, Lois might make an effort to seek Jane's input on something like the tactful phrasing of a letter and then take that advice. She might thank her secretary for providing insight as to the tactics of an opposing counsel with whom the secretary is familiar from prior cases.

What Enrollment Is Not

Enrollment is an act of communication that results in another person taking a path you have presented to him or her. The end result of enrollment is action. But this action is based on the other person's perception of the value in taking such action. We call this "committed action." Committed action is not taken from a sense of compliance, compulsion, or the lesser of two evils. It is taken based one's own enthusiasm for a course of action he thinks will further his own interests and get him what he wants. For instance, if I am speaking to my friend about going out to dinner, I communicate with her (listening and speaking) in such a way that she can see the value for herself in going out to eat. She is enrolled and thus takes action and comes to meet me.

In another instance, I have a potential client come in for a free consultation. After listening to her problem and asking questions so that I can fully understand, I convey what I can do for her in such a way that she signs my fee agreement and gives me a retainer. She has seen the value in retaining me and she has taken action based on that realization.

As you read this, you may be noticing that enrollment is

1. A mode of *communication*
2. where I come to fully understand the other person's desired result and
3. that person sees that what I am proposing will help her get her desired result
4. so that she *believes in the value* of what I am selling/presenting
5. to the degree that she *takes action* to utilize what I have presented as a way to attain her desired result.

Enrollment is distinct from

- Convincing
- Cajoling
- Harassing
- Pressuring

Enrollment is not "convincing." Many of us are adept at "getting people" to do what we want them to do. But that end result—the other person agrees to do what you want him to do (hire you, settle the case, etc.)—does not necessarily mean you have *enrolled* him in the outcome. You may have been so annoying and tenacious that he just gave in and said yes. The distinction between enrolling and convincing/cajoling/harassing/pressuring is not in the result—in both instances the person says yes. The distinction is whether the other person is invested in what you have enrolled him in or not. Does he truly see the value? Does he take ownership for getting to his result via your method?

Example

Imagine I have a busy friend who I call and invite to a Chinese restaurant for dinner. The following conversation ensues:

Friend: I am really too busy with my kids tonight and I do not have a reliable babysitter, but I would love to have you come over and have dinner with us.

Me: You know, you really work too hard and you deserve a break. Come on. You're no good to those kids if you don't get out once in awhile.

Friend: I guess you're right, but I don't have a sitter and Billy isn't feeling well.

Me: What about that girl who babysat last time? She might be available.

Friend: Well that's true. But the kids didn't like her very much.

Me: Good idea; you should call her.

Friend: Billy does have a cold though.

Me: What are you going to do for him at home? He'll get over it whether you are there or not.

Friend: You know; you are probably right.

Me: Great. So I will see you at 7:30.

Friend: Okay.

Do you think she is coming? Perhaps she is, but as you review the conversation, can you see that is not what she wants? She is not *enrolled* in meeting me at the restaurant. She is saying yes to me because it is easier than arguing. Also notice that this is entirely my agenda. I have decided we are going to a Chinese restaurant, so I am not at all curious about what would work best for her. This is a place where, if you listen closely, you will be able to tell that the person you are talking to may not be enrolled.

The next sign as to whether she is truly enrolled will be if she follows through or not. When people are not enrolled, they often will not do what they say they will. In order to predict whether a person is likely to follow through, see if they display some ownership for the promise. Here, you can tell that my friend has not seen the value in leaving her house and going to a Chinese restaurant. There is a good chance she is going to call me at 7 p.m. and tell me she couldn't get a sitter or Billy is too sick.

Is Enrollment the Same as Selling?

Enrollment is not necessarily distinct from "selling." It really depends on the type of "selling" one engages in. Many truly talented salespeople are actually engaged in what we have termed "enrollment." To the extent that we draw a distinction between selling and enrolling, we define selling as a "pitch" delivered by someone who does not truly listen and therefore does not fully understand what his customer wants or needs and does not alter his "pitch" to meet the customer's needs and desires. This is a common way of selling and it is important and useful to distinguish this from enrollment.

Breaking it Down

Enrollment consists of certain factors as stated above. The first is that the enroller listens very curiously and asks questions in order to understand exactly what the other person wants. Once you clearly understand what that person wants, you decide if you can provide it. If you can—if what you have fits with what they want—then you convey that. Here is where most "selling" misses the mark: The seller comes at the buyer with what the seller has. He does not spend the time to find out what the buyer truly wants. In most selling, the salesperson spends 80 percent of the time *telling* the customer what he has, and the customer speaks only 20 percent of the time. In contrast, the enroller only speaks 20 percent of the time and spends 80 percent of the time listening. And much of that 20 percent speaking is asking questions. In this way, the enroller fully comprehends what the other person wants; the other person sees that the enroller understands and cares about what he wants; and the enroller explains that his services will help that person get what he wants. And then, closing the deal is easy.

A Specific Model for Enrollment—REALITY

You cannot enroll if you cannot see reality. You must *clearly* see the other person's reality to enroll them in anything. Take the example of "enrolling" my friend in going out for Chinese food: if I had seen my friend's reality—that her son was sick, that she did not want to find a sitter, and did not want to leave the house—I would not have tried to convince her to go where *I* wanted to go. To do so ignores what she has said to me. I would have offered something that respected her reality at that moment.

You must understand REALITY if you are going to enroll someone in something, whether that is enrolling a client or customer into your business or enrolling your spouse or a friend in going out to dinner. This is a distinction from "selling," where we often talk *without* understanding what the other person's reality.

REALITY

R *apport*—Create rapport, build trust.

E *ngage*—Be genuinely interested and focused on the other person.

A *sk*—Ask questions to clarify the other person's desired outcomes.

L *isten*—Listen closely for what is important to him or her.

I *nternalize*—Understand the other person and what she wants and needs before you explain what you have. Be sure what you are offering fits the need.

T *each*—Show the other person that what you are offering will lead to the outcome they desire.

Y *es!*—Gain commitment and action.

The goal of enrollment is to show the other person that you understand his or her problems and issues and that you can support them with your service. You are not pushing your service on the other person; you are simply showing him that your service will assist him in achieving his goal. You are in partnership on his side. The REALITY model is not necessarily a linear process. As you progress through it, you may often need to go back to an earlier step in order to achieve your result. For instance, if you realize you are losing rapport, go back to that step and do what you need to rebuild that trust and rapport. If you get distracted, go back and re-engage with the other person. Remember: enrollment is all about partnership. It is a way to align with others to work toward and attain a mutually beneficial goal or result.

Pre-REALITY

Before you begin the process of enrollment, it is important to ask yourself *what do I want to enroll this person in*? In the earlier example, before I call my friend for dinner, I should determine if my goal is to simply have dinner with her, or if it needs to be Chinese food or a specific restaurant. Do I just want to get together with her? Since your goal is to enroll the other person in the value of doing something, you must first decide what that is.

When you are engaged in marketing conversations, the end goal of the enrollment discussion is to enroll the person in your value as an attorney and to build trust and establish your expertise so that you are the person they will call if they need an attorney and they will refer others to you. To enroll them in taking action, you must know what you are enrolling them *in*.

REALITY, In Depth

Mary

Mary is a family law attorney. Her practice has mainly focused on litigation, but recently she has been concentrating more on collaboration and mediation. This is the type of law that she feels fits her personality and she wants to move in this direction. A client comes into her office and says that she needs to hire a divorce attorney. The client, Suzette, is quite upset at Tom, her soon-to-be ex-husband. As is always important with enrollment, Mary's first question to herself is "what do I want to enroll this client in?" She decides that if it is best for Suzette, Mary would like to enroll her in collaboration or mediation rather than opting for litigation. But Suzette is very angry at Tom. Before Mary can enroll her in something other than scorched-earth litigation, she needs to employ the REALITY method. Otherwise, the two of them will often be at odds, with Mary trying to convince Suzette to do something, and Suzette feeling frustrated with her attorney.

Step One—(Attain and Maintain) RAPPORT

The first step, and an underlying requirement throughout the process of enrollment, is that you establish and maintain rapport. The discussion here will present the NLP (Neuro-Linguistic Programming) concept of rapport. This is perhaps the most important of the steps, so we will spend some time explaining it.

What is rapport?

From Webster's: Rapport—"Relationship, esp. one of mutual trust or emotional affinity."

From Wikipedia: Rapport is a term used to describe, in common terms, the relationship of two or more people who are *in sync* or *on the same wavelength* because they feel similar and/or relate well to each other.

The word "rapport" stems from an old French verb *rapporter* which means literally to carry something back. In the sense of how people relate to each other, this means that what one person sends out the other sends back. For example, they may realize that they share similar values, beliefs, knowledge, or behaviors around sports, politics or something else.

There are different ways to create rapport, from finding common likes and interests to mirroring physical posture and tone of voice.

Building rapport

Building rapport is one of the most fundamental sales techniques. In sales, rapport is used to build relationships with others quickly and to gain their trust and confidence. It is a powerful tool that veteran salespeople naturally employ, which allows them to close more deals with less effort.

How can you tell if you have rapport with another person?

_____

_____

_____

How can you tell if you have lost rapport with another person?

_____

_____

_____

Often, people's response to this question is the following: "I can feel when I am in rapport because I feel comfortable and confident, because the person is listening intently and maintaining eye contact. Often people can tell I have lost rapport when the other person breaks eye contact, turns away, seems agitated, or changes the subject." You will want to observe for yourself how you can tell whether you have rapport with another person. This is a very important first step. You will need to recognize when you have rapport and also when you have lost rapport and need to go back and regain it. You cannot enroll anyone in anything if you are not in rapport with him.

Methods of Building Rapport
Find Commonality
You can build rapport and create a sense of camaraderie and trust by finding something that you and the other person have in common. You can do this through identifying shared interests, shared likes and dislikes, and shared situations. This is often why people talk about sports or "the weather." There is a level of comfort in finding that others like what we like or have similar interests. Also, the way our minds work, we are more comfortable and trusting when our brains can agree with what we are hearing. For example, if it is unseasonably warm and I say, "Wow, it sure is hot today," I will gain rapport, as others know it is hot today (their minds say, "yes"). If however, it is unseasonably warm and I say, "I can't believe how chilly it has been lately," this will break rapport because my listener will be confused about what I am saying. Her brain will say, "No," which will prevent her from listening closely to me and also to some degree decrease her ability to trust me.

Physical Rapport—Mirroring
Mirroring involves getting in sync with the person you are enrolling on as many levels as possible.

Posture Mirroring: In this rapport-building technique, you match the other person's body language, not through direct imitation, but through mirroring the general message of their posture and energy. You can mirror another person's posture by sitting when they sit, standing when they stand, and holding your body in roughly the same position. For example, if they cross one leg, you might cross one leg. If they have their hand on the table, place your hand on the table. Do not mimic, but hold your body in generally the same position as theirs. One of Cami's clients reported having some of the most intimate and powerful conversations with her teenage son while driving in the car because the two of them were in physical rapport.

If you are uncomfortable or skeptical about this, we will tell you that physical rapport is a natural tendency for human beings. The next time you are sitting around a conference table or in an audience or with your family, look at body posture and note the "pockets" of physical rapport. Notice there will be groups of three or four people sitting or standing in a similar position. You will find this throughout the group. We have a natural and unconscious tendency to gain physical rapport with others. Knowing this, you can learn to consciously create physical rapport in order to allow others to feel more comfortable and trusting of you.

Tone and Tempo Mirroring: This involves matching the tone, tempo, inflection, and volume of another person's voice, and matching the way they speak. Again, actual mimicry will have the opposite effect! Also, you need not do this for long to have an effect. If you are soft-spoken and you encounter someone loud, you may raise your voice a bit—briefly and not too dramatically—to match them. If the other person speaks quickly, then you speak quickly. Again, only do this for a few sentences. It will be enough to gain rapport and have them become more comfortable with you. If you lose rapport, mirroring is a way to quickly restore it.

How does this relate to enrollment?

In its simplest form, enrollment is the skill of "pacing and leading." "Pacing" simply means to gain rapport. Once you gain rapport with another person and are "pacing" them, you can then "lead" them and they will tend to follow. In distance running, there is a person called a "pacer." If for example, you want to finish your marathon in four hours, you can follow someone who runs at the pace required to finish in four hours. In NLP terminology, you, the racer, are "pacing" with them, and they are "leading" you.

You can pace people anywhere. When you do, you create rapport with them, as described above. When you match someone's body language you are pacing with them. When you match their vocal tone, you are pacing. If they talk about golf and you join in the conversation about golf, you are also pacing. Pacing creates rapport.

In enrollment, we first pace in order to lead. As stated earlier, you gain rapport by doing something that causes the other person internally to say, "yes." Be sure it is something so obvious that they will agree. For example: "It is warm outside." If he agrees, he says, "yes" (whether out loud or only in his mind). You say, "This is a small room we are in," and the other person agrees—if only in his mind. If you can create a situation in which the other person's mind says "yes" to you at least three times in a row, then he or she will be very likely to say "yes" to the next thing you say or ask.

In other words, gaining rapport involves pacing, which then causes others to "follow." This technique is called "pace and lead." For example, if I want my son to read a particular book, I might begin by asking him about books he likes, and then discuss which of those I also like, and then segue into books I like which he might like, including the book I want him to read. At that point, he will be much more likely to want to read that book. As another example, if I want my spouse to get off the couch and come into the backyard with me, I might plop down on the couch next to him for a while, mirroring his body language and tone of voice for a while before suggesting, as I stand, that we venture into the backyard.

Leading

Once you gain rapport, others will actually change their behavior and follow your lead, as with the example of getting my spouse to come with me to the backyard. This is as subtle as leading another person from slumping into a more upright posture, or from speaking quietly to speaking more loudly. The attempt to lead is one way to test that you do indeed have rapport. If you begin leading and the other does not follow, you likely have lost (or perhaps had not gained) rapport. Being able to lead others through rapport makes it easier to achieve mutually desired outcomes, including reaching agreement or closing a deal.

Mismatching/Breaking Rapport

Gaining rapport is, of course, **a choice**. There may be some people with whom you would choose not to be in rapport. In this case, you have the choice of mismatching.

Mismatching allows you to break rapport in order to interrupt or avoid communicating. To mismatch, simply alter your body and/or voice to make them different from the other person's. This will subtly and unconsciously interrupt the flow of communication, giving you the opportunity to redirect the interaction.

Rapport

Mary has set her appointment with Suzette for 4 p.m., after she has her substantive work done for the day, and she clears her calendar for 2 hours, even though she does not believe it will take that long. She does this because she wants to be relaxed and be able to fully focus on Suzette, her body language and demeanor.

When Suzette comes into the office, Mary comes out from behind her desk and sits in one of two chairs that are arranged side by side. She offers Suzette the other. Because of the coaching she has received, Mary is conscious to work on attaining rapport before she focuses on anything else. Sitting side by side is the first matching technique that Mary uses to gain physical rapport. Initially in their conversation, Mary mirrors the way that Suzette is sitting in her chair, with one leg crossed and her body leaning slightly forward. Suzette is somewhat angry and her voice is fast and a bit loud. Gently, Mary also raises her voice a bit and speaks slightly faster. After a few sentences, Mary brings her voice back to its normal tempo and speed. As she does so, Suzette's voice also slows a bit (a first sign of rapport). Before delving into the substance of the case, Mary asks about Suzette's drive to the office and how it was to find parking. She comments on the weather and continues this "small talk" until she sees Suzette begin to nod and agree.

Step Two—ENGAGE

To engage is to be genuinely interested. It is important not only that you are *perceived* as interested and engaged, but that you actually *are* interested and engaged. There is little to gain when you go through the motions of appearing interested. People can tell. In order to truly engage, focus on the other person and do not multi-task during your conversation. Do not look at your phone. (Often in client meetings, the attorneys who Cami coaches go into a conference room, without their phone, so there will be no distractions at all.) Do what it takes to be truly interested in them, and let them know you are interested. This means a lot to people, will build trust and rapport, and will allow you to accurately hear the information you need.

Engage

Before Suzette came to Mary's office, Mary spent ten minutes thinking about how to show she is genuinely interested in Suzette's life and current circumstances. (We call this process "grounding.") She told herself to be curious about Suzette, to ask a lot of questions, and not to assume information about Suzette based on Mary's own "filter." (See chapter 8, Communication Skills for Lawyers, for info on "filter".)

Mary has already cleared her desk and her schedule. Her computer and phone are both off. (Note she does not put her phone on "vibrate" or leave the auditory indicator on her email. They are *off*.) She has made sure there will be no distractions or interruptions. She is not tired or distracted by what she will be doing later this evening. She has set the stage for being able to fully focus on Suzette and only Suzette.

Step Three—ASK [the right] Questions

Ask questions to clarify the desired outcomes. When you are having an enrollment conversation, you are talking to someone who *wants* something. And your goal is to show them that you can help them get what they want. Many salespeople are ineffective because they spend all their time showing what they have to offer and very little time, if any, asking what the other person actually wants. This is a mistake.

It is important to clearly understand what the other person really wants. Be **very** curious. Ask questions to find out what is important to this person. In this step it is important that you not come from your own agenda, but focus on the other person's. Listen reflectively. Understanding *their* agenda will assist you ultimately in showing them that what you have to offer (product or service) will support what they want.

Ask

Mary knows that, rather than having a particular line of inquiry, it is important to be normal and natural in her questioning. Because she spent time grounding to BE curious, she follows up on what Suzette says in a way that is truly curious and not forced or contrived:

Mary: What is the most important thing about this divorce?

Suzette: I want him to give me my fair share.

Mary: And what do you imagine that would be?

Suzette: [Explains.]

Mary: How will it be for you when that happens?

Suzette: I will feel supported by him.

Mary: How do you feel toward him right now?

Suzette: I am angry.

Mary: Why is that?

Suzette: [Explains.]

Mary is not interrupting or explaining; she is simply listening. Rather than tell Suzette why she should not be angry—which would only break rapport—she simply allows Suzette to talk.

Step Four—Really LISTEN

Eighty percent of the time, you should be listening. This is key. Go back to the chapter on communication for more tips and techniques on listening. Reflective listening is important to make sure you hear what the other person is actually saying, and to let that person know you hear her.

Listen

In reflective listening, Mary is not merely parroting back what Suzette says, but is articulating what she understands from Suzette, based not only on Suzette's words, but on her gestures, facial expressions, tone of voice, and body language.

Mary: What makes you concerned that Tom will not give you your fair share?

Suzette: Because he is a selfish bastard and I know he won't. He has always been selfish.

Mary: You are really angry at him.

Suzette: You bet I am.

Mary: And it sounds like he has done things in the past that make you concerned he might hide some of his assets. Is that accurate? [Mary is reading into what Suzette has said, and she asks Suzette if she is right in order to make sure she is on the right track]

Suzette: No, not hide assets, just not give me what he is supposed to. He'll just spend it and say he doesn't have any money.

Mary: So you don't think he will hide anything, but that he just won't give you what should be yours?

Suzette: Right.

Mary: So are you concerned that even if the court orders him to pay you, he won't?

Suzette: No. If the court orders him, he probably will. I just think he will fight me and the court will take his side and not give me enough money.

Mary: And then you won't have enough money to live on?

Suzette: Yeah, and I will have to work more and the kids will suffer.

Had Mary not listened reflectively, she may not have fully understood Suzette's concerns, and may have even taken unnecessary steps in the divorce.

Step Five—INTERNALIZE What You Are Hearing

In addition to being curious, asking questions, listening closely, and reflecting back, take a moment to consider what the other person really wants and ask yourself if this is something you can support or for which you can provide assistance. If you are unsure, ask questions to clarify. Be sure that what the other person wants is something you can really help them with.

Internalize

Mary has learned that Suzette wants to have enough money to support herself and the children without having to work more. Mary knows that Suzette can get what she wants through collaboration or mediation, so she continues with the enrollment conversation. Had Suzette said that her goal was to make Tom "pay" for having cheated on her or that she wanted sole custody of the children, then Mary might have reconsidered her attempts to enroll Suzette in collaboration or mediation.

Step Six—TEACH the Person How What You Have Will Help

All of the prior steps are mainly focused on listening and gaining information. We do this first. Then at the teaching point we show the person how we can help them achieve the outcome they want. This only works if you are very clear on what it is they want. Let them know *how* your product or service can support them in achieving their result by *referring back to what they said they wanted* and tying the two together. This is the part where you get to talk.

Teach

Now that Mary is clear on what Suzette wants, Mary explains how collaboration/mediation will help Suzette to achieve that:

Mary: The law is pretty clear that each party to a divorce gets 50 percent of the community assets and the person with less income—which is you—typically gets some type of support. And since Tom also has an attorney, he will know all of that. I have looked at your community assets and each of your incomes. You can spend a lot of time and money fighting or you can sit down with each other and we can figure out a settlement that will enable you to not have to work much more, if at all, but will give you enough money to raise the kids. In the long run this will be a lot cheaper, thereby saving money for you and the kids, and will make it more likely Tom will make the payments, as it will be something he agreed to. We may have to figure out some plans regarding the children and custody and visitation, but the goal will be to make you financially secure once the divorce is final.

Step Seven—Listen for "YES"

This step is about generating commitment and action. Once the other person agrees that you can help them, you still need to be sure they will take action. Ask the other person, "What will you do and by when?" Have them be clear. This is a very important part; it separates "enrollment" from "a nice conversation." And you also must commit to what *you* will do and by when. Be sure to follow through and do what you say you will do. And be sure to follow up with what the other person has promised. "Yes," is what you want; but by itself, "yes" is not enough. You must generate *action*.

Yes

Suzette agrees that maybe it is a good idea to engage in collaboration/mediation. At this point, Mary asks her to take certain action toward that goal. She suggests the parties exchange financial information and agree on a time to meet to discuss settlement. Once Mary has suggested particular action to Suzette, Mary can gauge how committed Suzette is to working toward a settlement by whether Suzette agrees to take particular action by a particular date. If Suzette is committed, it will be demonstrated both in her agreement to take action toward settlement *and* by her actually taking the actions that she has promised. (In the end, what a person is committed to can only be accurately assessed by what she actually does. Action is the only true indicator of commitment. See chapter 4, Are You Committed?) If she is not yet enrolled, she will balk at Mary's suggested action and Mary will need to go back to earlier parts of the REALITY model. If that happens, Mary will ask more questions about Suzette's hesitation. She will reflect back what she hears to Suzette. And if Mary still feels collaboration/mediation is best for Suzette, she will then take the information Suzette has given her and tell Suzette how this will achieve Suzette's stated needs, moving again through the REALITY process and ultimately asking that Suzette commit to taking some action toward settlement if Suzette wants to go this route.

Use this model to enroll new clients into hiring you; to enroll your partners into going a certain direction in the practice; to enroll your associates in getting work done in a particular fashion and by a particular time; and even in enrolling your children in cleaning their rooms.

Homework

1. Practice each element of REALITY separately. Spend a week on each element. For example, spend one week just on rapport. Spend another week on listening (see chapter 8). Spend another week on asking meaningful questions, and so on.
2. After you have practiced the elements of REALITY, practice the art of enrollment. Start easy. Enroll the cashier at Starbucks into giving you the perfect cup of coffee. Enroll your spouse into going out to dinner. Make it harder – enroll your kids in

cleaning their rooms; enroll your secretary into finishing a particular job by a particular time.

3. Teach this technique to other attorneys in your office. Practice and talk to them about what is working and not. Use this technique to bring more clients into your firm.

Chapter 11

Trust in our Profession

"Trust is the glue of life. It's the most essential ingredient in effective communication. It's the foundational principle that holds all relationships."
Stephen Covey

Why Read This Chapter?

1. You are aware of the common perception of lawyers regarding integrity and trustworthiness and you would like to stand out from the crowd.
2. You have noticed distrust in your office—people not sharing information; being afraid to tell the truth; saying only what they think you want to hear.
3. You have seen behaviors in your office that may break trust[1] with you and/or your clients—people who are late to meetings; who do not fully disclose the truth; who manipulate the information they have.
4. You have been engaging in behaviors that you think may break trust with others - sometimes not telling the full truth; being late to meetings; gossiping.
5. You do not feel you can always trust yourself. You make agreements with yourself—to exercise more, eat better food, get more rest—that you find yourself breaking. (Note: while we will not specifically talk about self-trust in this chapter, it is an important concept that affects your ability to build trust with others. If you do want to work on the concept of self-trust, you can use all of the following tips with yourself as well as with others.)
6. You often feel distrustful of others.

---

1.   In this chapter, we will use the terms "build trust" to refer to behaviors that have the greatest likelihood of having others trust you; and "break trust" to mean behaviors that cause others to lose trust in you in some way.

Trust in the Legal Profession

How does the public generally perceive lawyers? You know the jokes: we are not seen as very trustworthy or even honest. How does this perception affect you as an attorney? Do clients trust us? Do judges? How about opposing counsel? Where are the stereotypes controlling and where is trust built or broken based on what we *do*?

A study by the ABA addresses these questions. Published in 2002, it found that while Americans believe lawyers are knowledgeable about the law and can help clients navigate the system, and while the majority of those surveyed were satisfied with their lawyers' service, Americans believe lawyers are greedy, manipulative, and corrupt. Consumers tell stories of lawyers who misrepresent their qualifications, overpromise, are not upfront about their fees, charge too much for their services, take too long to resolve matters and fail to return phone calls.[2] This indicates a general lack of trust in attorneys by the public.

How can you as an individual (or as a firm) build trust with your clients in a culture where attorneys are often not trusted just as a matter of course?[3] First, you must be aware—aware that this is the perception, aware of what **you** do that breaks trust with people, and aware of the actions **you** can take to build trust.

Trust has many more aspects than you might imagine. Most people know that failure to keep agreements and outright lying cause distrust. But there are many more, often subtle, ways to break, and conversely to build, trust with others. You may be surprised.

Foundational Thoughts on Trust

Trust is a key component in relationships. We will start by briefly examining how most people view trust.

Simple Trust

Most people do not think about trust until it is gone. Usually, we trust others on some level from the time we meet them until the time that trust is broken. This tends to be unconscious or at least subconscious on some level. Once we stop trusting someone, it is very difficult, if not impossible, for them to rebuild our trust. Cami often illustrates this based on the "circle of trust" philosophy in the movie, "Meet the Parents." As described by Jack Byrnes (Gaylord Focker's father-in-law), you are either in the circle, or you are out of the circle. And once you are out, there is no coming back in. Most people subscribe to this philosophy, whether consciously or not. We may let people into the circle fairly easily, but once they are out, it is nearly impossible for them to get back in.

---

2.   LEO J. SHAPIRO & ASSOCS., PUBLIC PERCEPTIONS OF LAWYERS CONSUMER RESEARCH FINDINGS (2002) (prepared on behalf of Section of Litigation, ABA).

3.   Many of our suggestions are adapted from Stephen M.R. Covey's THE SPEED OF TRUST and from Solomon and Flores' BUILDING TRUST—IN BUSINESS, POLITICS, RELATIONSHIPS AND LIFE.

What causes people to kick others out of their circle of trust varies from person to person. Some people will stop trusting you if you are late for a meeting one time. Some will stop trusting for consistent lateness over a period of time. Some people do not care if you are late, but will kick you out of their circle if they realize you have lied to them or manipulated the truth, or if they realize you have taken advantage of them or a situation. For some, you have to do something they consider to be "big," like stealing money from them. We all have different standards, some based on timeliness, some based on truthfulness, and some based on emotional components, such as whether we can share our feelings with others without fear they will repeat it or ridicule us.

The main hallmarks of simple trust are (1) most people choose whether to trust or not somewhat unconsciously; and (2) once trust is lost, it is nearly impossible to regain.

Accountable Trust

"Accountable trust," is a different concept from how most people view trust. As you know from reading the accountability chapter, the concept of accountability is (1) we are responsible for our results; and (2) we have far more choices and control over our results than we believe we do. The concept of accountable trust is likewise based on choice: we can choose whether to trust others, and—importantly for this chapter—can choose to engage in the behaviors that will build or break trust with others. Unlike simple trust, accountable trust puts the onus upon us to consciously take action to build trust with others.

As part of the concept of simple trust, we tend to believe that people will trust us or not and there is little we can do to change this; but accountable trust means that we always ask what more we can do to build trust with the other person. Under the concept of simple trust, we believe that lawyers have a poor reputation and there is nothing we can do about that, but accountable trust has us determine how we can stand out from other attorneys in this regard. Accountable trust gives us more choice in the situation. This is a powerful concept because when trust is absent from a relationship (whether with a client, judge or spouse), the relationship does not function well, if at all. So having more choice is a good thing.

There are two sides to accountable trust: (1) We can consciously choose to trust or distrust others; and (2) We can consciously choose behaviors that will build trust with others. In this chapter we will focus on the latter.

Take a moment now to answer the following self-assessment questions. They are designed to raise your awareness of your own beliefs about trust. When you clarify your own views on trust, you will be more able to see how others might view trust as well. This is a good starting point for learning how to consciously build trust with others.

Your Current Beliefs About Trust

1. How do you define trust?

_____

2. Who do you trust the most? Why?

_____

3. Who do you trust the least? Why?

_____

4. Who are you certain trusts you? How do you know?

_____

5. What causes you to stop trusting others?

_____

6. What action(s) do you believe you regularly take that build(s) trust with others?

_____

7. What action(s) do you believe you regularly take that break(s) trust with others?

_____

The Basic Behaviors that Build and Break Trust

Following are the major behaviors that either build trust with others, or that break trust with others. Trust-building and trust-breaking behaviors are two sides of the same coin. For example, if I tell the truth and people know this, it builds trust. If I do not tell the truth and people know this, then it breaks trust.

1. Keep Your Agreements

We start with this behavior because it is the most obvious. Along with being accountable (see below), doing what you say you will do—keeping your promises—is one of the quickest ways to build trust. And not doing what you say you will is definitely the quickest way to break trust. This is clear to most people. So why do so many of us break trust in this way?

First, we often do not appreciate what constitutes an agreement. (This is ironic, as lawyers often are intimately involved in determining when agreements have been made.) For our purposes, an agreement and a promise are the same thing even though a "promise" often carries more emotional weight. For purposes of building and breaking trust, a promise or an agreement is anything you say you will do for another person. (Note that all of the trust behaviors may be applied to building trust with oneself. As stated above, we will not discuss this concept in detail in this chapter, but we encourage you to use all of these tips to increase your trust with yourself. In this context a promise could also be anything you agree to do for yourself.)

To reiterate, anytime you say you will do something for someone else, you are making an agreement. Under this definition, it doesn't matter if the entire agreement is stated by the other person and you simply say "OK." It doesn't matter if you don't really want to do what you are asked to do. It doesn't matter if in your mind you are thinking "if I have time" or "I will try." If you say "okay" or "yes" or even "I guess," you have made an agreement. This includes things like, "I'll call you later today," "I'll get milk on the way home," and "You'll have the brief by Friday." It includes situations in which you say, "Sure I'll do that," without thinking about what you are committing to and because saying "sure" is the quickest way to move on from the conversation and you were only half listening anyway. This is important to know because if you don't follow through, the other person will believe you have broken an agreement, which of course, breaks trust with them.

To build and maintain trust with others you *must* keep your agreements.

Example

If you tell your opposing counsel that you will have a response to the settlement offer by the end of the week, then give him a response to the settlement offer by the end of the week. Tell your client you have made this agreement and that you intend to keep it. Because many attorneys are so lax regarding their agreements with opposing counsel, actually keeping your agreements will build trust very quickly. This includes being on time for depositions and returning telephone calls promptly. If my opposing counsel knows that he can trust me to do what I say I will do, he is much more likely to trust me when I give him information about the case and when I request an extension on discovery responses.

It also doesn't matter if you think it is just a "small agreement." In fact, this is the area where trust is created and/or broken most often, because throughout the day we make many "small" agreements. We heard a story once about a teenager who was relating her lack of trust in her parents. When asked why she did not trust them, she recalled times when she had asked them if they would take her to the mall and they said, "Sure, later," but they did not take her; nor did they even acknowledge that they had broken the agreement. Telling your teen you will take her to the mall is an agreement. And although it may seem like a "small" agreement to the parents, not following through breaks trust with the child. **The consequence of broken agreements is broken trust.** This is true whether the agreement is to finish a big, time-sensitive project by a certain date or to go get coffee for someone. While breaking the first agreement may engender a greater reaction and upset and have greater long-term consequences than breaking the second, they both break trust.

Often, Cami has her clients keep a "promise log" for a week, in which they record all of the promises they make to others and to themselves. Then they keep track of those promises they kept and those they did not. They are surprised to see how often they don't keep their promises. This is a great exercise for learning how many promises you make each day and noting those you keep, and those you break—sometimes without even thinking about it. Further tips to keeping agreements are these:

- **Be aware and conscious when you are making an agreement**, or even when you are making a statement that could be interpreted by another as an agreement.
- **Write down all agreements you make**, even those you think of as the "small" ones (like being home for dinner at a particular time or reading to your child before bed), at least until you get good at keeping your agreements.
- **Calendar the date on which you have agreed to deliver** on any agreement (again, even reading to your child at night).
- **Own up when you do not keep your agreements**—admit that you made a mistake and do not try to hide, deny, or make excuses for the failure. Then, figure out what you did that led to the broken agreement and decide to do something different next time.
- **Say, "No," more often.** Train yourself to only agree to do something if you are certain you will do it. Try saying, "Let me check and see if I have the time and I'll get back to you later today." (Remember this is also an agreement. So be sure to get back to this person today.) Checking to be sure you can keep your promise before you make it will also build trust, sending the message that the agreement is important to you.

2. Communicate Clear Expectations

This second behavior—communicate clear expectations—relates closely to the first, which is to keep your agreements. People who make agreements with one another are often not on the same page as to what the agreement is. "Communicate clear expectations" means tell the other person what you expect; ask questions; and be sure you understand what they expect of you.

Have you ever had an experience in which you made an agreement with another person, believing they would complete something by a certain time, but they did not? And when you asked about it, you discovered they thought the project was due on a different date? This is an example of neither party communicating clear expectations.

Have you ever thought you were producing exactly what was requested but when you delivered, you discovered it was not what the requester had in mind? As we have established, when we make any kind of agreement, we will build or break trust based on whether we deliver. So when you make an agreement (no matter how large or small) check in with the other person; say, "Here is what I am agreeing to do for you." Find out if you are both on the same page. Do not agree unless you are clear that you can meet the expectations.

Mary

Mary has just substituted into a case and has received about twenty boxes of documents from former counsel. Mary tells her associate to go through the boxes and determine what discovery has been done on the case. Two days later, the associate is still going through the boxes. Appalled, Mary asks her associate what he has been doing all this time. It turns out that most of the documents were produced in response to discovery, and the associate has been cataloguing everything. He is on box 9. Mary is furious; all she wanted the associate to do was spend an hour or two listing depositions that had been taken and how many types of written discovery requests had been served. The associate believed he had been asked to go through the documents that had been produced and describe them. Obviously, neither party understood the other's expectations.

Another aspect of communicating clear expectations is to include the terms of fulfillment and *the date or time by when* you or the other person will deliver. When you do not state the timeline, the other person is likely to infer one and may not communicate that to you. So when you say to your client, "I will research the law on that and get back to you," he may assume the additional "later today" or "by the end of the week." He may believe you are promising to finish by a certain time. But in your mind, you may be thinking, "I have other things to do right now. Trial is not for two months. I will get it to him in a few weeks." Or you may have no idea when you will do it, just before it "needs" to be done in your mind. But when the client's assumed deadline passes, he believes you have broken an agreement, even if you do not see it this way. This affects his trust in you regardless of whether you believe you had an agreement. As such, communicating timelines *clearly* to people will ultimately build trust with them—as long as you keep them!

When someone agrees to deliver a project for you, ask them "What are you agreeing to do?" Tell them, "I just want to make sure we are on the same page." If there is any doubt as to the expectations, or if the agreement requires certain specifics, it is useful to put the agreement in writing. This works well with secretaries and other support staff, as well as with clients and even opposing counsel. It may take some time to jot down the particulars in writing, but much more time is spent—and wasted—in trying to regain another's trust again after you lose it.

3. Be Accountable

As we address in depth in another chapter, accountability is "the ability to account for the choices I have made and am making." It is **not** about pointing fingers at the circumstances or other people. In *any* situation, you can find your own involvement and your own choices. Focus on your choices, not the circumstances. When you own up to your results (especially when they are different from what you promised) this builds trust. If you are late and you were stuck in traffic for fifteen minutes because of an accident, do not blame the accident. Say, "I am late. I broke my agreement to be here at 2 p.m." Own that. Then say, "I did not leave early enough to arrive on time if I encountered an accident. Next time I will because you are important to me and I want to meet with you." In this example, you build trust when you acknowledge you had an agreement to arrive at a particular time and you take ownership for the fact that you were late, rather than blaming outside sources or relating a reason, story or excuse.

Furthermore, this way of talking and of looking at situations will assist you in learning from your mistakes so you won't continue making them. For example, if you believe the traffic accident *made you late*, then rather than confronting your own failure to leave early enough to deal with unforeseen circumstances, you will continue to find yourself late whenever there is an accident or traffic is bad. However, when you look at your own involvement in the situation, you have the opportunity to change it so you will be on time in the future (even when there is an accident!), which also builds trust.

We discuss accountability throughout this book, as we believe it is the cornerstone for a successful practice, a successful business and a successful life.

Example

Have you ever heard an attorney who has just been chastised by the judge blame his or her secretary for the error? Think about how you would perceive that attorney. It is hard to trust someone who blames others for their mistakes, especially when done to avoid responsibility. The accountable, and trust-building, mindset is this: when your secretary miscalendars something or serves the wrong party or neglects to attach the exhibits to your motion, you are accountable for that mistake. It will build trust with others when you "own" the mistake. Take responsibility for it. Knowing and acknowledging that what happens in your office is ultimately your responsibility will build trust with others. Obviously as part of your accountability—learning from your mistakes and not making them again—you also need to determine if you have been clear with your secretary as to what she was supposed to do, if she needs more training, and then ultimately if she is the right secretary for you.

4. Be Honest, Upfront and Open

Most people recognize that honesty is a foundational tenet of trust. Yet we tend to create a lot of exceptions about what "honesty" really means. Note, for example, the "white lie." Being upfront means telling the truth even when—particularly when—it may have adverse consequences. A great trust-builder is telling the truth even when it does not benefit you, and particularly when it harms you. Tell your client the value of the case. Tell him the true chances of success. Tell your client if you think you may not be the right attorney for this case.

Speak directly. Do not beat around the bush or leave a mistaken impression. Lawyers are often seen as "slick" because we are so good at arguing and framing situations to favor our side that we sometimes talk this way to our clients, and even our friends, spouses and children.

Use language clients understand. When we talk over their heads, it breaks trust. You may have "technically" told them the truth, but if they do not understand the ramifications of what you are saying or how it actually affects them, you are not helping them to trust you.

We are professionals with our own language that lay people often do not understand. Think about visiting a doctor and complaining of an ailment and having the doctor recite in technical medical terms what might be wrong with you; you leave knowing nothing more about your condition than when you went in. We are more likely to trust the doctor who speaks clearly and in simple language, translating medical terms into words we understand. The same is true with clients and attorneys. Help them understand. They will trust you more.

Be transparent. Transparency is defined as being clear or readily understood. Tell people what you know, even the parts you are not required to reveal. Encourage your clients to do the same.

Steph: I have a story I like to tell my clients to encourage them to tell the truth, *especially* when it makes them look bad. Many years ago, I represented the defendant in a trial that largely came down to who was telling the truth. After losing a motion for nonsuit, I began putting on my defense. During cross-examination of my client, opposing counsel asked how the client had obtained certain information. The client paused, then threw up her hands in a gesture of surrender and answered the question. The judge looked at the client, and then at me and said, "Do you realize she has just admitted to a crime?" I immediately stood up and shouted, "Objection. Fifth Amendment. Move to strike!" or something like that. The judge shook his head, sustained the objection, struck the testimony, and shortly thereafter took a break. When the judge returned, he stated he had reconsidered the motion for nonsuit, found it meritorious, and granted it. Trial was over, and my client had prevailed. Leaving aside the authority of the court to grant a motion for nonsuit after the defense had begun its case-in-chief, the moral of the story (or so I believe) is that when the judge realized the client would admit to a crime in order to uphold her oath to tell the truth, he realized the client's version of the facts was the correct one, and that she had not done what the plaintiff had accused her of doing.

Where are you hiding the truth or protecting yourself? Where are you less than transparent? We build trust when we tell the truth, particularly when it makes us look bad or is embarrassing or could lead to an unfavorable outcome. We also build trust when we reveal our motives and explain why we are doing what we do. This makes it possible for others to verify what we are reporting. Tell your clients the weaknesses in the case so they can make intelligent decisions about how or whether to move forward. When you make a strategic decision in the case, involve the client in that decision, explaining the reasons and the strategy behind it, the possible advantages and pitfalls, and even the thought process behind the decision. Full disclosure regarding your approach to the case builds trust.

5. Acknowledge and Fix Your Mistakes

Do you ever try to hide your mistakes? Think back to a situation in which you have done this (of course we all have); and reflect for a moment on your motivation for doing so. We always have a reason for doing what we do; we always have a positive intention. So ask yourself: at that time, what were you afraid of? What were you trying to gain? What was your positive intention?

Here are some questions to ask yourself to increase your self-awareness of where you might be seeking to protect yourself by hiding your mistakes:

When have I shied away from admitting an error? Who was involved? Why did I do it?

Without judging myself, what can I learn about where I tend to hide or deny (or simply not mention) mistakes I have made?

In order to change your trust-breaking behaviors, it is important to know what motivates you to engage in them in the first place. Begin observing yourself neutrally and without judgment, and notice where you are not completely honest, particularly regarding your mistakes and what you perceive as your shortcomings. What have you done or not done that you have not revealed to your client? To an associate? To your spouse?

Cami: I worked with an attorney who inadvertently sent an e-mail to a third party that contained certain information about a client. The information was not overly important, but of course it was confidential. When the attorney realized what he had done, he immediately contacted the third party and had them destroy the e-mail, but then he agonized over it for days. He did not want to tell the client what he had done, reasoning that trust would be broken when the client realized he had made this mistake and had revealed her information. But this attorney had as one of his long-standing goals to increase his perception as a person who could be trusted, and he decided to take a chance and do what he believed to be "the right thing." Even though the client whose information was shared never would have discovered what happened, the attorney told her. It took a great deal of courage for him to do this. This client told her attorney that his revealing his error actually made her trust him more because she never would have known about it had the attorney not told her. As a result, this client knows that she will always get the truth from her attorney, even when that truth is not in the attorney's favor or potentially makes the attorney look "bad."

Admitting mistakes builds trust. This is particularly true in a situation such as the example above where you would not be "caught" if you did not reveal what had happened. When you make a mistake, apologize immediately and without excuses. On the other side, be open to forgiving others when they make mistakes. When you make it easy for them to apologize and admit their mistakes, you pave the way for them to be honest with you about their own shortcomings, thus creating open, honest and trusting relationships.

The next step is to fix your mistakes. Once you realize your mistake, do what you can to rectify the situation. In the foregoing example, even though there was little to "fix", because no direct harm had come from the inadvertent disclosure, the attorney assured his client that he had contacted the third party to whom he had sent the information and told her to delete it. He also decided to double-check the address every time before sending an email to one of his clients. He also asked his client what else, if anything, he could do to fix his mistake.

One of the biggest challenges attorneys face is completing tasks by the time we promise to finish them. When we realize we will not be done on time, we often say nothing, hoping the other person will not notice. But even if the other person does not say anything to you about having taken an hour, a day, or even a week longer than you said you would to finish the work, acknowledging that you have broken your agreement with them goes a long way toward building trust. It shows the other person that you are conscious of your word and do not let things "slide." Certainly, if you don't meet your deadline and don't say anything and the other person **does** notice, you **will** break trust by not saying anything.

Steph: I once worked with an attorney who would regularly promise to get me his research by a certain date and then two days later would still be working on it. He did not understand my concern and did not view these lapses as broken agreements ("You don't even need it until next week," he would complain). As a result, I did not trust him. It would have been different if he had come to me and acknowledged that he had not finished by the time he said he would; or if he admitted that he frequently overpromised and had unrealistic expectations about how long things would take; or had I seen that he was taking steps to correct the situation. But his failure to even acknowledge there was a problem and his insistence on blaming me for being so "demanding" made him untrustworthy to me. I stopped working with him.

6. Being Respectful Builds Trust

What does respect mean to you? Like beauty, it is often in the eye of the beholder. Take a moment and consider the following:

1. **How do you define respect?**

---

2. **How do you know when you receive respect or disrespect?**

---

3. **How do you know when you are treating someone with respect or disrespect?**

How does respect build trust? Of all of the behaviors mentioned in this chapter, this one is likely the least obvious. You might think that even if you are disrespectful to your client, if you do a good job for him, he will still trust you. And he might. But the truth is that people trust in different ways and for different reasons. There are a myriad of ways that people experience trust. For many people, being treated respectfully causes them to put their faith in you—to trust you—far more than if you simply do a good job for them. When your clients believe you *truly* and *genuinely* care about them and their case, and not merely about the revenue it might generate for you, they will be far more loyal to you and will trust you more.

Each of the trust-building behaviors in this chapter will set you apart from other attorneys (and most other people) if you apply it consistently. For attorneys, this one is particularly important. Consider the 2002 ABA study cited at the beginning of this chapter, regarding the public perceptions of lawyers. Attorneys are often seen as caring only about the bottom line. We often don't return phone calls or keep our clients informed. The frequency of this complaint shows how much it means to clients to feel like they are important—to be treated with respect.

Be respectful to everyone, not just judges and clients, but court staff, opposing parties and opposing counsel. You will set yourself apart and build trust when you treat **everyone** with respect. Our clients are watching us. Be a zealous advocate, but do not use "zeal" to justify disrespect. Treating anyone with disrespect breaks trust not only with that person but with others who witness you. Sometimes clients expect us to be "mean" to opposing counsel and may even be disappointed when we are respectful. Be cautioned against falling into this trap. As with all the behaviors listed in this chapter, how you act with *everyone* will build or break trust with those around you. People know internally (even if not consciously) that if you behave a particular way with someone else, you will behave that way with them. Even if you are typically respectful to a client, if you are disrespectful to others in his presence, it can break trust with him. This is an important point to learn about trust—people watch your behavior and do not necessarily distinguish how you treat them from how you treat others.

As such, it is also important to show respect to your opposing counsel. Not only do you build trust with that counsel, but you also distinguish yourself from others in the profession who are not as respectful. You will also reduce your stress level and make it more likely that opposing counsel will treat you with respect and even cooperate when you need something from him or her.

Steph: Many years ago I was involved in a very contentious case in which opposing counsel was bombarding me with motions and discovery. Two weeks before Christmas, that counsel served me with three separate motions that were calendared for hearing just after New Year's. When I asked for a brief continuance, so I did not have to spend the Christmas holiday working on oppositions, the answer was no. I thus moved for a continuance. On December 21, the hearing was held, at which time the court granted the continuance. As we were leaving the courthouse, opposing counsel was visibly fuming over the loss of a perceived advantage. I quietly got her attention and said, "Have a Merry Christmas." The attorney looked at me sternly, assuming it was a joke. I repeated, "It's the holidays; have a really nice Christmas." Then I smiled and walked off. From that time forward, opposing counsel was no longer snide, and the last-minute motions became less frequent. Once the case was over, opposing counsel was friendly when we saw each other, and even referred a few cases to me. This is the power of trust-building through respect.

7. Be Loyal

In *The Four Agreements*, Don Miguel Ruiz calls this habit "being impeccable with your word."

Loyalty is similar to respect; it involves being respectful of others when they are not present. Being loyal means only speaking about others as if they were present. Don't badmouth others. Don't gossip. This can be one of the hardest habits to break. But when you complain *to* one person about another, it sends the message you will also complain *about* that person when he or she is not around. This erodes trust. Whether you are talking about one client to another, to one attorney about another, to a client about an attorney or an attorney about a client, you are sending a message that your habit is to gossip about people. The listener knows that you will eventually talk about her. And when a person knows you may talk about her behind her back, she will not feel safe talking to you. This will substantially reduce the strength of the relationship.

Do not disclose private information about others. This includes more than just the ethical dictates that all attorneys are bound to uphold. Do not tell your wife that your secretary is having an affair. Do not tell your brother that your best friend just lost her job. In all areas, talking like this breaks trust. It not only breaks trust with the person listening to you, but if the subject of your gossip discovers what you have said about him or her, that person also will not trust you.

Some people feel a powerful drive to talk about others. In some contexts, it can be a way of gaining rapport with the listener, and we may forget that our gaining rapport in the moment comes at a cost. Not only is it disrespectful and disloyal to the subject of the gossip; the listener will also trust you less. Sometimes it's hard to know what is acceptable to discuss. One rule is to simply not talk about other people. This avoids the "slippery slope" of even starting to gossip. Another rule is to only speak as if the subject of your conversation was listening to you. Would that person be okay with you telling another that his son won first place in the chess tournament? Probably. Would he be okay with you telling others that he has started drinking heavily? Perhaps not. Use this test to determine what to say.

Mike

Mike noticed a surprising change among some of his partners. One of them was having an affair that everyone knew about and which the partner did not try to hide. There was much office conversation about this among the other partners and the staff, and Mike was repeatedly given the opportunity to join in the conversation. But it was important to him not to gossip. He thus not only removed himself from some interesting conversations; but every day he had to have the courage to say, "I am not willing to talk about this." It made him feel like a bit of an outcast and some of the other partners (and even staff members) would rib him about it, but he just kept refusing to talk about the affair. And he felt much better about himself for not participating in the conversation. Eventually people stopped talking about it in front of him.

Being loyal also includes giving credit to others when they are not present as much as when they are. If someone congratulates you for a good result that was not solely your effort, it will build trust if you name and praise those who contributed. If you were the leader of a successful group effort, be sure to give credit to everyone involved. This builds trust not only with those who hear you speak, but also with those whom you have praised when they were not present.

8. Be Results-Oriented

How often do you say you "tried" when you failed to deliver? Eliminate this word from your vocabulary and tell the truth about your results. Look honestly at what you have produced and distinguish your results—what you actually accomplished—from your stories of how you tried to accomplish the result. Were you on time to this meeting? "One minute late" is a result, as is being "on time" and being "three minutes early." Start getting very clear about the results you are generating. "I was stuck in traffic" is a story. "I am late" is the result.

Often we get stuck in our reasons, stories and excuses and do not even acknowledge the results. Part of what builds trust with others is to tell the truth about your results. Tell the client that you did not get the settlement letter out yesterday, as promised, but that you are working on it right now and that you will send it today before the close of business. Don't tell him you will send it by noon if you aren't absolutely sure you will finish it by then. And don't tell him how you were working on it yesterday but then got a frantic call from another client and had to deal with that crisis all afternoon. That is a story and an excuse. It breaks trust to play the victim and blame your circumstances for your results. Letting go of the stories you tell is also immeasurably beneficial in changing your results.

Your clients are looking at your results. They do not care about your process, the actions you took to "try" to get the result, or all the other work you have to do. They care about the result: did you do what you said you would do for them when you said you would do it? If you don't deliver a result, communicate in a way that lets your client know you will make changes in order to follow through in the future. Clients put a lot of faith and trust in us. We need to assure them that their trust is not misplaced. One way of doing this is by being results-oriented: by delivering the results that you promise; and by speaking in terms of results and not in terms of actions taken toward results.

Speaking in Terms of Results	
The Results	The Reasons, Stories, and Excuses
I was late.	I am sorry; traffic was awful.
The award is less than we thought it would be.	The judge didn't understand this case. I've said it before. He should really step down from the bench.
I was unable to get the depo date changed.	Opposing counsel is a jerk; he just wants to run up the fees in this case.
I know that I promised to get the brief to you by 5 p.m. Friday. I am not done yet.	I worked until 11 p.m. every night this week and came in at 6 a.m. every morning. I just have too much to do.

Underpromise and overdeliver. People determine whether they can trust you based on the ultimate outcome and not all the work you did to "try" to get there. "Trying," storytelling, and excuse-making breaks trust.

In short:

- Deliver results
- Speak in terms of results and tell the truth about your results
- Be accountable when you do not deliver your results and make needed changes so you can deliver next time

9. Improve Yourself

No one can ever know "everything" about a given topic. We are less likely to trust people who act as if there is nothing left for them to learn. Always be in a learning mode. Set aside a regular time daily, weekly, and monthly to educate yourself in any and all different areas of life, particularly in your area of law or business. Read about new developments in the law. Read topics that would be of interest to your particular clients. Read business-building articles and blogs.

Why does this improve trust? For one thing, it shows people you are aware that you don't know everything. So when you tell them you **do** know the answer, they are more likely to believe you. Also, when people stop learning, they are, or at least appear to be, closed to new possibilities and information. This can also cause a break in trust because clients and others may not trust that you will be open to their ideas or their perspectives.

Constant learning sets you apart and generates trust because it shows others that you are wise enough to know what you do not know, and knowledgeable enough to know where to go to get the answers.

Example

A deputy police officer once related that he had great respect and trust for his sergeant because the sergeant read the paper every day cover to cover. It was important to the sergeant to stay current on local and national news at all times. The deputy felt that the sergeant's taking ownership for knowing what was going on, not just locally but nationally, showed that he cared about his community and his world—that he was open to information and took his job seriously. He was perceived as one who would go above and beyond the basic job requirements to do the best he could for his community and his deputies, including reading the entire newspaper (and getting up early enough to do so).

10. Say What Is So

Take your head out of the sand. Look around right now and notice where you are denying reality. We all have some level of denial in some areas of our lives and we all do it for various reasons. Become aware of your reasons. What are you ignoring and why? Answer the following questions with whatever comes to mind. The answers do not need to make sense; honest responses will provide you with valuable information. You can analyze the "whys" of your denial later.

1. What am I pretending not to know in my firm?

_____

_____

_____

2. What am I not acknowledging in the way I manage my time?

_____

_____

_____

3. What am I not paying attention to in my family?

_____

_____

_____

4. What else am I ignoring right now?

_____

_____

_____

When you have your answers to these questions, or whenever you learn something you would rather not know about, learn to face it head-on. This means asking the tough questions, usually of yourself, and becoming aware of what you are doing and what is going on around you. Robert Frost said, "The best way out is always through." The more we ignore the difficult issues and try to go around them, the more they recur.

Hank

Hank had a new associate that he really liked. But on Mondays the associate would come in late and looking tired or ill. Sometimes on Thursdays or Fridays he would be late as well. Every so often, the associate would get "food poisoning" and not come in at all. Then for weeks at a time the associate was bright, chipper, on time, and full of energy. One evening Hank called the associate at home and the associate was not speaking coherently and slurring his words. The next day, the associate could not come to work because of "stomach flu." Eventually Hank had to admit to himself that his associate was an alcoholic who was either going to have to get some help or could no longer work at the firm. Hank really liked the associate, who did excellent work when he wasn't drinking, and was reluctant to finally acknowledge that the man was a potential liability for the firm. But once he admitted to himself what was happening, he could face it head on; he approached the associate, confronted the situation and put some boundaries in place. This was a better result than continuing to ignore it.

Additionally, be honest with others about what you are seeing. If you have a client or an associate who is habitually late, tell him that it makes it difficult for you to trust that he will show up when he says he will. You don't have to be blunt or rude, but at the same time, do not sugarcoat your information; you want him to get the message. He may not want to hear the truth, but he *will* know you as someone who can be trusted to tell the truth. He will never have to wonder whether you are bothered by something because you will have a reputation for saying what is true.

Steph: At the very beginning of my career, I had a secretary who could be fairly blunt. One day, after I had related being upset at something opposing counsel had said, my secretary turned to me and said, "You take things too personally." Of course, I took this very personally and marched into my office and shut the door. But after I had simmered down, I thought about it and realized that I *did* take things too personally, and that this would not bode well for a lengthy legal career. From that time, I took what others said to me far less personally, and I have always remembered this important bit of information. Ultimately, I was grateful to have a secretary who told me the truth.

Being aware and saying what is so builds trust, with others and with ourselves. Talk about trust and those things that break it and build it. Look at the communication chapters and the chapter on building rapport (enrollment) for the best ways to get your message across so others can hear and understand you.

11. Listen

One of the habits in Stephen Covey's 7 *Habits of Highly Effective People* is "seek first to understand and then to be understood." Simply stated, people will not listen to you until they feel heard. When people feel heard by you, they trust you more. Why? For one thing, when you are listening deeply, you are not pushing your own agenda; you are interested in what is important to them. It is easier to trust someone who is interested in what you want than someone who doesn't seem to care. Additionally, when people believe you are truly listening to them, they trust that you understand their concerns. If you do not listen, or appear not to listen, you may be the most intelligent, creative, or aggressive lawyer, but your clients will not necessarily trust you to do what is in their best interest.

Another benefit of listening closely is that people will not seek advice from you until they feel like you are hearing them. In this way, listening closely will assist you with "client control." If you *truly* hear your client and she feels heard by you, she will also be more likely to listen to you and to take your advice. Note that when people are speaking with high emotion and/or repeat themselves and their points, they are typically not feeling heard. When you really hear them, the emotion and repetition will typically dissipate.

Here are ways to begin consciously listening:

- **Take time**—focus on your speaker and do not do anything else while listening (for example, looking at your computer screen, your phone, people walking by);
- **Tune in**—focus your attention on your speaker and let go of the judgmental, evaluative, or just plain distracting thoughts in your head;
- **Ask questions**—be genuinely curious what your speaker wants to convey to you. This can also help you let go of judgment and evaluation;
- **Tell the speaker what you heard him say**. It is useful to repeat back, in your own words, what you have heard. This is sometimes called "reflective listening." In doing so, you may be surprised how often you do not understand fully what another is communicating.

Example

JoAnne, the client, is upset: "You never return my calls and I am sick of it!"

"Okay; let's talk more about that," says her attorney.

"I called you yesterday and the day before and I have not heard back from you."

"It sounds like this is very important to you, JoAnne, and that when I don't get back to you right away, you feel like you can't reach me," replies her attorney.

"That's true; and I really need to tell you something."

Note in this exchange the attorney simply listened. He did not defend himself or try to make her wrong saying that it had only been forty-eight hours, or make excuses for why he hadn't called back. He listened for what was the problem and she calmed down. If you can set aside your ego, your judgment, assessment and opinion, you can hear people and they will ultimately listen to you. Had the attorney immediately tried to get across how busy he was, JoAnne would **not** have listened. And she likely would have stayed angry Now that she is feeling the attorney hears her, they can decide how to proceed in the future when JoAnne calls.

All of this listening should be done *before* you make your point. You will be amazed how much more open others are to listening to you if they believe you have truly listened to them.

12. Trust Others

It may seem counterintuitive, but extending trust to others will make them trust you more. Additionally, people will typically act how you expect them to act. When we distrust someone, he or she is less likely to keep agreements with us. There is no reason for others to act in a trustworthy way if they know we do not trust them. This is especially true of children and teens, but it extends to clients, opposing counsel, and others in the office. Therefore, when we extend trust to others, they are more likely to keep their agreements. Think about this in your personal life and in your practice.

There is of course a distinction between choosing to extend trust for the sake of the relationship, and trusting blindly. We are not advocating the latter. Blind trust is when you close your eyes to the truth. Examples are when someone has embezzled from you but you re-hire them, or when your spouse has lipstick on his collar and you ignore it. That is blind trust. When we say, "Choose to trust others," we are talking about conscious trust: allowing others to act how they act, trusting that they will act honestly or appropriately, but noting where they do not and then doing something about it. This is distinct from either requiring someone to earn your trust, or conversely trusting them blindly. It is a conscious choice that seeks areas where trust can be extended, taking into account past behavior and the risk of trust being broken.

Where have you extended trust, even though there was a risk involved and been pleasantly surprised?

_____

_____

_____

We tend to trust or distrust unconsciously, or at least subconsciously, based on our emotions and a desire not to get "burned" again. Trust is best if it is a conscious act—a choice you make as to whether to trust or not trust another person. As we stated in the beginning of this chapter, this is accountable trust. The behavior of trusting others is that of trusting accountably. Choose to trust others when you think that is best for the relationship.

Steph: Typically, I require retainers for hourly work, particularly with new clients. But once the retainer is gone, I usually do not require additional retainers, as long as subsequent bills are paid and within a reasonable time. I am up front with my clients about this, because I trust them to pay my bills as they become due, without the requirement of a retainer. Most clients respond favorably to this, appreciating the trust I place in them and the freedom of not having to pay additional retainers. For those who do not pay invoices on time, I require additional retainers or, in some instances, cease representation. Sometimes I will continue representation, with the understanding that the client will pay what they can when they can, and I trust them to be honest about their financial situation. At the same time, I am not blind to the possibility that I simply may not be paid, and I enter this situation consciously.

13. Talk About Trust

This is a topic that is rarely addressed. Yet some of the most valuable information you can convey in a relationship is what causes you to trust and not trust the other person. Tell people when you trust them and why. Tell them when they have broken agreements with you and the effect it has on you. Invite others to tell you what makes them trust and not trust you, and how you can be more trustworthy in their eyes. This can have incredible benefits in a family, and it is also essential in the workplace. This is a great topic for an attorney meeting and with support staff. You may be surprised what you learn.

Conclusion

The vast majority of attorneys are of good moral and ethical character. We do what we believe is right, we act ethically, and we believe we are trustworthy. Yet people often approach us expecting something else. How can we change this view? Our advice is to use the above behaviors, choosing one to work on each day for one week, and then move on to the next one. Practice them. Put up sticky notes by your computer reminding you to work on them. Use the concepts and the behaviors with clients, your children, your spouse, opposing counsel, judges, colleagues, and especially with yourself. Talk to people about trust and see what you learn.

Homework

1. Work with one trust-building behavior per week, under the following format:
   a.   Monday morning, choose your trust-building behavior. Write it somewhere you will see it every day.
   b.   Write down what that behavior means to you.
   c.   At the end of each day, look back and see where you applied this behavior consciously and/or unconsciously, and record it in your journal. Write what you learned about yourself and where you will make changes to be more effective with this tip the next day.
2. Work with a group—your family or law firm, for example—teaching, learning, and reviewing these concepts.
3. Keep a "promise log" for one week. This is a simple piece of paper divided into two columns. In the first column, write every promise you made to anyone that day. In the second column, write whether you kept that promise or not. At the end of the week, look for patterns. In what situations and with what people do you normally keep your promises? When do you tend to break them?
4. After your week of observing your promises, decide what you can do to improve your level of promise keeping. Then implement that behavior.

Afterword

Now What?

Now that you have finished this book, what will you do with the information? You have a toolkit containing many tools that, if you use them, will transform the way you practice law. But this is key: you must use them. Many people read books that contain information on how to improve their businesses and their lives. Then they put down the book and expect to somehow retain what they have read. But that is not how the human mind works. Cami's workshops on this material are filled with experiential learning—practices, games, activities—to assist in internalizing the information. To *internalize* means to absorb the information; to learn it like the back of your hand; to be able to access it when you need it. You will have *internalized* when you are talking to an upset client and you immediately begin to reflect back what you are hearing. You will have *internalized* when you recognize a distraction or an urgency and realize it is not *your* urgency, and that immediately addressing it is not the best use of your time, but you find a way to set it aside to deal with in a proactive fashion later. You will have *internalized* when you have a decision to make and you ask yourself, "How can I make this decision based on my purpose?"

It is important to remember this tenet:

"I hear and I forget. I see and I remember. I do and I understand."

Confucius

You cannot fully understand the information in this book without taking action on the material.

If you wanted to build a tree house, we could offer you the hammer, saw, drill, and screwdriver, and we could write a book telling you how to use the tools to build a tree house. But until you pick them up and begin to experiment and put them to use, *your tree house will not get built.*

So use your tools. Here are different options:

1. If you have simply read the book and not done any of the exercises, go back through now, chapter by chapter, and do the homework. Spend a month on each chapter, fully committing yourself to the homework and to *internalizing* the concepts.
2. If you've gone through and done the homework, you are much closer to internalizing the tools. Mastering these tools is a lifelong endeavor. One never arrives at

flawless communication. One is never as fully accountable as one might be. There is always room for improvement. So now you have done the homework, look at your practice and ask where the next area of improvement lies. You might go back to chapter 2 and develop a new well-formed outcome for whatever is next in your practice and life. When you decide what your next goal is, ask which chapter applies and go through it again. **This book is meant to be a reference resource**—not just an interesting read—go back to it often. Keep it near you all the time. Use it!

3. Get an accountability partner, or a group of partners and study the book. Do the homework together. Find a group of attorneys who would like to learn to practice law in a new way. Go to http://www.mclarencoaching.com/coaching-for-attorneys/ and learn about Cami's Coaching for Attorneys class series to further internalize these tools.

4. Look into hiring a professional coach to help you move to the next level.

5. Always be in the mindset of *kaizen*—continuous and never-ending improvement.

6. Whatever you do, never stop.

That Which Is Not Acted upon Is Not Learned.

To the journey,
Cami & Steph

Glossary of Terms

Accountability: The ability to account for one's choices and results. Ownership of the results we have created and the ability to acknowledge they are based upon choices we made, whether consciously or unconsciously. (Found in chapter 3, Accountability; and throughout the book.)

Acknowledge: Look for, notice, and draw attention to (1) what one has done that one is proud of; (2) what was challenging, yet one completed; and (3) what one has simply completed. A process to do at the end of something—the end of a project, the end of a day, the end of a week, the end of anything that is closed down or completed. It allows us to feel good and, importantly, to move on. (Found in chapter 6, the Case for Self-Maintenance.)

Agenda: Similar to a goal or objective, though often one we are so attached to that it is hard to see the agendas of others. In this book, the term is used in reference to the goal or objective of a conversation, and the question for effective communication is, "What is the other person's agenda and how does it match my own?" (Found in chapter 10, the Art of Enrollment.)

Assumption: An interpretation one makes about a person, thing or situation that one then believes, without direct knowledge of its truth. We make assumptions to fill in the blanks of our actual knowledge. For example, "I know he was angry with me because of the look on his face and the tone of his voice." In the context of accountability, we use the term "assumption" to describe, in part, what motivates us to make certain choices. We often make choices based on unconscious or partly-conscious beliefs, attitudes or assumptions. (Found in chapter 3, Accountability.)

Attitude: A way of approaching and viewing the world that is habitual and often unconscious. For example, one may have an overall pessimistic or optimistic attitude toward life and the experiences that arise. In the context of accountability, we use the term "attitude" to describe, in part, what motivates us to make certain choices. We often make choices based on unconscious or partly-conscious beliefs, attitudes, or assumptions. (Found in chapter 3, Accountability.)

Belief: A thought one thinks over and over again, finally believing to be true. For example, one might believe himself to be "shy." Another might say she is "outgoing." One who holds a belief that he is shy, consistently sees evidence proving he is shy and continues to act in accordance with the belief, avoiding situations that might be challenging for a shy person. In the context of accountability, we use the term "belief" to describe, in part, what motivates us to make certain choices. We often make choices based on unconscious or partly-conscious beliefs, attitudes or assumptions. (Found in chapter 3, Accountability.)

Choices, non-working: Those that create results one does not want. A behavior, action, decision, or choice that produces an outcome one does not desire. (Found in chapter 1, Taking a Stand.)

Choices, working: Those that create results one wants. A behavior, action, decision or choice that produces an outcome one desires. (Found in chapter 1, Taking a Stand.)

Chunking: A way of breaking large tasks into smaller, more manageable pieces. This is an NLP concept based on the premise that the human mind conceptualizes tasks in various sizes of information. In chunking, we acknowledge that different people feel more comfortable with different sizes of information or tasks on their way to completing a larger task. By "chunking," we take a task that feels overwhelming and break it down into smaller tasks or steps (i.e., chunks). We continue breaking it down until we have reached chunk sizes that feel most comfortable to us as individuals. (Found in chapter 7, Managing your Time and Energy.)

Circumstances: External factors; things that happen to us, and outside us, over which we have little or no control. (Found in chapter 3, Accountability.)

Coaching: The practice of partnering with and supporting others in a way that allows them to discover and employ their own resources and to reach their objectives. (Referenced throughout the book.)

Comfort Zone: The set of circumstances, behaviors, and actions that are most familiar and involve the least amount of risk. A way of living that avoids discomfort or risk. It reinforces the status quo and is unlikely to produce change. A comfort zone may not literally be comfortable, as for example, where one habitually works "too much." It does not feel fulfilling or comfortable, but it avoids the risk of doing something different, trying something new. (Referenced throughout the book.)

Commitment: The state of being bound emotionally or intellectually to an ideal or course of action. To commit is to obligate or bind oneself to follow through to a particular result. We can only know what we are committed to by looking at our actions; we do not evidence commitment by talking about a desired result, but by whether, and the extent to which, we take action to manifest that result. (Found in chapter 4, Are you Committed?)

Commonalities: Capitalizing on what you have in common with another person in order to generate rapport. This might be subject matter (i.e., love of baseball) or observation of something jointly experienced (i.e., the weather). (Found in chapter 10, the Art of Enrollment.)

Conflict: An unresolved clash in the way that two or more people see the world or a particular situation. Conflict may be uncomfortable but it provides an opportunity to obtain greater understanding of another's world view, belief system, or filter. (Found in chapter 8, Communication Skills for Lawyers.)

Drift: A common and mainly unconscious way of approaching the world, one's life and one's practice. An individual drift is one that tends toward an "auto-pilot" approach to life and work, and which fosters mediocrity. When operating from a personal drift, one does not consciously assess and make choices, but instead unconsciously reacts to what is around him based largely on a habitual response. A group drift is a common way of approaching the world, our lives and our practice, based on common beliefs and perceived limitations. An example of a group drift may be, "we are too busy to be on time for meetings." This is not literally what we say, but an underlying belief or attitude that keeps us from changing the behavior. (Found in chapter 1, Taking a Stand, and throughout the book.)

Ecology: The NLP concept that all things in one's life and practice are connected and that we cannot effectively make lasting change in any part of our lives or practice until we have determined and acknowledged the effect the change will have on our lives or practice as a whole. (Found in chapter 2, Creating a Well-Formed Outcome.)

Excuses: Circumstances that one focuses on in order to escape accountability for failing to bring about a promised or desired result. For example, "I was late because the traffic was so bad," is an excuse in which one points to the traffic as a way to avoid taking accountability for failure to bring about the result of being on time. (Found in chapter 3, Accountability.)

Experience: One's overall perception of an event, made up of how one sees, hears, and feels about the event. For example, "what was your experience of the conversation?" (Referenced throughout the book.)

Feedback: Webster's defines as, "Return of a portion of the output of a process or system to the input, esp. to maintain performance or to control a system or process; return of data about the result of a process." Feedback is anything outside oneself that provides information about one's actions. All feedback is information for the system. For example, tripping while walking down the street is feedback; a conversation with someone resulting in her being upset is feedback; if I say I will bring in ten new clients this month and I bring in five, that is feedback. Feedback is a valuable learning device that we all too often ignore. (Found in chapter 8, Communication Skills for Lawyers.)

Feedback loop: A model of human communication that acknowledges people do not communicate based solely on what is said, but also based on each person's interpretation of what is said. For example, when one person speaks, the other person hears through his or her filter and interprets the meaning of the speaker's words. As such, when the listener responds, it is not necessarily to what the speaker said, but to how the listener interpreted what the speaker said. Similarly, when the listener responds, the original speaker also applies an interpretation and responds based not necessarily on what that person meant, but on her interpretation of it. And so on, resulting in an ongoing loop. (Found in chapter 8, Communication Skills for Lawyers.)

Filter: A way in which one sees the world based on one's upbringing, culture, experiences, and goals. (Found in chapter 8, Communication Skills for Lawyers.)

Intention: The statement of one's commitment; and subsequently following through with dedicated action *until the result is generated.* It is not simply a statement of what one "wants," but what one will generate through committed action. (Referenced throughout the book.)

Judgment: Although not defined this way in the dictionary, this term is commonly used to mean a negative assessment. As used in this book, it means assessing something as good or bad, as opposed to simply viewing it objectively. The term is found in the accountability chapter and referenced as a way of viewing a situation or feedback we are given that makes it hard for us to learn from it. For example, if I judge myself as stupid for forgetting to bring certain work home, it is hard for me to learn from the situation and make the necessary changes in the future. (Referenced throughout the book.)

Life Balance: This is a very personal assessment of whether all the areas of importance in one's life are in a similar level of fulfillment. The question is **not** whether one is spending the same amount of time in each area, but whether he or she feels each area is receiving enough attention. It is a way of determining whether one is expending more effort in one area of life that is causing another area to be neglected, creating a sense of being "out of balance." (Referenced throughout the book.)

Map: Our view of the world based upon our beliefs, experiences and backgrounds. Our map is a filter or an interpretation. Commonly it is so engrained that we do not realize it as an interpretation, but believe it to be true. Our maps are as individual as we are. The phrase "the map is not the territory" means that we do not see reality; we see our interpretation of reality. (Found in chapter 8, Communication Skills for Lawyers.)

Mirroring: In developing rapport, the reflection of another's tone, rate of speech, or physical behavior, in order to create a sense of connection. For example, one might mirror another's posture by adopting a similar stance; or mirror one's tonality, by speaking similarly. (Found in the chapter 10, the Art of Enrollment.)

Multi-tasking: Doing more than one thing at a time. Also known as "doing several things poorly." (Found in chapter 7, Managing Your Time and Energy.)

Neutrality: Objectivity; non-judgment. In this book, often used to describe the element of accountability by which we look at our results and choices with the sole objective of learning from them and without berating or judging. (Found in chapter 3, Accountability and chapter 5, Values-Based Living.)

NLP: Neuro-linguistics programming. A discipline that enables people to unblock the structures of human communication and human excellence, allowing them to think, communicate and manage themselves, and others, more effectively. NLP explores the relationships between how we think (neuro), how we communicate (linguistic) and our patterns of behavior and emotion (programs). (Referenced throughout the book.)

NLP presupposition: Within the discipline of NLP, these are principles that we recognize are in effect at all times. When we acknowledge and act according to the presuppositions, we are more effective. For example, it is useful in understanding another person, to pre-suppose that "the map is not the territory," (i.e., that people respond to their view of the world and not to reality itself). Understanding and acknowledging the presuppositions in dealing with others can greatly improve how we communicate. (Referenced through-out the book.)

Obstacles: Internal barriers or patterns of thought or behavior that get in the way of performing at our best and generating the results and changes we want. (Found in chap-ter 4, Are You Committed?)

Pacing/leading: "Pacing" is generating rapport through establishing commonalities with another person (see mirroring, commonalities). After pacing, one can "lead" the other person in a different direction, and because we have gained rapport with the other person, that person will tend to "follow." This is a great tool in enrollment. (Found in chapter 10, the Art of Enrollment.)

Paradigm: (a) A framework containing the basic assumptions, ways of thinking, and methodologies that are commonly accepted by members of a community; (b) a cognitive framework shared by members of any discipline or group, (i.e., a company's business paradigm); (c) a typical view of a situation, often shared by the group. For example, in Chapter 7 on time management, we note a common paradigm among attorneys that the only way to stay on top of everything is to work hard, fast, and late into the night. We suggest a different time management paradigm is to look closely at the choices we make as attorneys and to fit different tasks into our days in a different order or system, thereby getting more done more effectively. (Found in various chapters, and especially chapter 7, Managing Your Time and Energy.)

Patterns: Behaviors and results that are repeated throughout one's life and practice. Recognizing them is often the key to making change to attain our goals. For example, if you want to be perceived as reliable and you have a pattern of being late to meetings, you may realize on further reflection that you are late most the time in other areas, and that changing that behavior and developing a new pattern of punctuality will have far-reaching effects and lead to greater reliability. (Found in chapter 3, Accountability.)

Rapport: Synchronization of thoughts, feelings or actions between two or more people that evokes a feeling of affinity or trust. (Found in chapter 10, the Art of Enrollment.)

Reaction: An *unconsciously* chosen and often automatic behavior in a given situa-tion. Contrast it with "response," which is a *consciously*-chosen action. A reaction may be termed "knee-jerk" due to its automatic and unconscious nature. (Found in chapter 5, Values-Based Living; chapter 6, the Case for Self-Maintenance; and chapter 7, Managing Your Time and Energy.)

Response: A *consciously* chosen behavior in a given situation. A response, as opposed to a more automatic and *unconscious* "reaction," is more likely to be in keeping with our goals and intentions. (Found in chapter 5, Values-Based Living; chapter 6, the Case for Self-Maintenance; and chapter 7, Managing Your Time and Energy.)

Reflective listening: Paying close attention to another's words and body language in order to understand the meaning of the communication, and indicating that understanding back to the other for confirmation or correction. (Found in chapter 8, Communication Skills for Lawyers.)

Resourcefulness: The ability to recognize, find, and then employ internal and/or external support in order to handle a situation effectively. (Found in chapter 4, Are you Committed?)

Result: An outcome. A result is anything—the house you live in, whether you are married, how much money you make, whether you were on time to work—that occurs or is present in your life. The result is typically feedback on the effectiveness of your actions or behavior. (Referenced throughout the book.)

SMART goal: A common method of goal setting involving a process by which the person setting the goal clearly delineates the way in which the goal is **specific, measurable, aligned** with his or her purpose and vision, **risky** (outside his/her comfort zone in some way), and **time-based** (including a deadline for completion). (Found in chapter 2, Creating a Well-Formed Outcome.)

Values: Internal guiding principles, consciously articulated. In this book, we suggest these principles be used to make decisions and take actions in all aspects of life. (Found in chapter 5, Values-Based Living.)

Victim/victimhood: The opposite of accountability, this is the practice of looking outside ourselves at factors we cannot control in order to find excuses as to why we do not have the results we say we want. (Found in chapter 3, Accountability.)

Well-Formed Outcome (WFO): An NLP process that enables one to fully flesh out a goal, including the necessary action steps, thereby making it clear and easier to attain. (Found in chapter 2, Creating a Well-Formed Outcome.)

Bibliography

- Joseph O'Connor, *An Introduction to NLP* (1998).
- Steven Keeva, *Transforming Practices* (1999) (an ABA Journal Book).
- Michael Gerber, *The E-Myth Attorney* (2010).
- Jay Foonberg, *How to Start and Build a Law Practice* (2004) (ABA).
- Jeffrey Gitomer, *The Little Black Book of Connections* (1999).
- Stephen Covey, *The Seven Habits of Highly Effective People* (1990).
- Stephen Covey and A. Roger and Rebecca Merril, *First Things First* (1994).
- Mehmet Oz & Michael Roizen, *YOU: Staying Young* (2007).
- Robert Cooper, *The Other 90%: How to Unlock Your Vast Untapped Potential for Leadership and Life* (2002).
- Richard Carlson, *Don't Sweat the Small Stuff, and It's all Small Stuff* (1997).
- Napolean Hill, *Think and Grow Rich* (1937).
- Janet Atwood & Chris Atwood, *The Passion Test* (2006).
- Jon Kabat-Zinn, *Wherever You Go, There You Are* (1994)
- Jerry Hicks & Esther Hicks, *The Astonishing Power of Emotions* (2008).
- Jon Kabat-Zinn, *Full-Catastrophe Living* (1990)
- David Allen, *Getting Things Done* (2002).
- Gary Harper, *The Joy of Conflict Resolution* (2004).
- Rick Warren, *The Purpose-Driven Life* (1997).
- Martha Beck, *Finding Your Own North Star* (2001).
- Stephen Covey, *The Speed of Trust* (2006).
- Robert Solomon & Fernando Flores, *Building Trust: In Business, Politics, Relationships and Life* (2003).
- Don Miguel Ruiz, *The Four Agreements* (1997).

Index